UNION STATION

oni
PRESS

UNION STATION™

Written by
ANDE PARKS

Illustrated by
EDUARDO BARRETO

book design by
KEITH WOOD

edited by
JAMIE S. RICH

special thanks to
GORDON PURCELL

"To Cynthia, who makes everything possible."
– Ande Parks

"To my kids, Andrea, Guillermo, Diego,
and Laura, and to my parents."
– Eduardo Barreto

published by
JOE NOZEMACK

associate editing by
JAMES LUCAS JONES

ONI PRESS, INC.
6336 SE Milwaukie Avenue, PMB30
Portland, OR 97202
USA

www.onipress.com

First edition: October 2003
ISBN 1-929998-69-4

1 3 5 7 9 10 8 6 4 2

PRINTED IN CANADA

ACT I

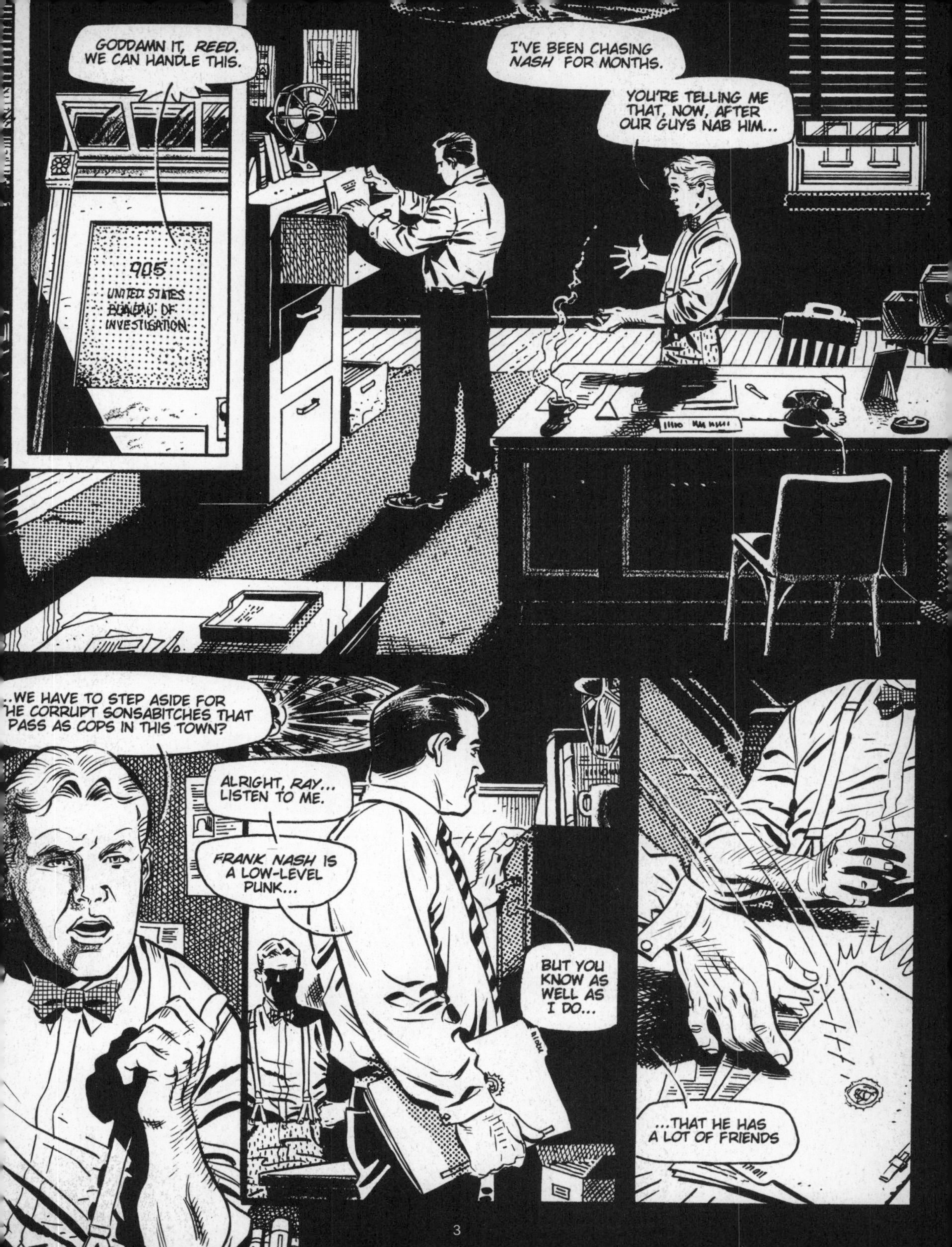

GODDAMN IT, REED. WE CAN HANDLE THIS.
905
UNITED STATES BUREAU OF INVESTIGATION
I'VE BEEN CHASING NASH FOR MONTHS.
YOU'RE TELLING ME THAT, NOW, AFTER OUR GUYS NAB HIM...
..WE HAVE TO STEP ASIDE FOR THE CORRUPT SONSABITCHES THAT PASS AS COPS IN THIS TOWN?
ALRIGHT, RAY... LISTEN TO ME.
FRANK NASH IS A LOW-LEVEL PUNK...
BUT YOU KNOW AS WELL AS I DO...
...THAT HE HAS A LOT OF FRIENDS

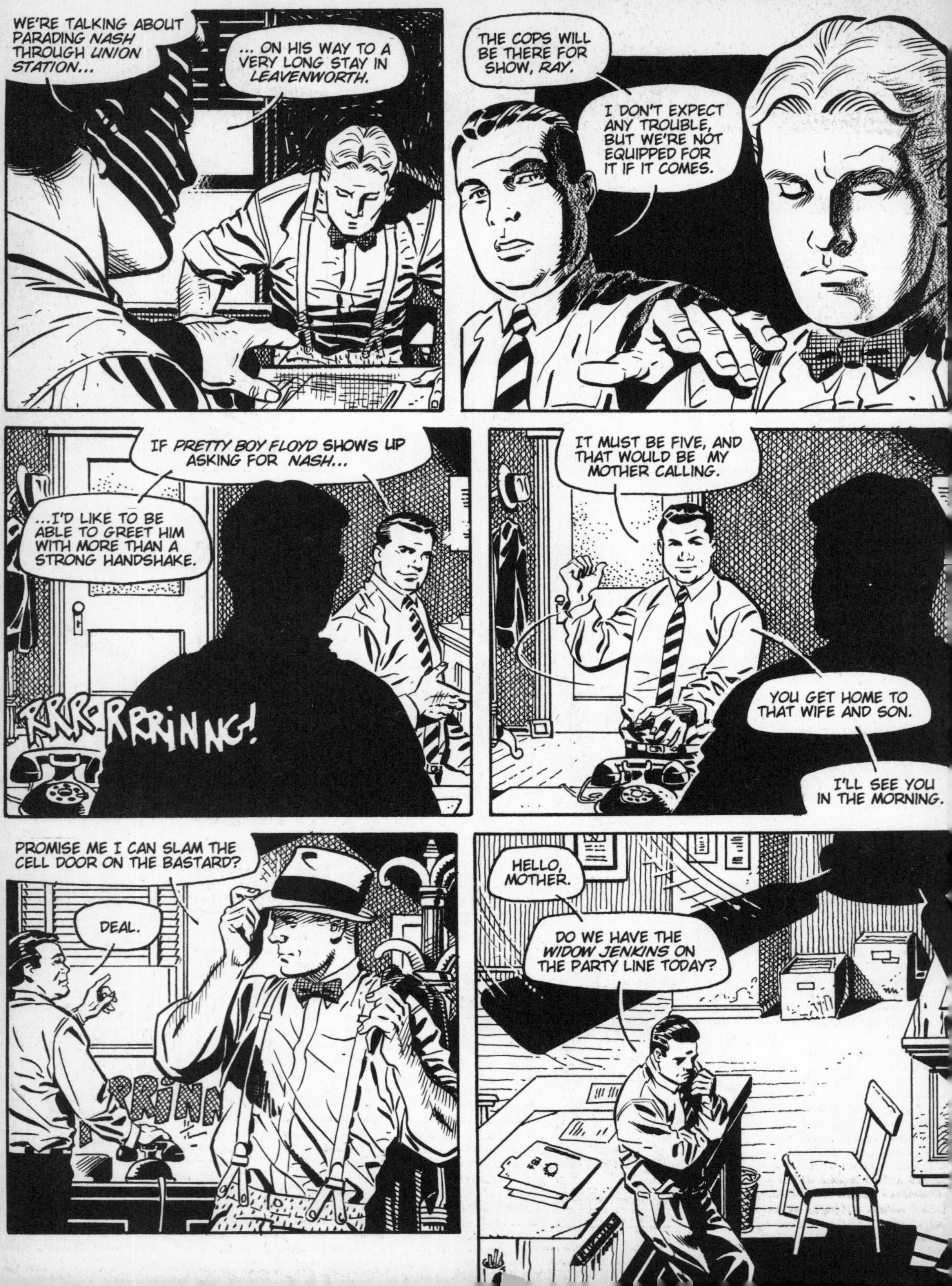
WE'RE TALKING ABOUT PARADING NASH THROUGH UNION STATION...
... ON HIS WAY TO A VERY LONG STAY IN LEAVENWORTH.
THE COPS WILL BE THERE FOR SHOW, RAY.
I DON'T EXPECT ANY TROUBLE, BUT WE'RE NOT EQUIPPED FOR IT IF IT COMES.
IF PRETTY BOY FLOYD SHOWS UP ASKING FOR NASH...
...I'D LIKE TO BE ABLE TO GREET HIM WITH MORE THAN A STRONG HANDSHAKE.
RRR-RRRING!
IT MUST BE FIVE, AND THAT WOULD BE MY MOTHER CALLING.
YOU GET HOME TO THAT WIFE AND SON.
I'LL SEE YOU IN THE MORNING.
PROMISE ME I CAN SLAM THE CELL DOOR ON THE BASTARD?
DEAL.
HELLO, MOTHER.
DO WE HAVE THE WIDOW JENKINS ON THE PARTY LINE TODAY?

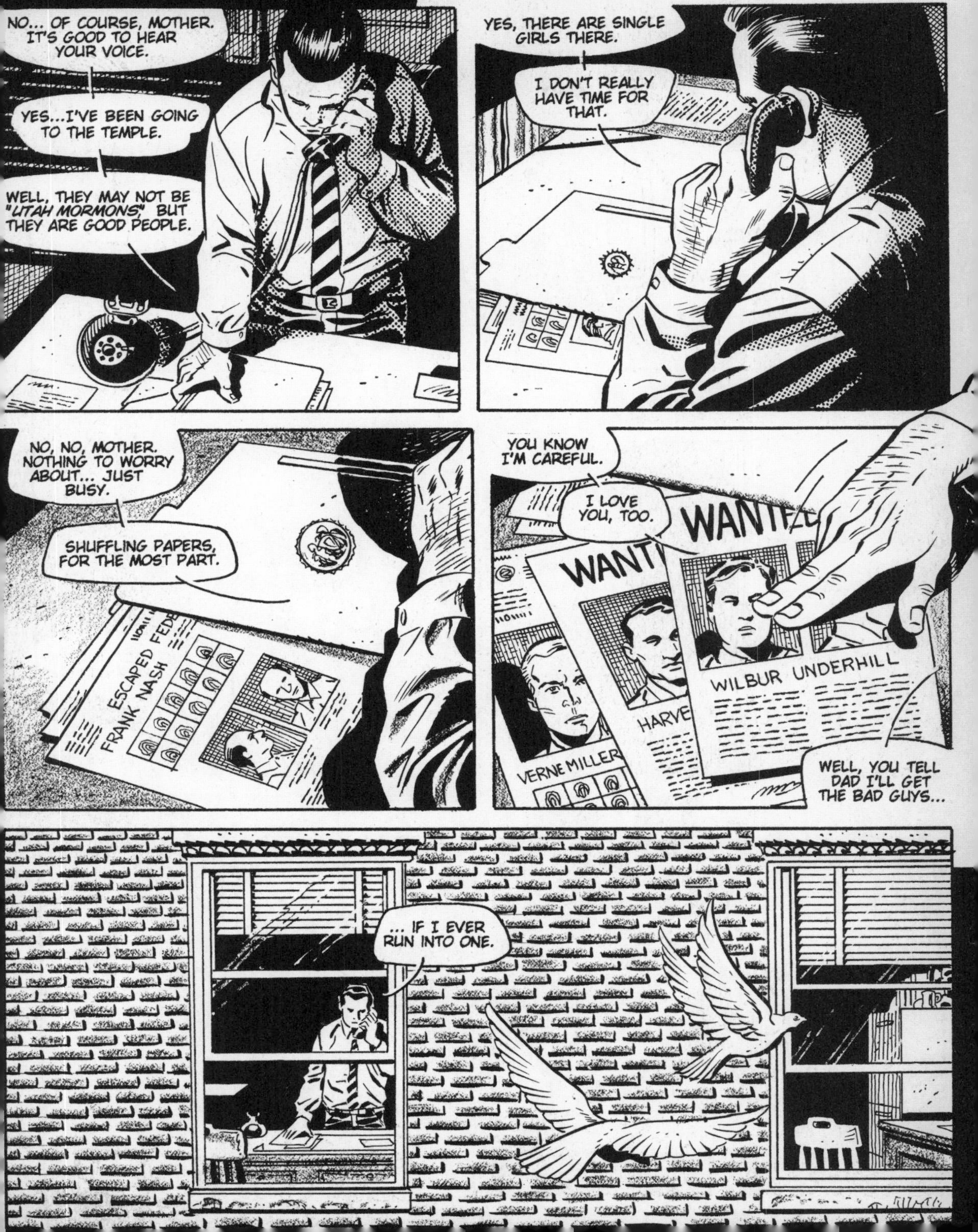
NO... OF COURSE, MOTHER. IT'S GOOD TO HEAR YOUR VOICE.
YES...I'VE BEEN GOING TO THE TEMPLE.
WELL, THEY MAY NOT BE "UTAH MORMONS," BUT THEY ARE GOOD PEOPLE.
YES, THERE ARE SINGLE GIRLS THERE.
I DON'T REALLY HAVE TIME FOR THAT.
NO, NO, MOTHER. NOTHING TO WORRY ABOUT... JUST BUSY.
SHUFFLING PAPERS, FOR THE MOST PART.
ESCAPED FEDE
FRANK NASH
YOU KNOW I'M CAREFUL.
I LOVE YOU, TOO.
WANTE
WANT
WILBUR UNDERHILL
HARVE
VERNE MILLER
WELL, YOU TELL DAD I'LL GET THE BAD GUYS...
... IF I EVER RUN INTO ONE.

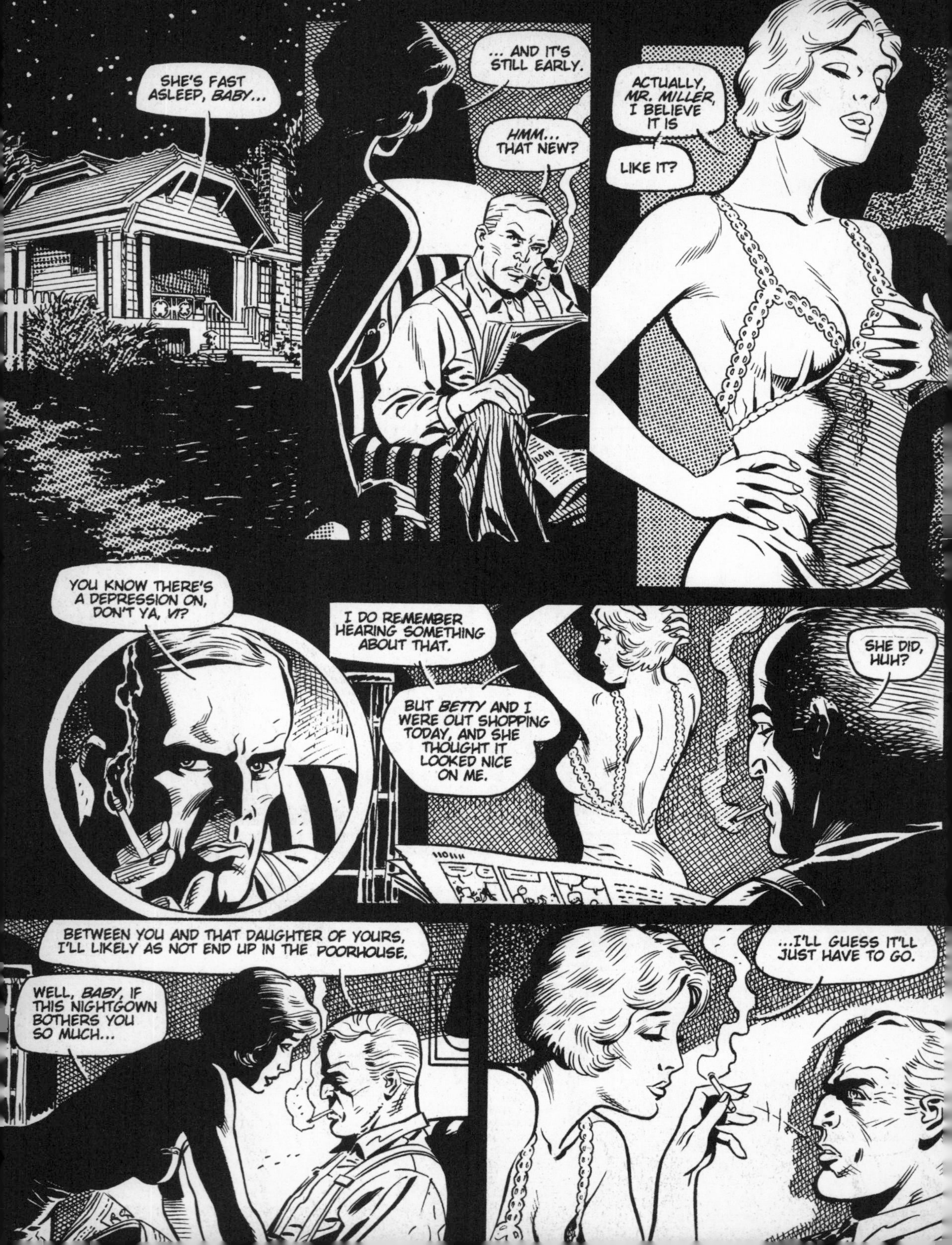
SHE'S FAST ASLEEP, *BABY*...
... AND IT'S STILL EARLY.
HMM... THAT NEW?
ACTUALLY, *MR. MILLER*, I BELIEVE IT IS
LIKE IT?
YOU KNOW THERE'S A DEPRESSION ON, DON'T YA, *VI*?
I DO REMEMBER HEARING SOMETHING ABOUT THAT.
BUT *BETTY* AND I WERE OUT SHOPPING TODAY, AND SHE THOUGHT IT LOOKED NICE ON ME.
SHE DID, HUH?
BETWEEN YOU AND THAT DAUGHTER OF YOURS, I'LL LIKELY AS NOT END UP IN THE POORHOUSE.
WELL, *BABY*, IF THIS NIGHTGOWN BOTHERS YOU SO MUCH...
...I'LL GUESS IT'LL JUST HAVE TO GO.

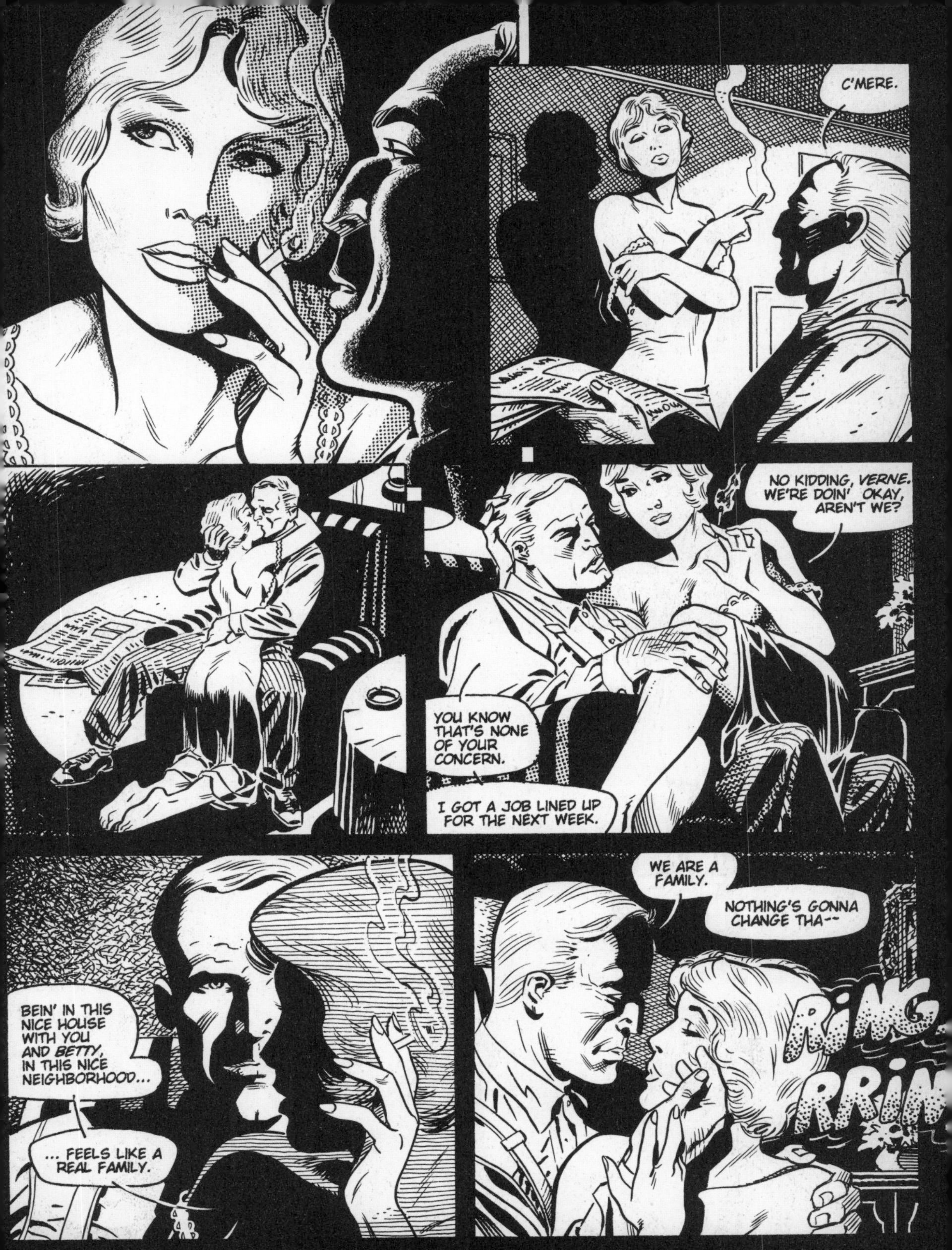
C'MERE.
NO KIDDING, VERNE. WE'RE DOIN' OKAY, AREN'T WE?
YOU KNOW THAT'S NONE OF YOUR CONCERN.
I GOT A JOB LINED UP FOR THE NEXT WEEK.
BEIN' IN THIS NICE HOUSE WITH YOU AND BETTY, IN THIS NICE NEIGHBORHOOD...
... FEELS LIKE A REAL FAMILY.
WE ARE A FAMILY.
NOTHING'S GONNA CHANGE THA--
RING
RRIN

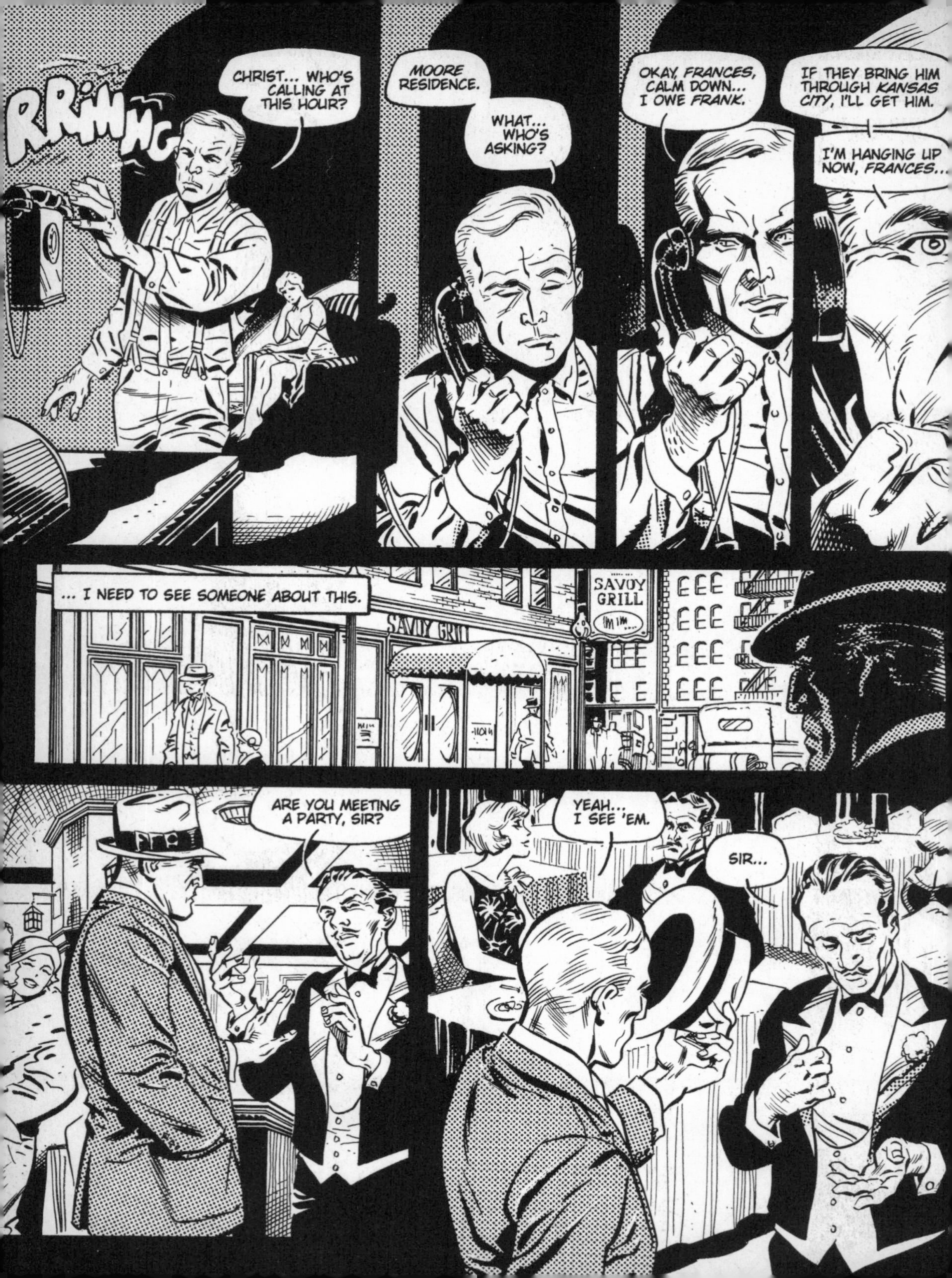
RRiNNNG
CHRIST... WHO'S CALLING AT THIS HOUR?
MOORE RESIDENCE.
WHAT... WHO'S ASKING?
OKAY, FRANCES, CALM DOWN... I OWE FRANK.
IF THEY BRING HIM THROUGH KANSAS CITY, I'LL GET HIM.
I'M HANGING UP NOW, FRANCES...
... I NEED TO SEE SOMEONE ABOUT THIS.
SAVOY GRILL
SAVOY GRILL
ARE YOU MEETING A PARTY, SIR?
YEAH... I SEE 'EM.
SIR...

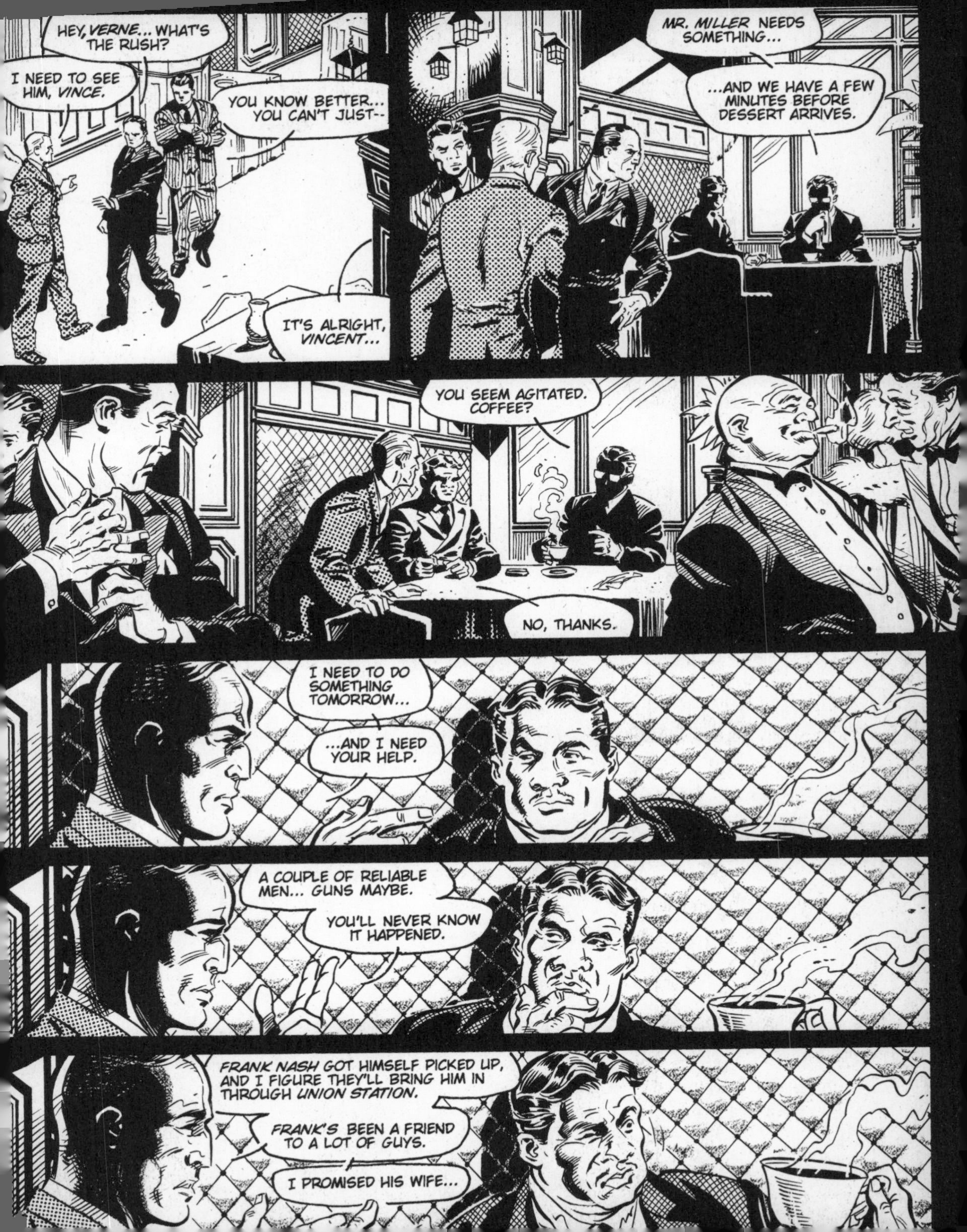
HEY, VERNE... WHAT'S THE RUSH?
I NEED TO SEE HIM, VINCE.
YOU KNOW BETTER... YOU CAN'T JUST--
IT'S ALRIGHT, VINCENT...
MR. MILLER NEEDS SOMETHING...
...AND WE HAVE A FEW MINUTES BEFORE DESSERT ARRIVES.
YOU SEEM AGITATED. COFFEE?
NO, THANKS.
I NEED TO DO SOMETHING TOMORROW...
...AND I NEED YOUR HELP.
A COUPLE OF RELIABLE MEN... GUNS MAYBE.
YOU'LL NEVER KNOW IT HAPPENED.
FRANK NASH GOT HIMSELF PICKED UP, AND I FIGURE THEY'LL BRING HIM IN THROUGH UNION STATION.
FRANK'S BEEN A FRIEND TO A LOT OF GUYS.
I PROMISED HIS WIFE...

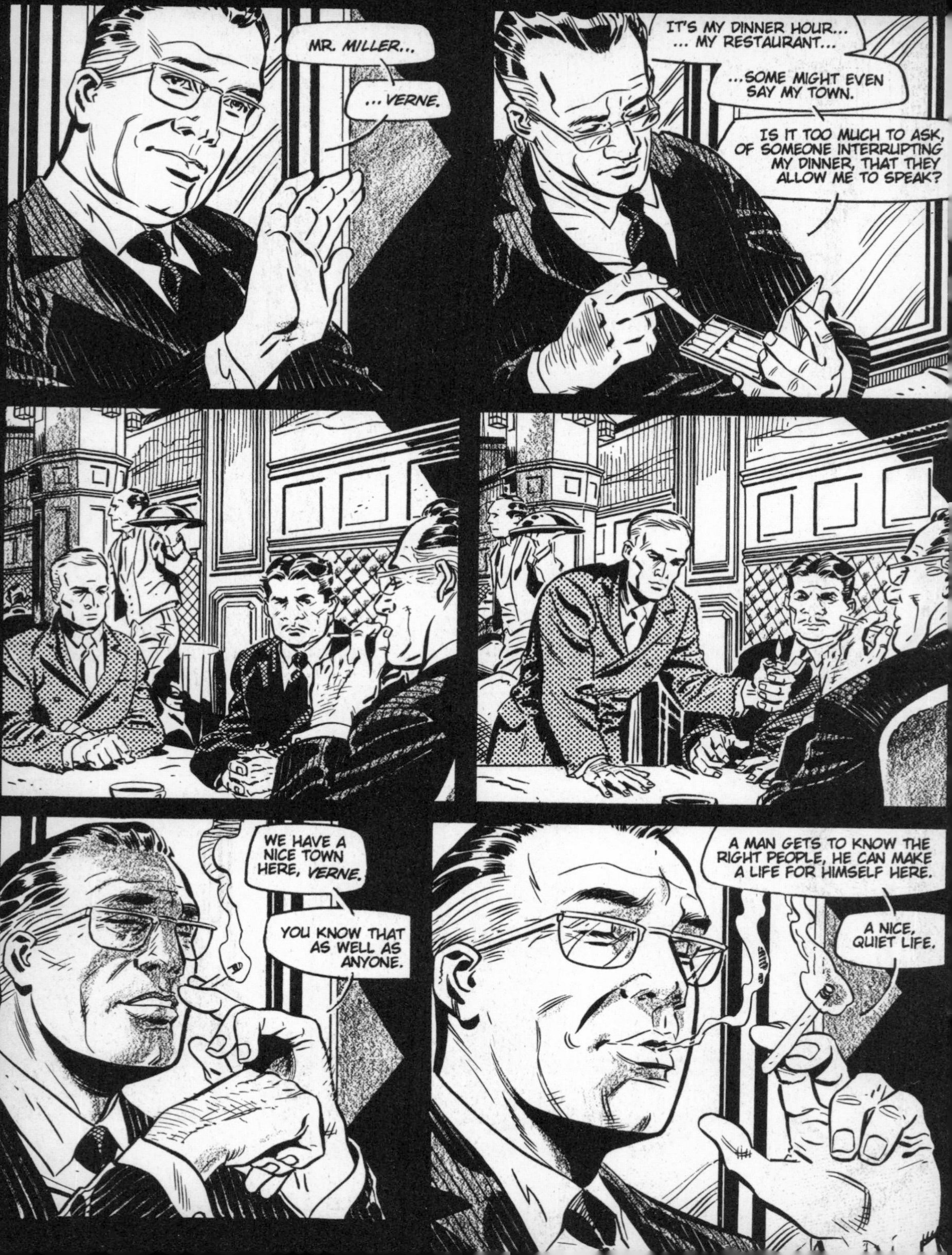
MR. MILLER...
...VERNE.
IT'S MY DINNER HOUR... ... MY RESTAURANT...
...SOME MIGHT EVEN SAY MY TOWN.
IS IT TOO MUCH TO ASK, OF SOMEONE INTERRUPTING MY DINNER, THAT THEY ALLOW ME TO SPEAK?
WE HAVE A NICE TOWN HERE, VERNE.
YOU KNOW THAT AS WELL AS ANYONE.
A MAN GETS TO KNOW THE RIGHT PEOPLE, HE CAN MAKE A LIFE FOR HIMSELF HERE.
A NICE, QUIET LIFE.

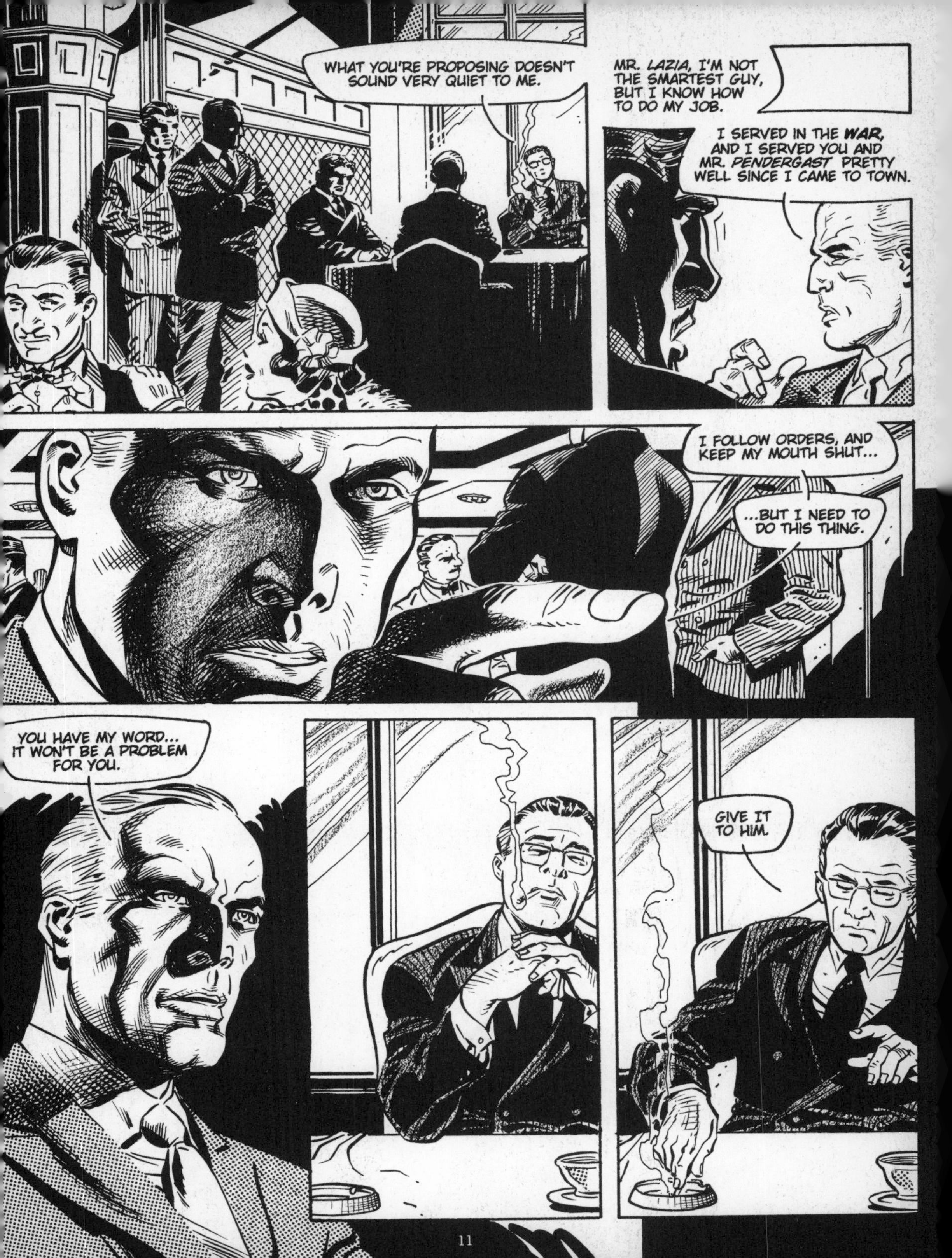
WHAT YOU'RE PROPOSING DOESN'T SOUND VERY QUIET TO ME.
MR. LAZIA, I'M NOT THE SMARTEST GUY, BUT I KNOW HOW TO DO MY JOB.
I SERVED IN THE WAR, AND I SERVED YOU AND MR. PENDERGAST PRETTY WELL SINCE I CAME TO TOWN.
I FOLLOW ORDERS, AND KEEP MY MOUTH SHUT...
...BUT I NEED TO DO THIS THING.
YOU HAVE MY WORD... IT WON'T BE A PROBLEM FOR YOU.
GIVE IT TO HIM.

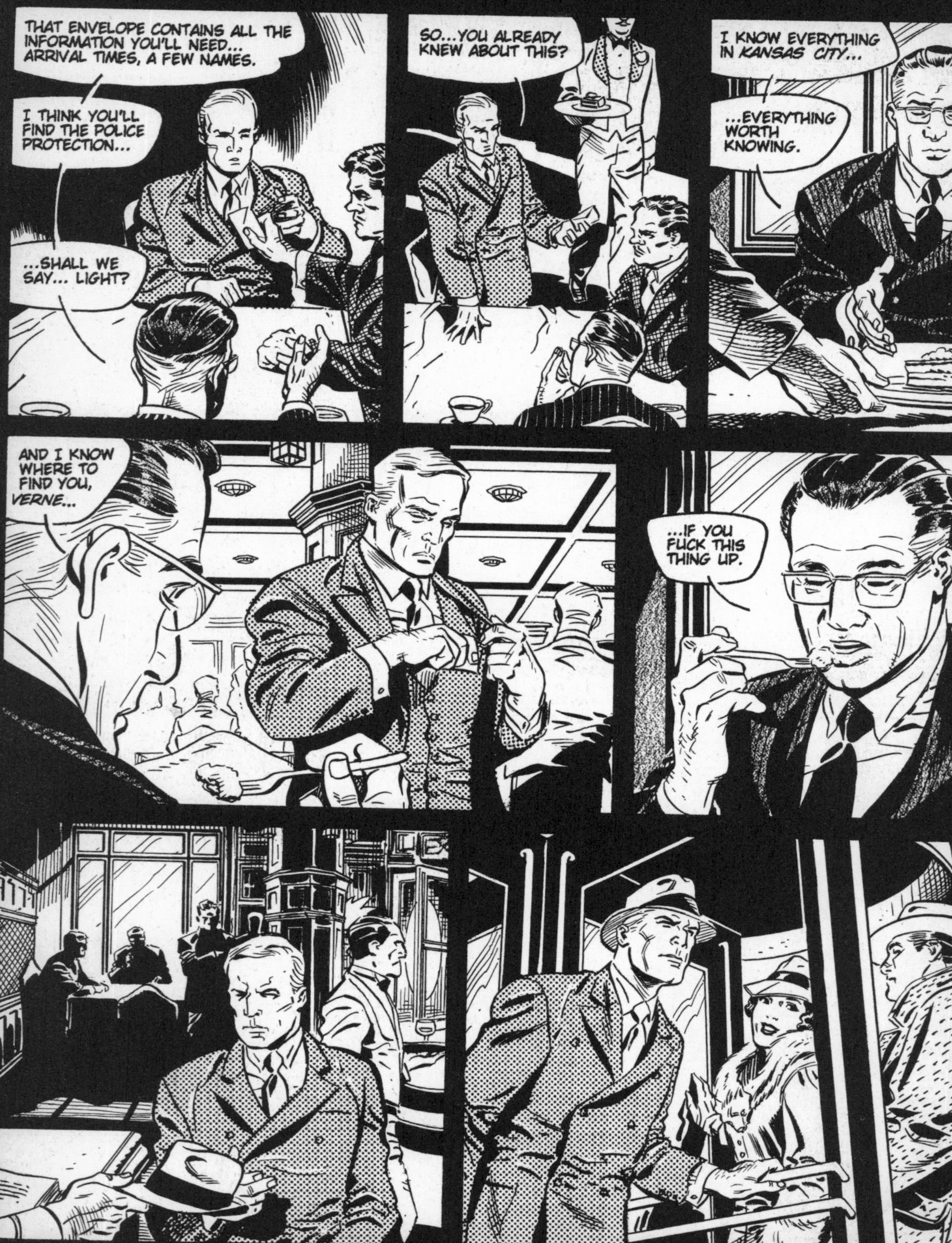
THAT ENVELOPE CONTAINS ALL THE INFORMATION YOU'LL NEED... ARRIVAL TIMES, A FEW NAMES.
I THINK YOU'LL FIND THE POLICE PROTECTION...
...SHALL WE SAY... LIGHT?
SO...YOU ALREADY KNEW ABOUT THIS?
I KNOW EVERYTHING IN *KANSAS CITY*...
...EVERYTHING WORTH KNOWING.
AND I KNOW WHERE TO FIND YOU, *VERNE*...
...IF YOU FUCK THIS THING UP.

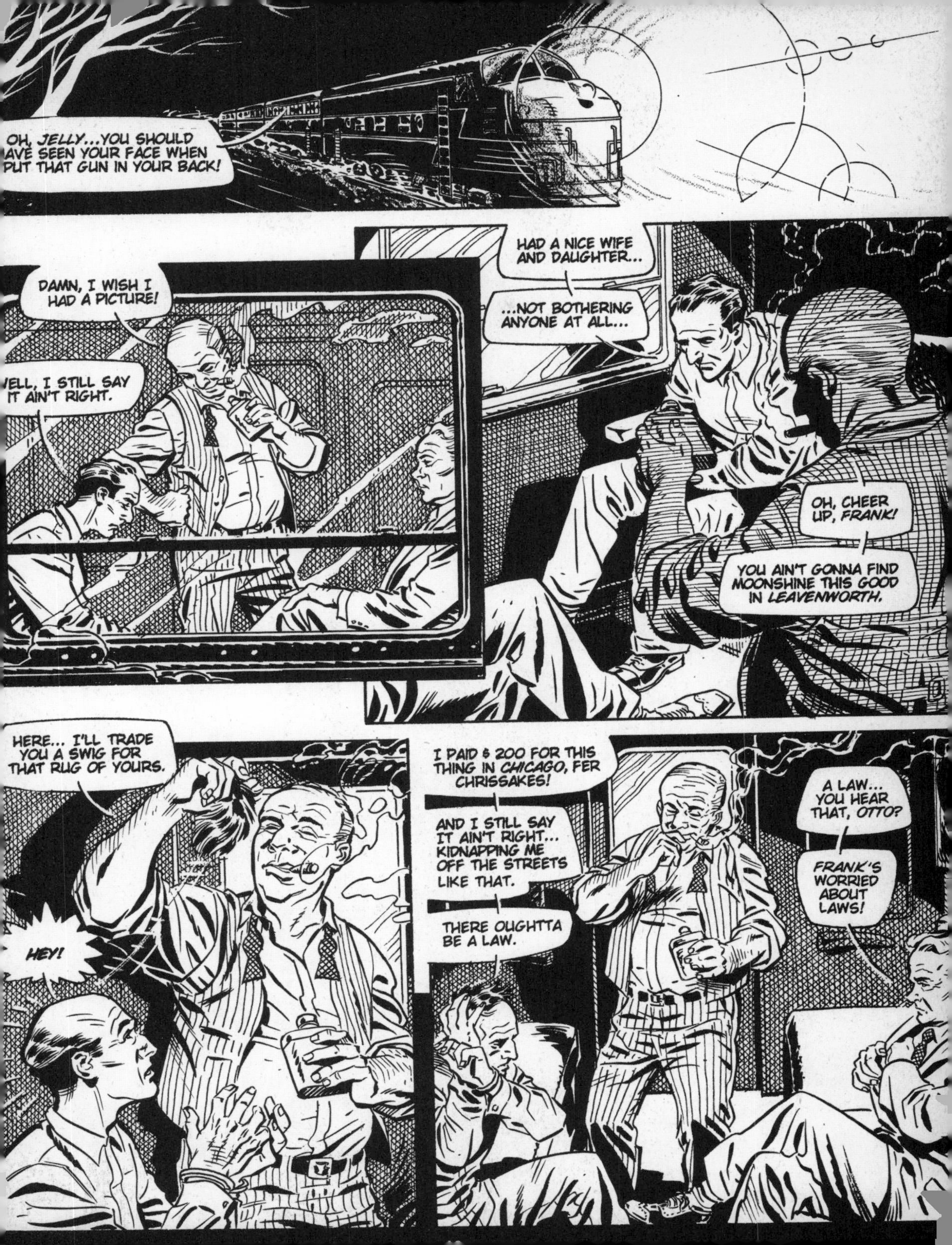

OH, JELLY...YOU SHOULD
AVE SEEN YOUR FACE WHEN
PUT THAT GUN IN YOUR BACK!
DAMN, I WISH I HAD A PICTURE!
WELL, I STILL SAY IT AIN'T RIGHT.
HAD A NICE WIFE AND DAUGHTER...
...NOT BOTHERING ANYONE AT ALL...
OH, CHEER UP, FRANK!
YOU AIN'T GONNA FIND MOONSHINE THIS GOOD IN LEAVENWORTH.
HERE... I'LL TRADE YOU A SWIG FOR THAT RUG OF YOURS.
HEY!
I PAID $ 200 FOR THIS THING IN CHICAGO, FER CHRISSAKES!
AND I STILL SAY IT AIN'T RIGHT... KIDNAPPING ME OFF THE STREETS LIKE THAT.
THERE OUGHTTA BE A LAW.
A LAW... YOU HEAR THAT, OTTO?
FRANK'S WORRIED ABOUT LAWS!

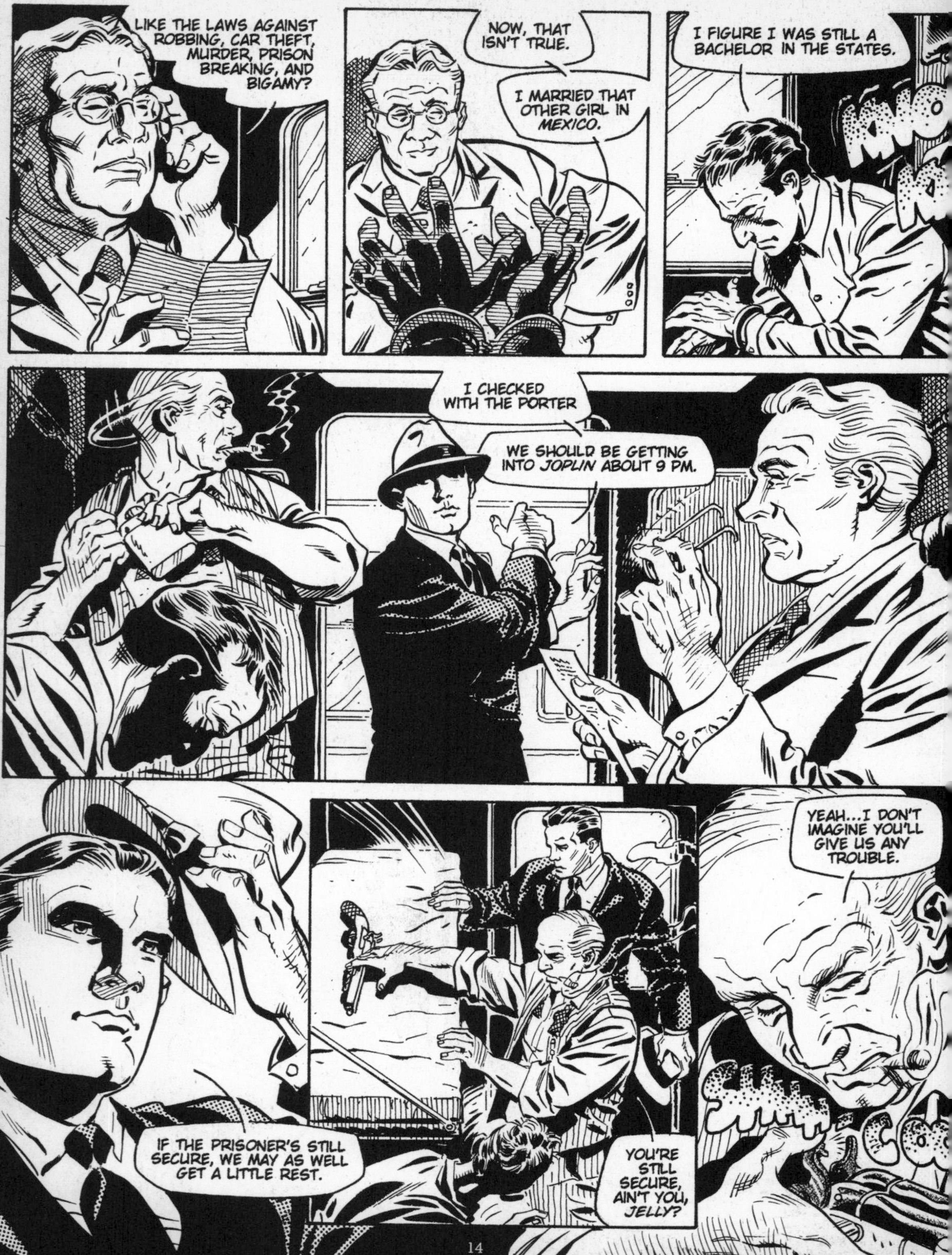

LIKE THE LAWS AGAINST ROBBING, CAR THEFT, MURDER, PRISON BREAKING, AND BIGAMY?
NOW, THAT ISN'T TRUE.
I MARRIED THAT OTHER GIRL IN MEXICO.
I FIGURE I WAS STILL A BACHELOR IN THE STATES.
I CHECKED WITH THE PORTER
WE SHOULD BE GETTING INTO JOPLIN ABOUT 9 PM.
IF THE PRISONER'S STILL SECURE, WE MAY AS WELL GET A LITTLE REST.
YOU'RE STILL SECURE, AIN'T YOU, JELLY?
YEAH...I DON'T IMAGINE YOU'LL GIVE US ANY TROUBLE.

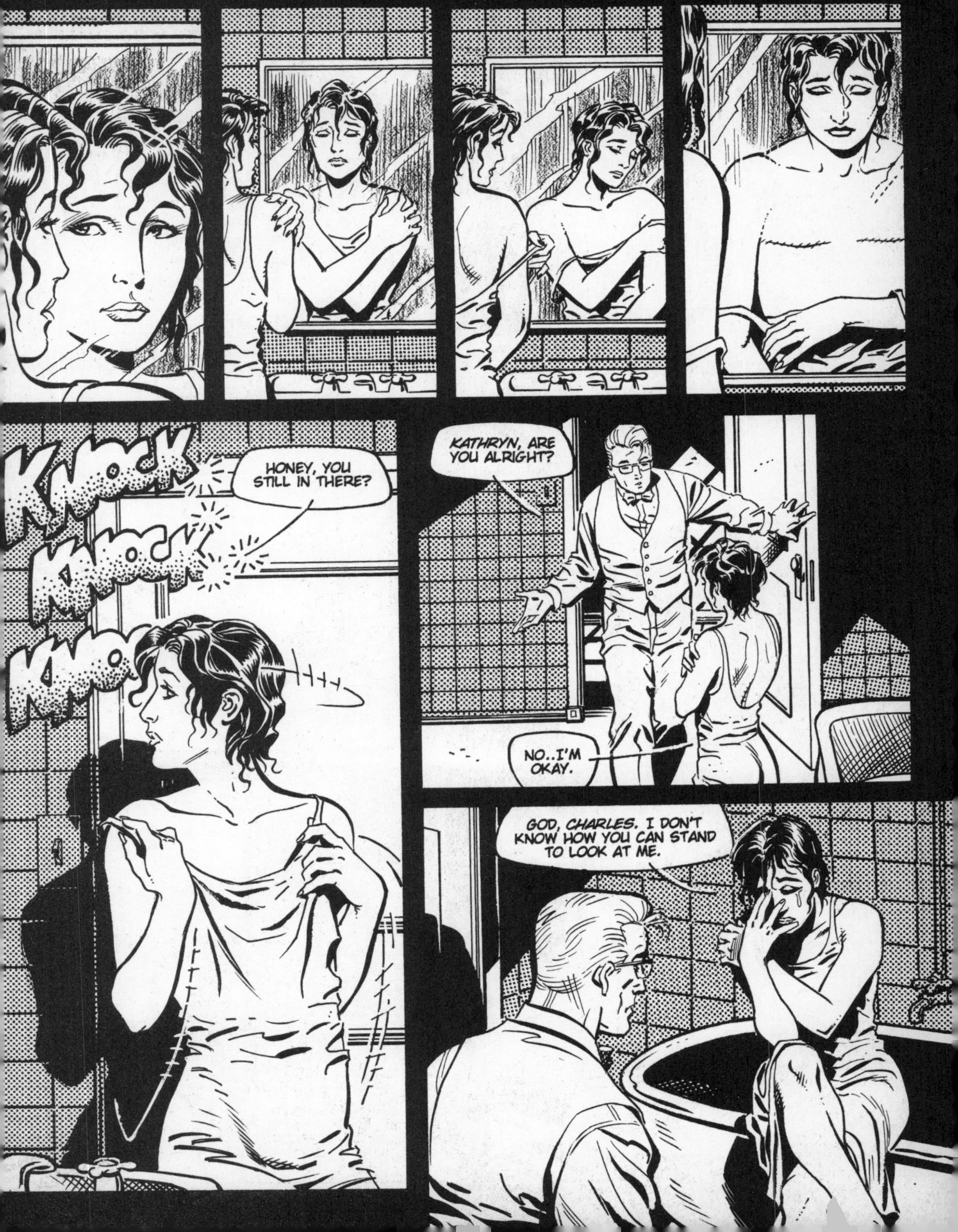
KNOCK
KNOCK
KNOC
HONEY, YOU STILL IN THERE?
KATHRYN, ARE YOU ALRIGHT?
NO...I'M OKAY.
GOD, CHARLES. I DON'T KNOW HOW YOU CAN STAND TO LOOK AT ME.

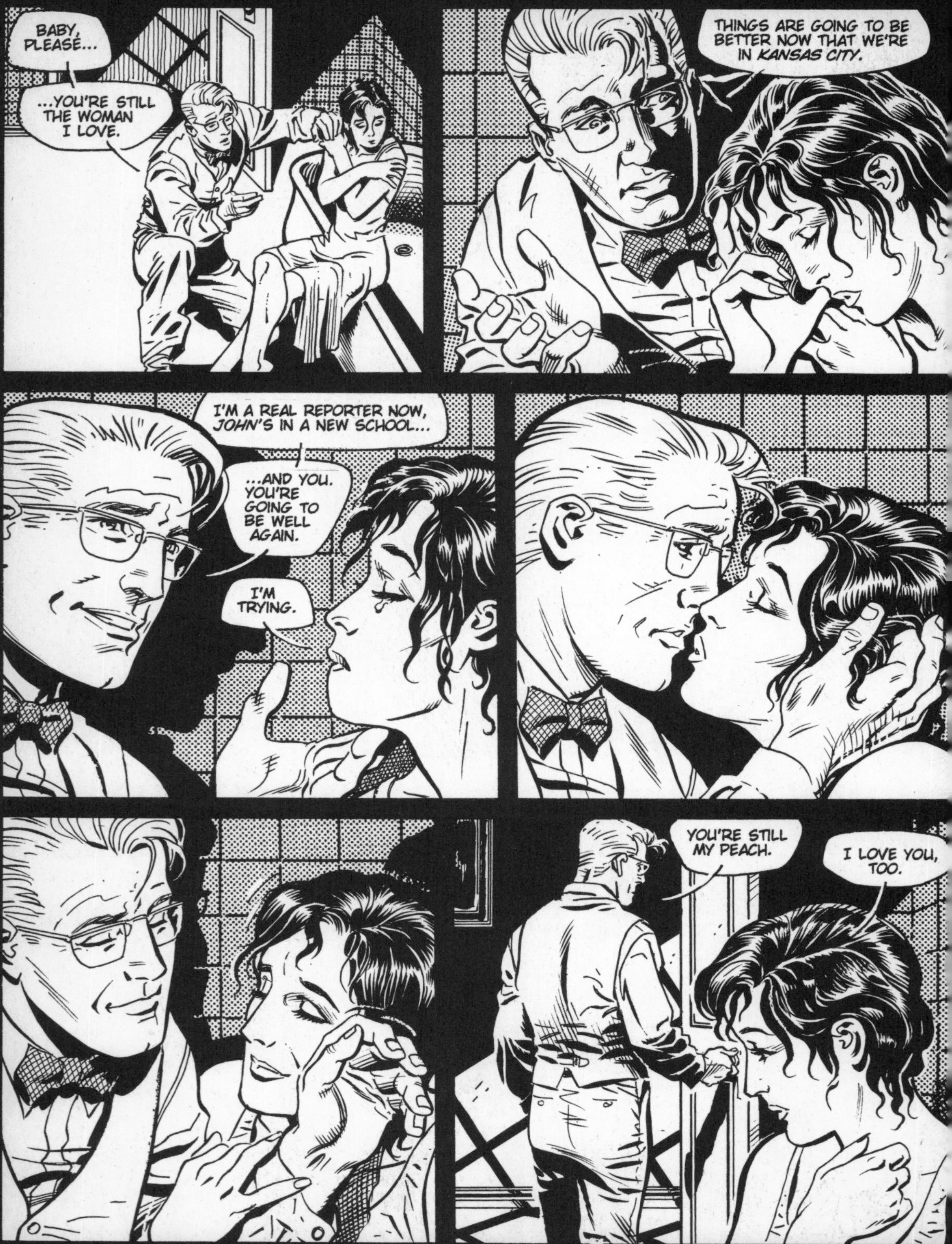
BABY, PLEASE...
...YOU'RE STILL THE WOMAN I LOVE.
THINGS ARE GOING TO BE BETTER NOW THAT WE'RE IN *KANSAS CITY*.
I'M A REAL REPORTER NOW, *JOHN'S* IN A NEW SCHOOL...
...AND YOU. YOU'RE GOING TO BE WELL AGAIN.
I'M TRYING.
YOU'RE STILL MY PEACH.
I LOVE YOU, TOO.

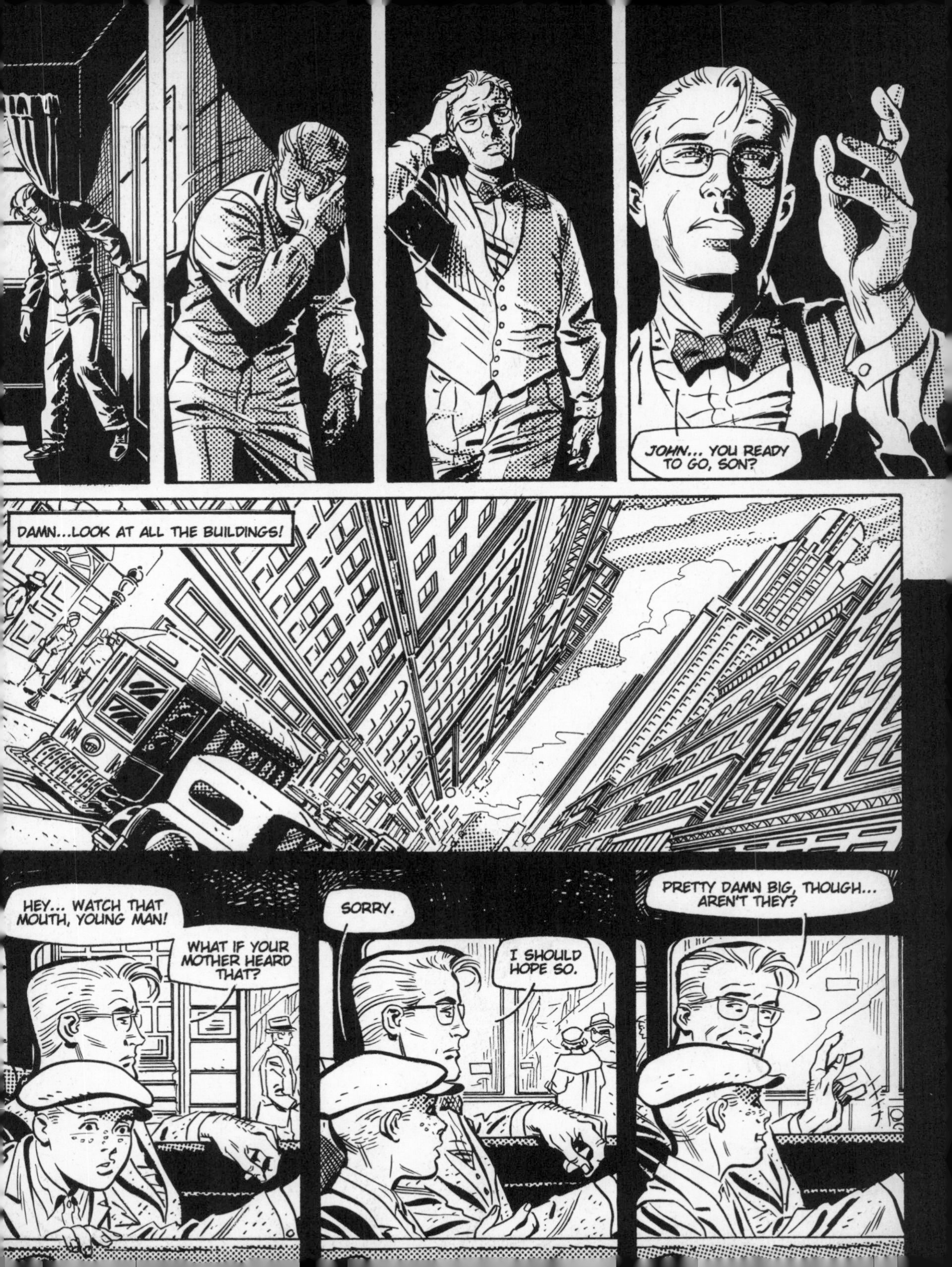
JOHN... YOU READY TO GO, SON?
DAMN...LOOK AT ALL THE BUILDINGS!
HEY... WATCH THAT MOUTH, YOUNG MAN!
WHAT IF YOUR MOTHER HEARD THAT?
SORRY.
I SHOULD HOPE SO.
PRETTY DAMN BIG, THOUGH... AREN'T THEY?

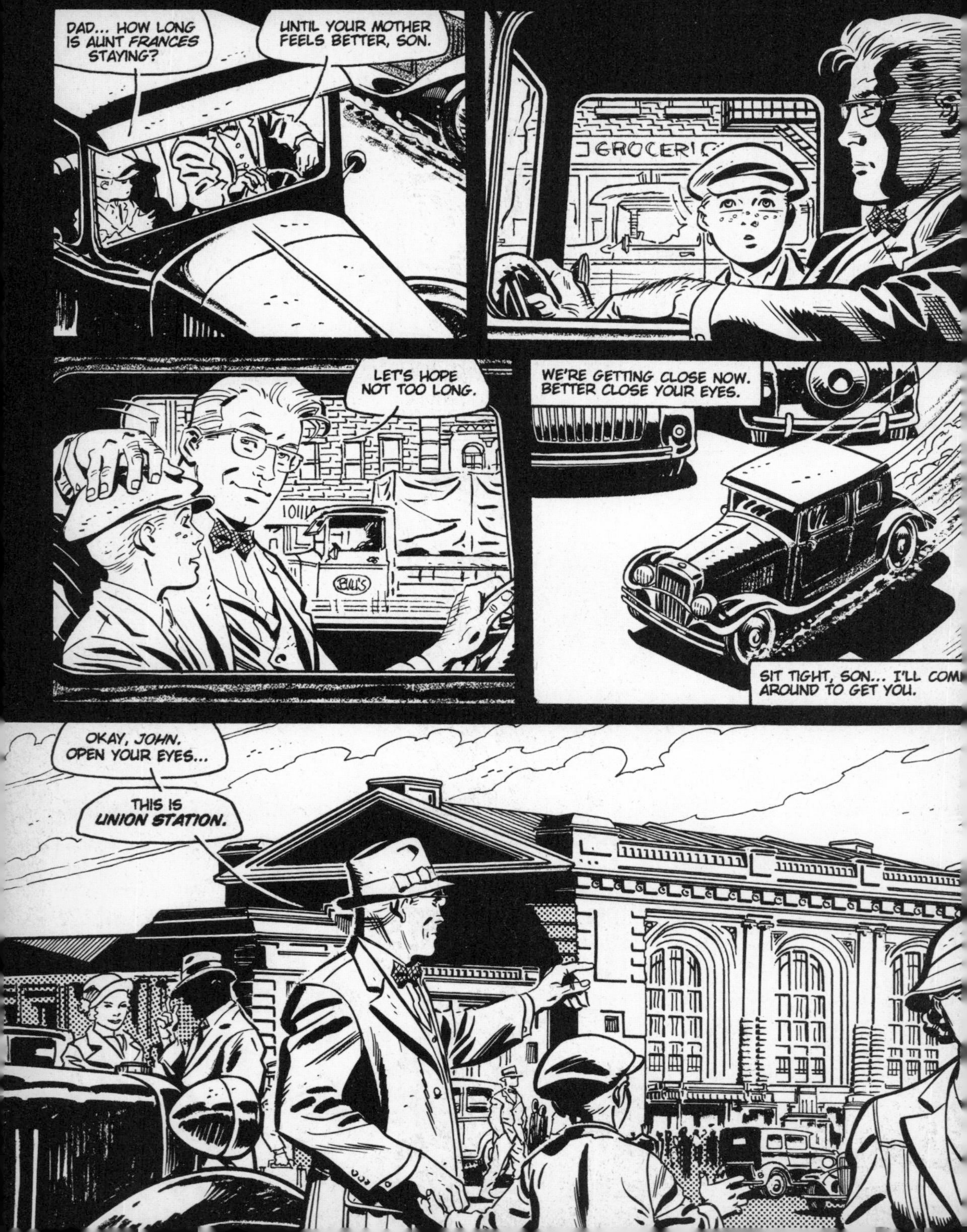
DAD... HOW LONG IS AUNT FRANCES STAYING?
UNTIL YOUR MOTHER FEELS BETTER, SON.
GROCERI
LET'S HOPE NOT TOO LONG.
BILL'S
WE'RE GETTING CLOSE NOW. BETTER CLOSE YOUR EYES.
SIT TIGHT, SON... I'LL COM
AROUND TO GET YOU.
OKAY, JOHN. OPEN YOUR EYES...
THIS IS UNION STATION.

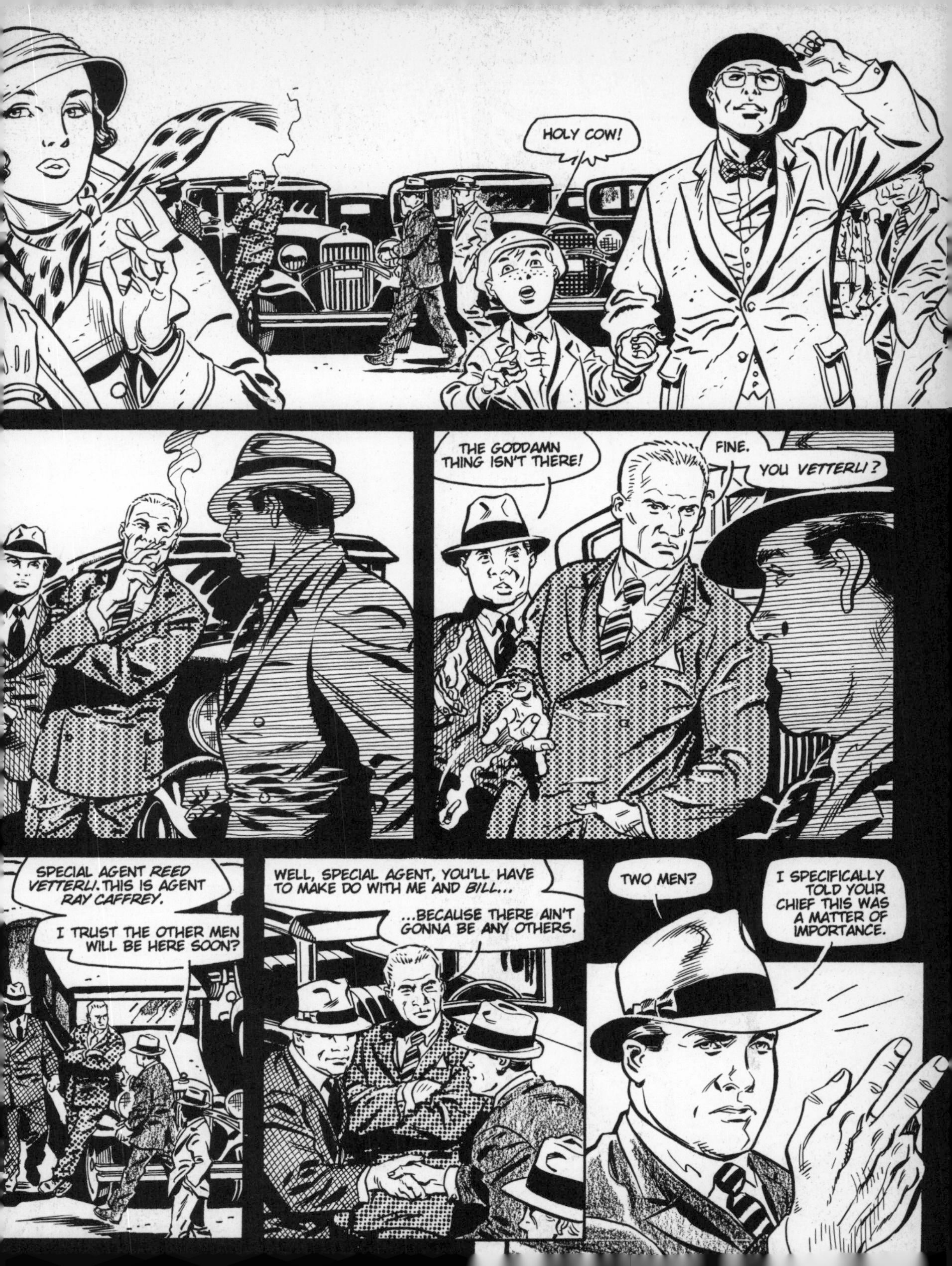

HOLY COW!
THE GODDAMN THING ISN'T THERE!
FINE.
YOU VETTERLI?
SPECIAL AGENT REED VETTERLI. THIS IS AGENT RAY CAFFREY.
I TRUST THE OTHER MEN WILL BE HERE SOON?
WELL, SPECIAL AGENT, YOU'LL HAVE TO MAKE DO WITH ME AND BILL...
...BECAUSE THERE AIN'T GONNA BE ANY OTHERS.
TWO MEN?
I SPECIFICALLY TOLD YOUR CHIEF THIS WAS A MATTER OF IMPORTANCE.

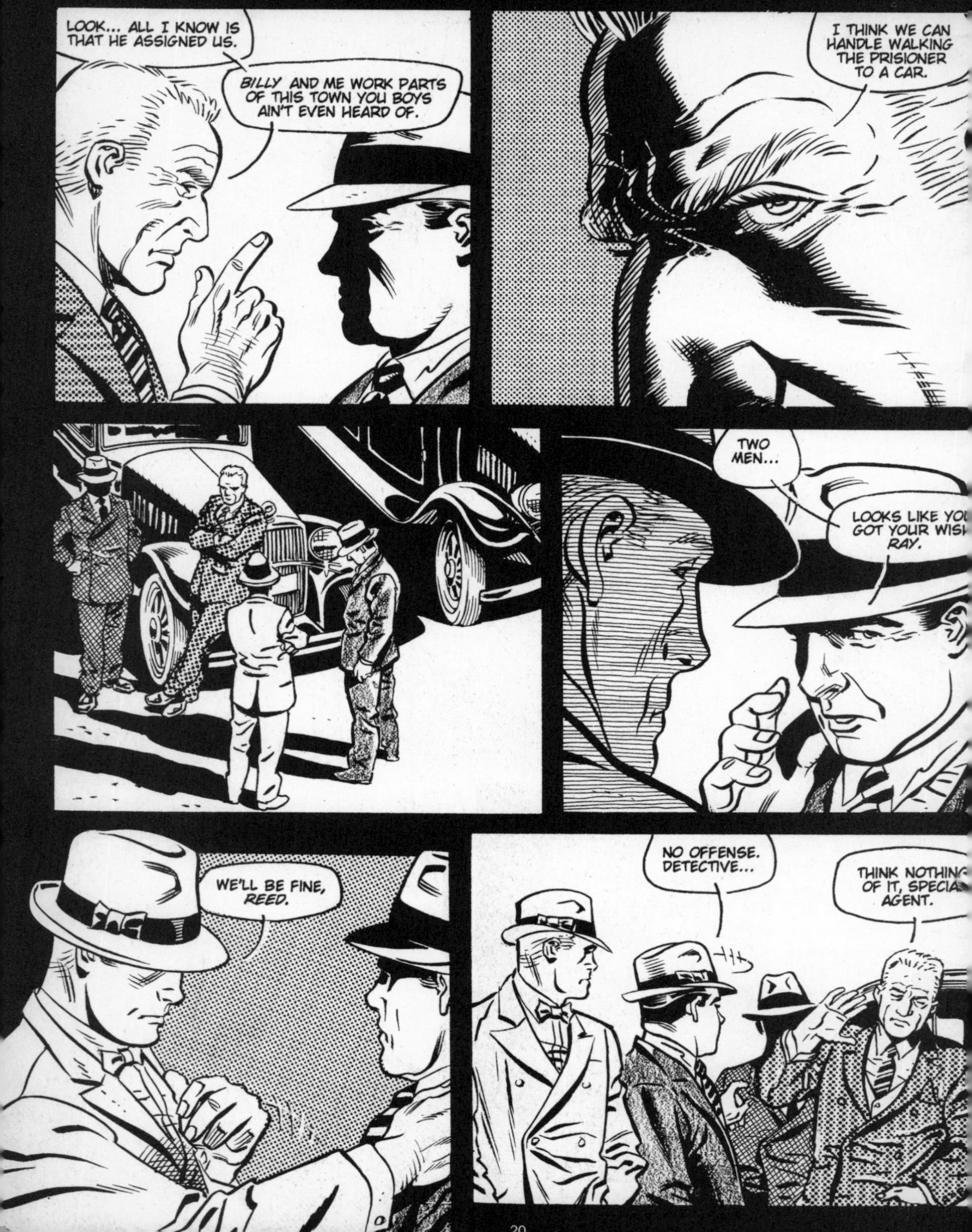
LOOK... ALL I KNOW IS THAT HE ASSIGNED US.
BILLY AND ME WORK PARTS OF THIS TOWN YOU BOYS AIN'T EVEN HEARD OF.
I THINK WE CAN HANDLE WALKING THE PRISIONER TO A CAR.
TWO MEN...
LOOKS LIKE YOU GOT YOUR WISH RAY.
WE'LL BE FINE, REED.
NO OFFENSE. DETECTIVE...
THINK NOTHING OF IT, SPECIAL AGENT.

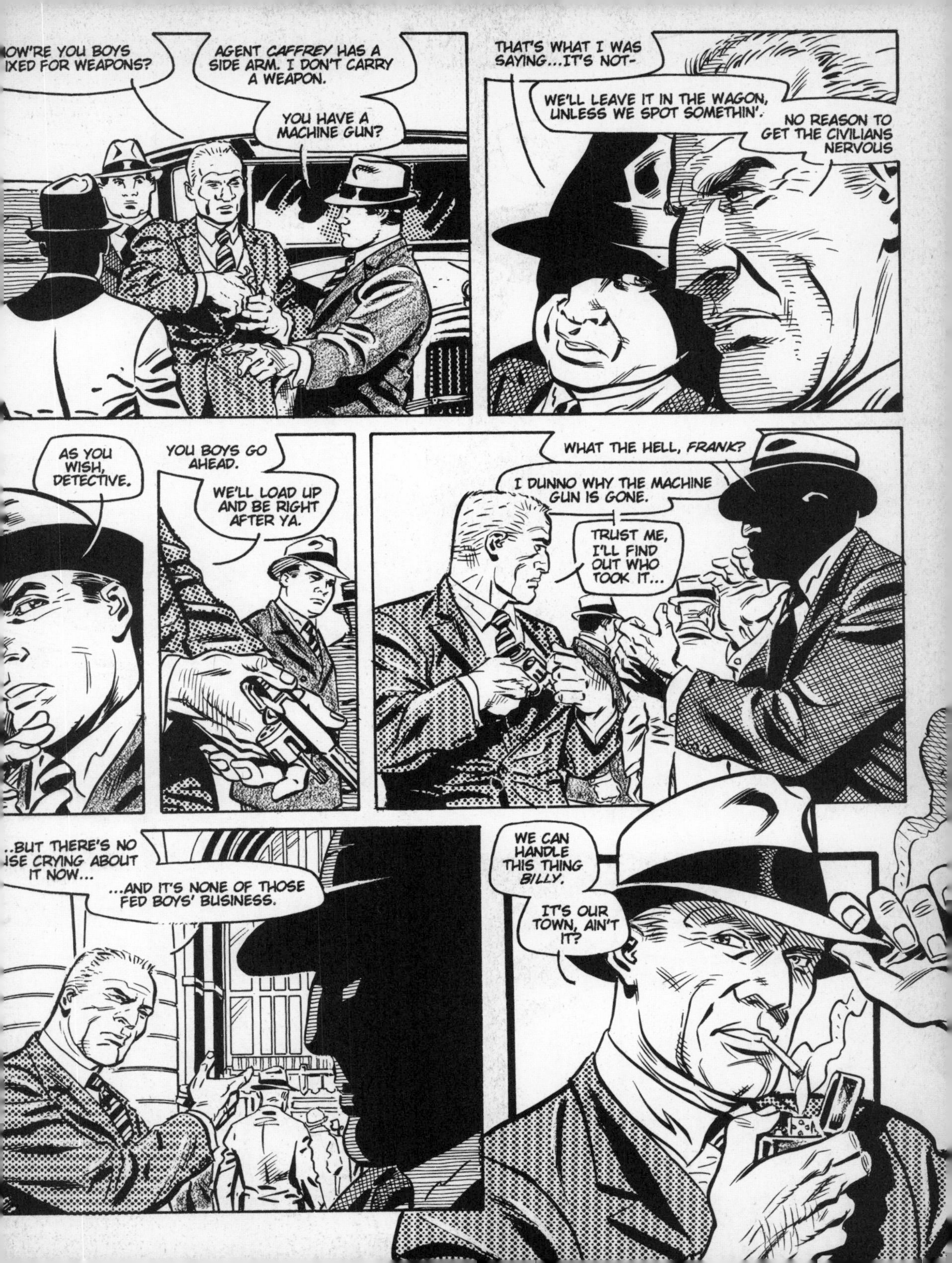

OW'RE YOU BOYS IXED FOR WEAPONS?
AGENT CAFFREY HAS A SIDE ARM. I DON'T CARRY A WEAPON.
YOU HAVE A MACHINE GUN?
THAT'S WHAT I WAS SAYING...IT'S NOT-
WE'LL LEAVE IT IN THE WAGON, UNLESS WE SPOT SOMETHIN'.
NO REASON TO GET THE CIVILIANS NERVOUS
AS YOU WISH, DETECTIVE.
YOU BOYS GO AHEAD.
WE'LL LOAD UP AND BE RIGHT AFTER YA.
WHAT THE HELL, FRANK?
I DUNNO WHY THE MACHINE GUN IS GONE.
TRUST ME, I'LL FIND OUT WHO TOOK IT...
..BUT THERE'S NO ISE CRYING ABOUT IT NOW...
...AND IT'S NONE OF THOSE FED BOYS' BUSINESS.
WE CAN HANDLE THIS THING BILLY.
IT'S OUR TOWN, AIN'T IT?

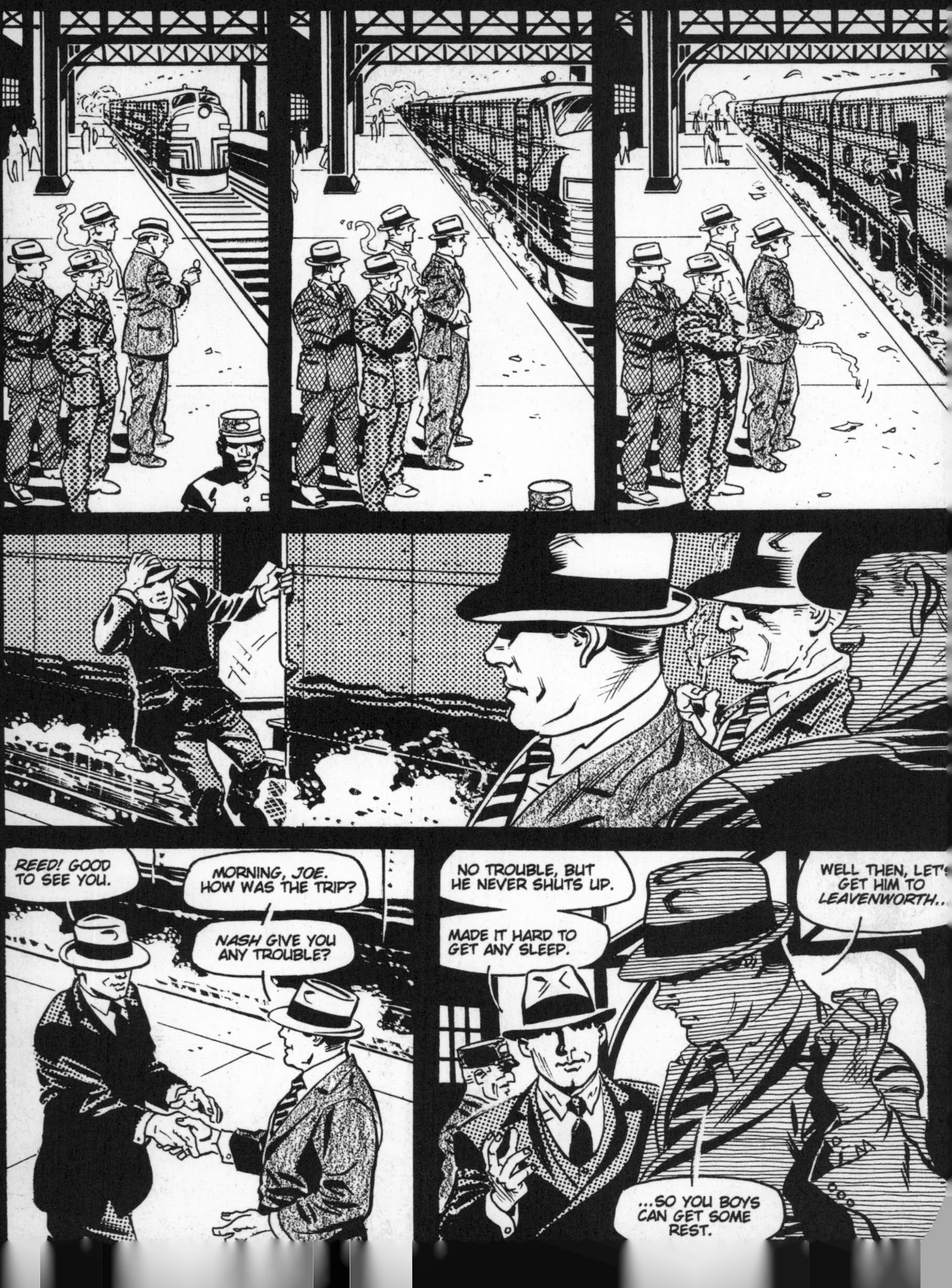

REED! GOOD TO SEE YOU.
MORNING, JOE. HOW WAS THE TRIP?
NASH GIVE YOU ANY TROUBLE?
NO TROUBLE, BUT HE NEVER SHUTS UP.
MADE IT HARD TO GET ANY SLEEP.
WELL THEN, LET'S GET HIM TO LEAVENWORTH...
...SO YOU BOYS CAN GET SOME REST.

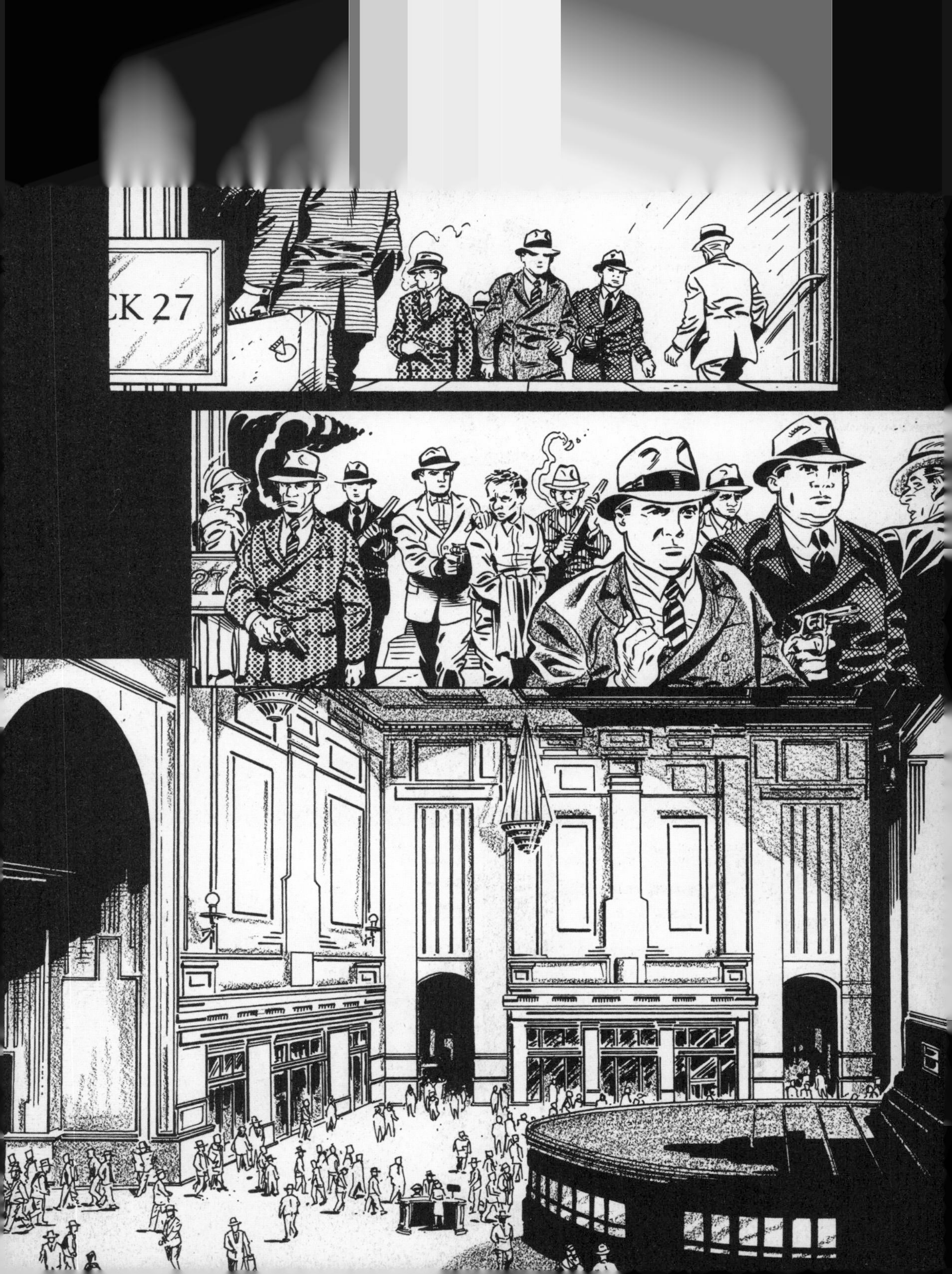

CK 27

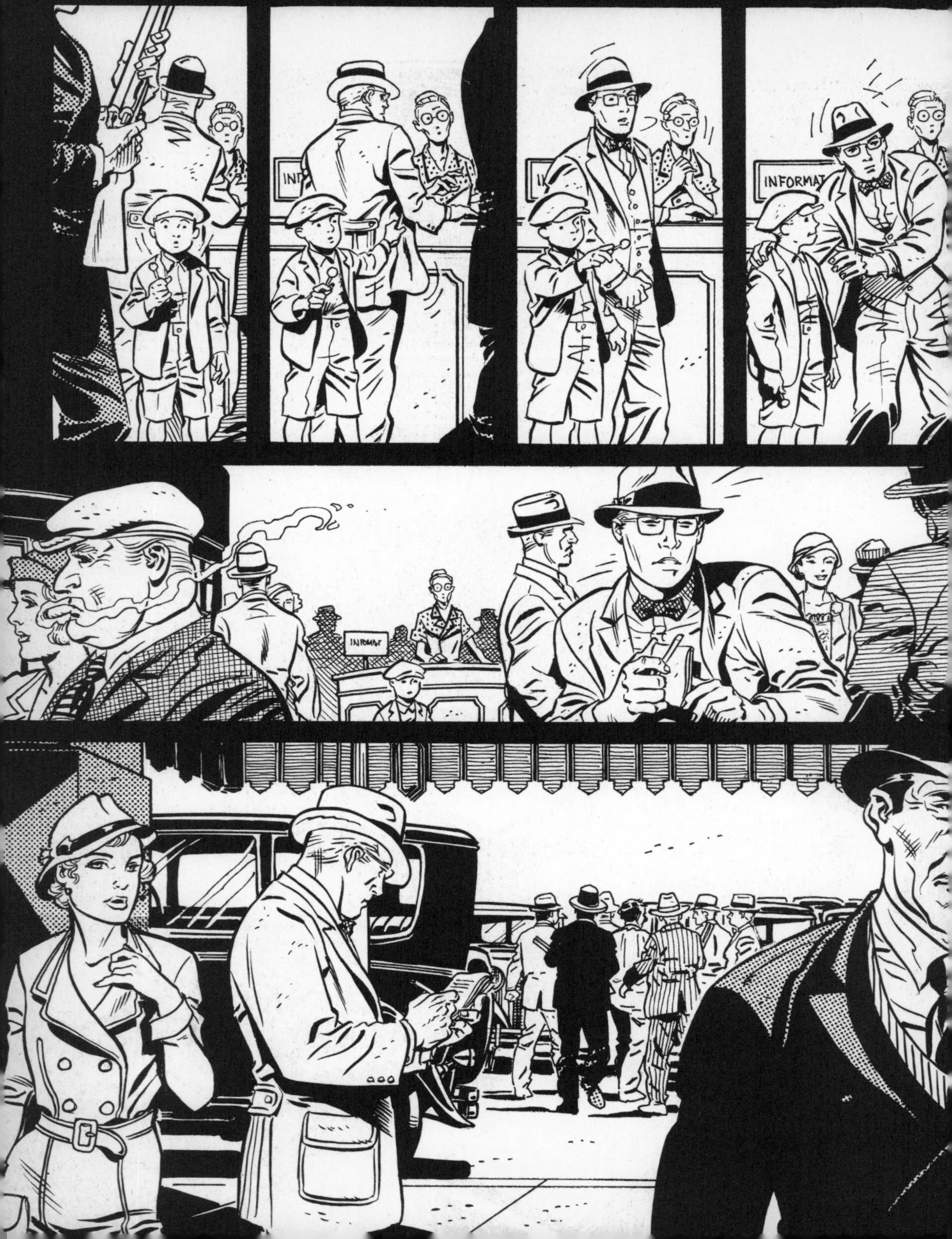
INFORMAT

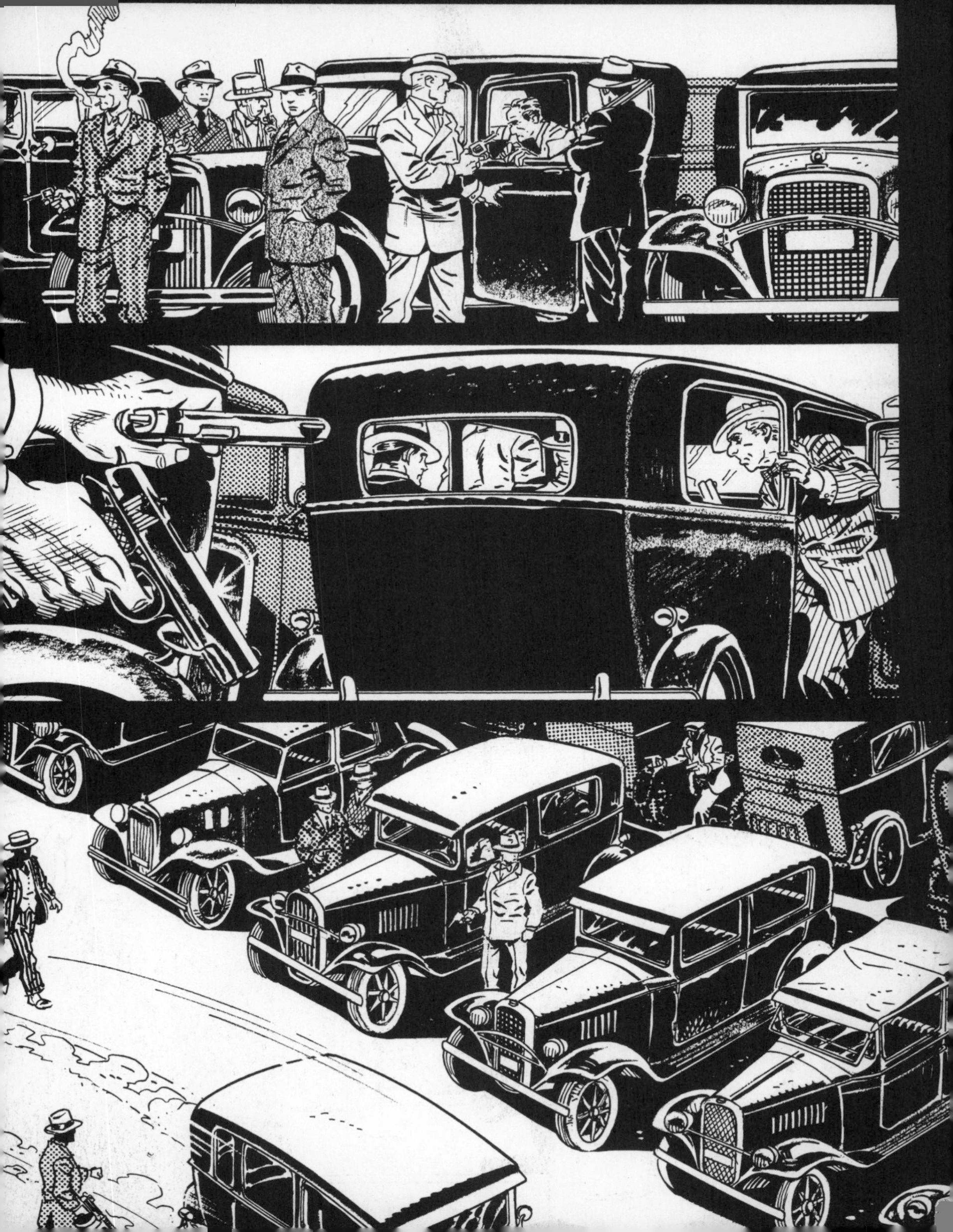

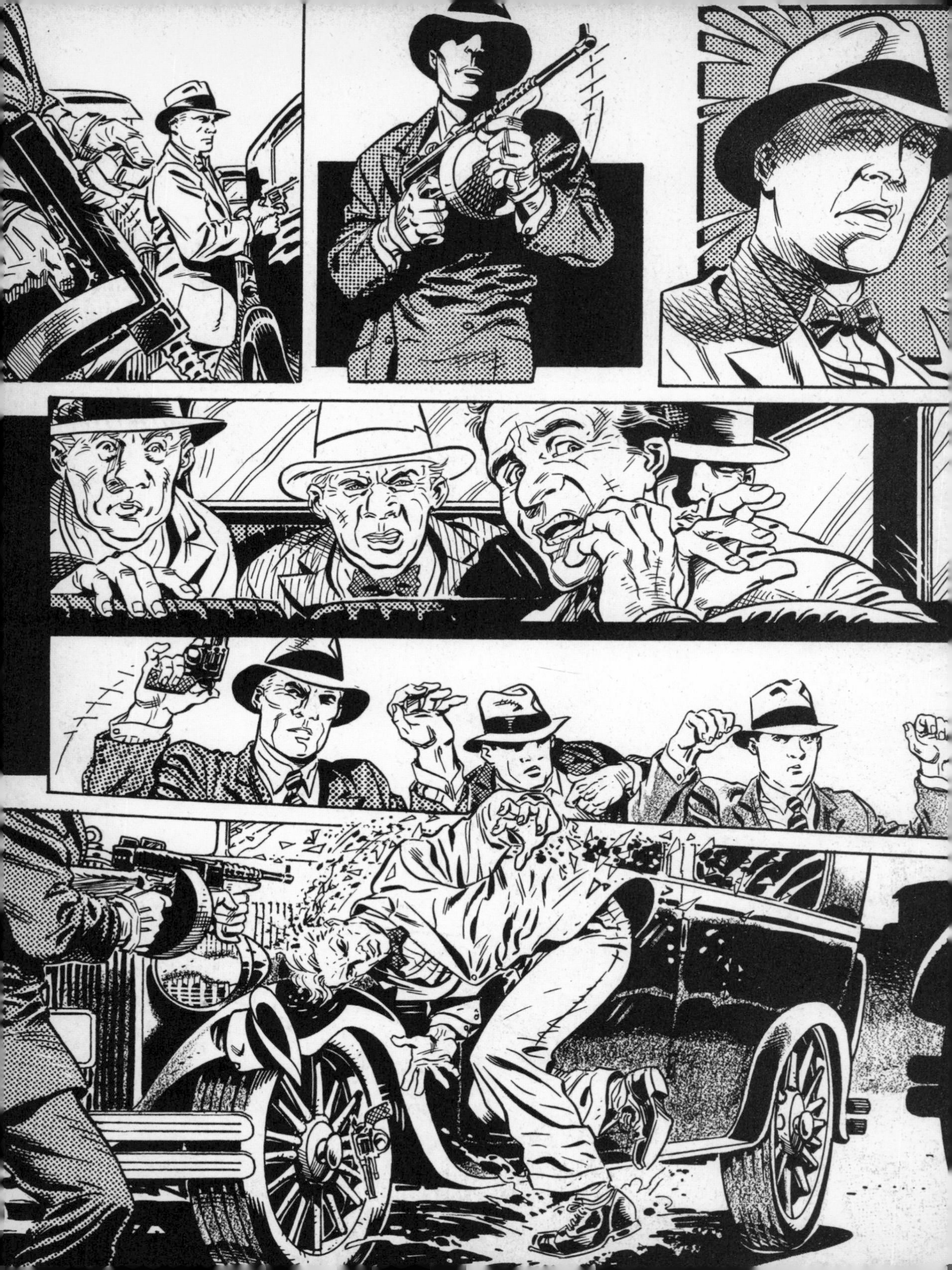

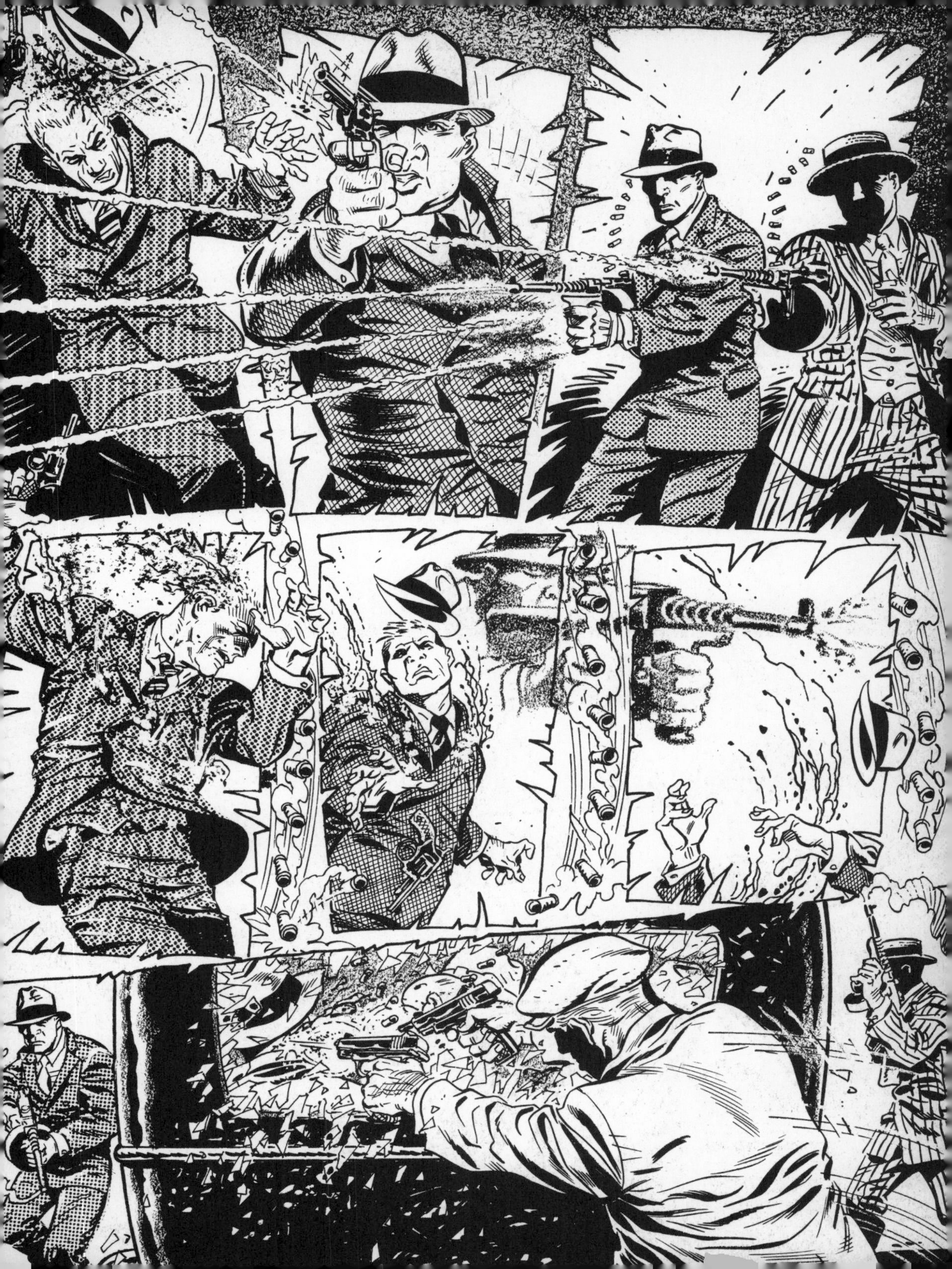

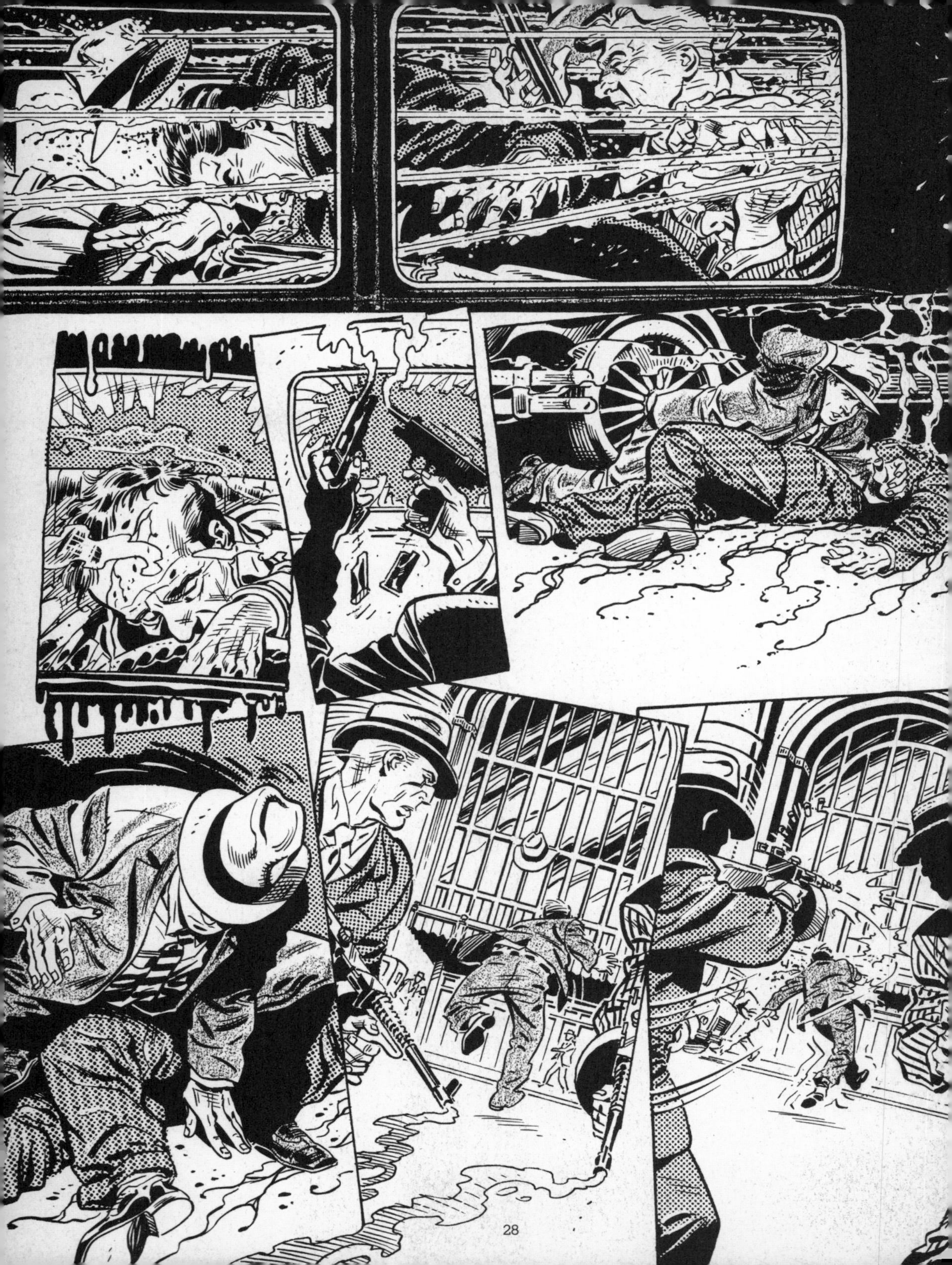

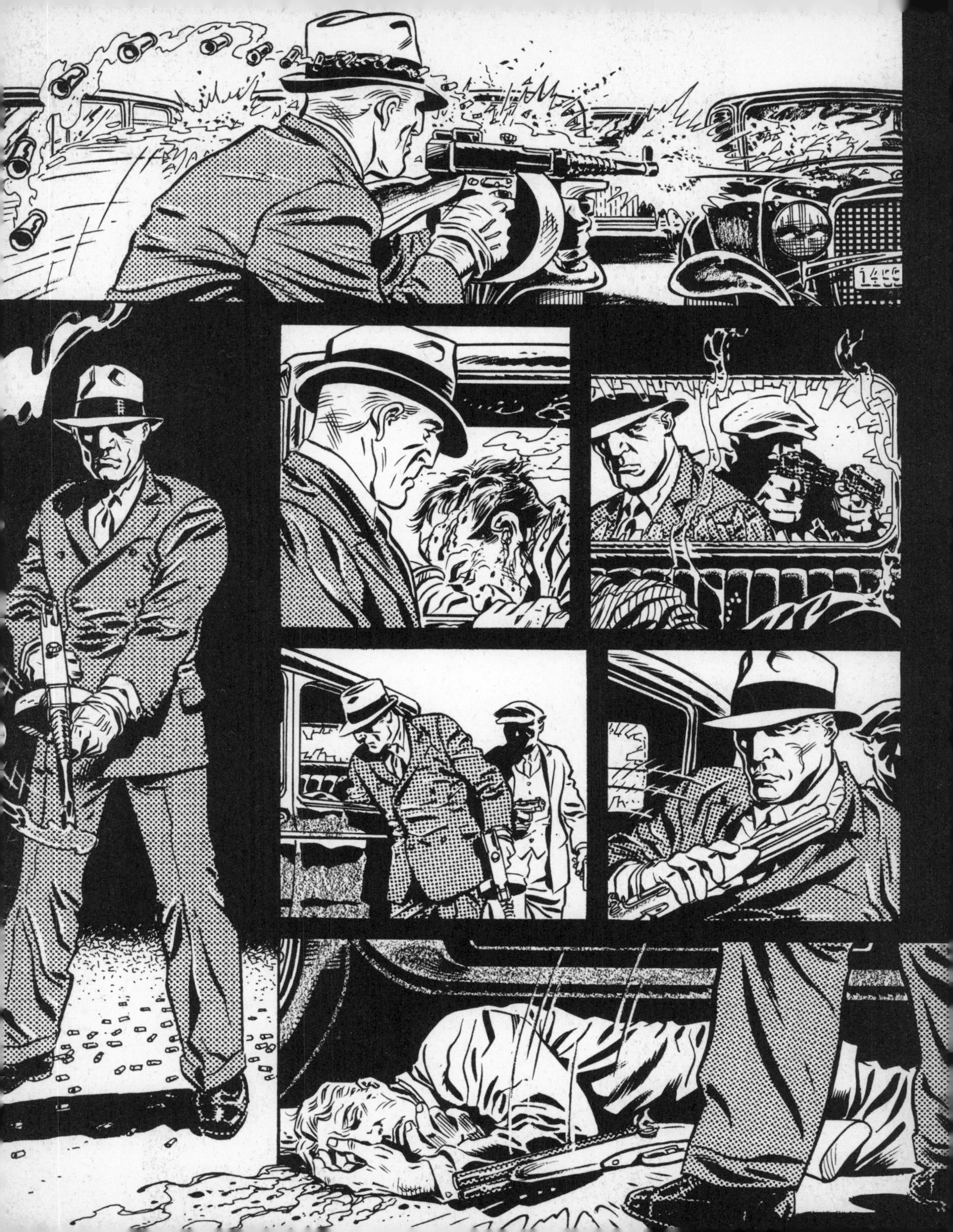

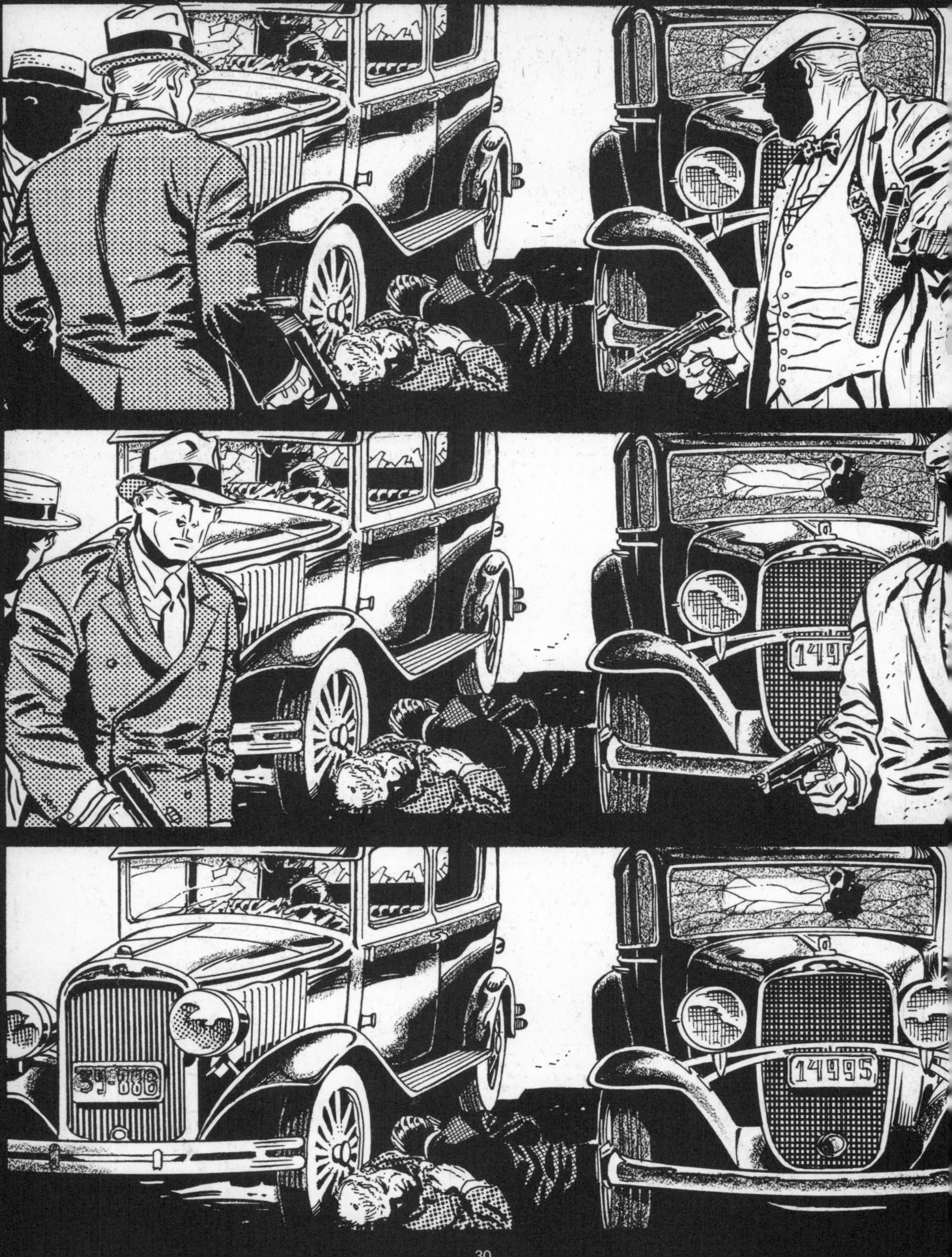
14995

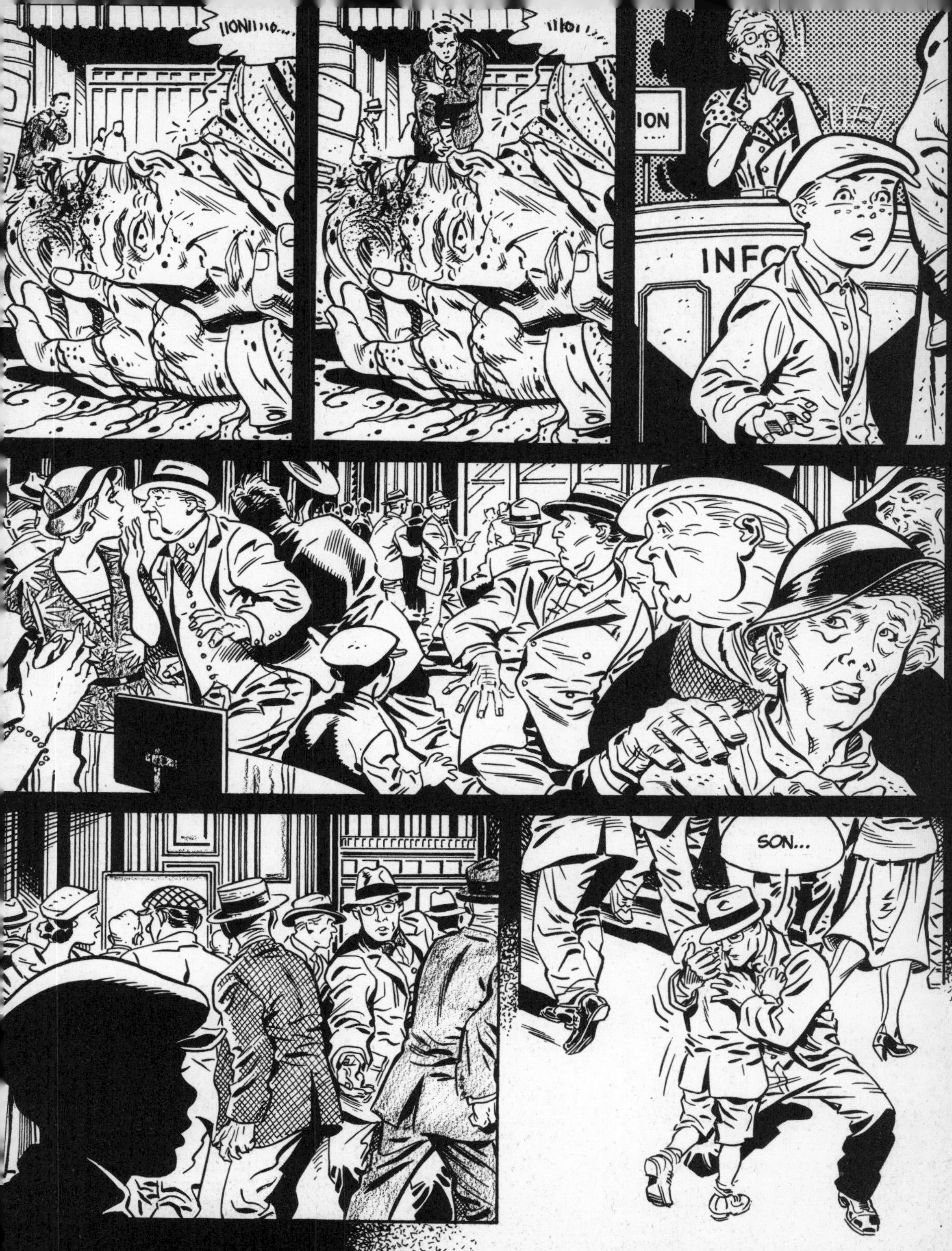
ION
INFO
SON...

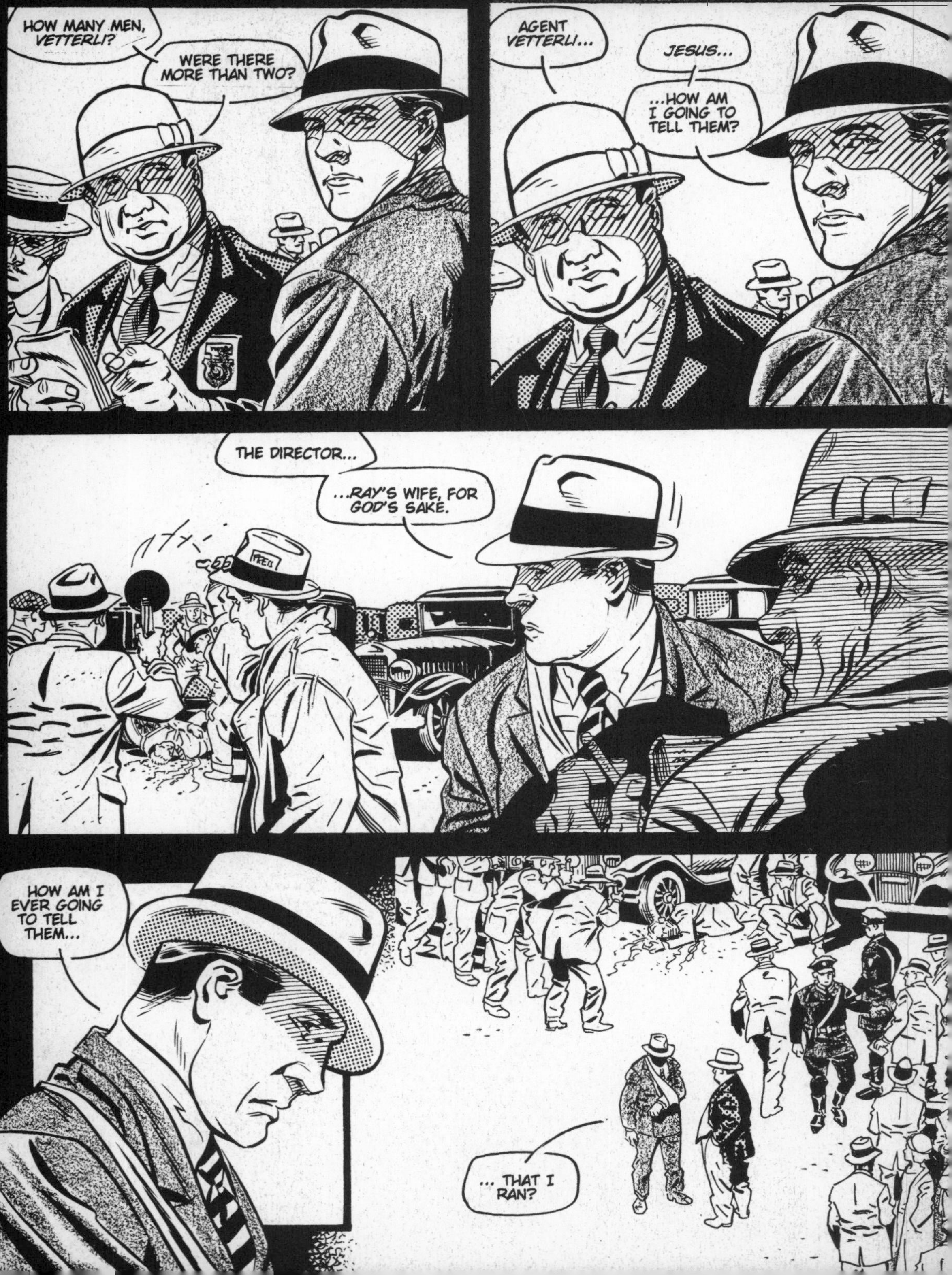
HOW MANY MEN, VETTERLI?
WERE THERE MORE THAN TWO?
AGENT VETTERLI...
JESUS...
...HOW AM I GOING TO TELL THEM?
THE DIRECTOR...
...RAY'S WIFE, FOR GOD'S SAKE.
HOW AM I EVER GOING TO TELL THEM...
... THAT I RAN?

ACT II

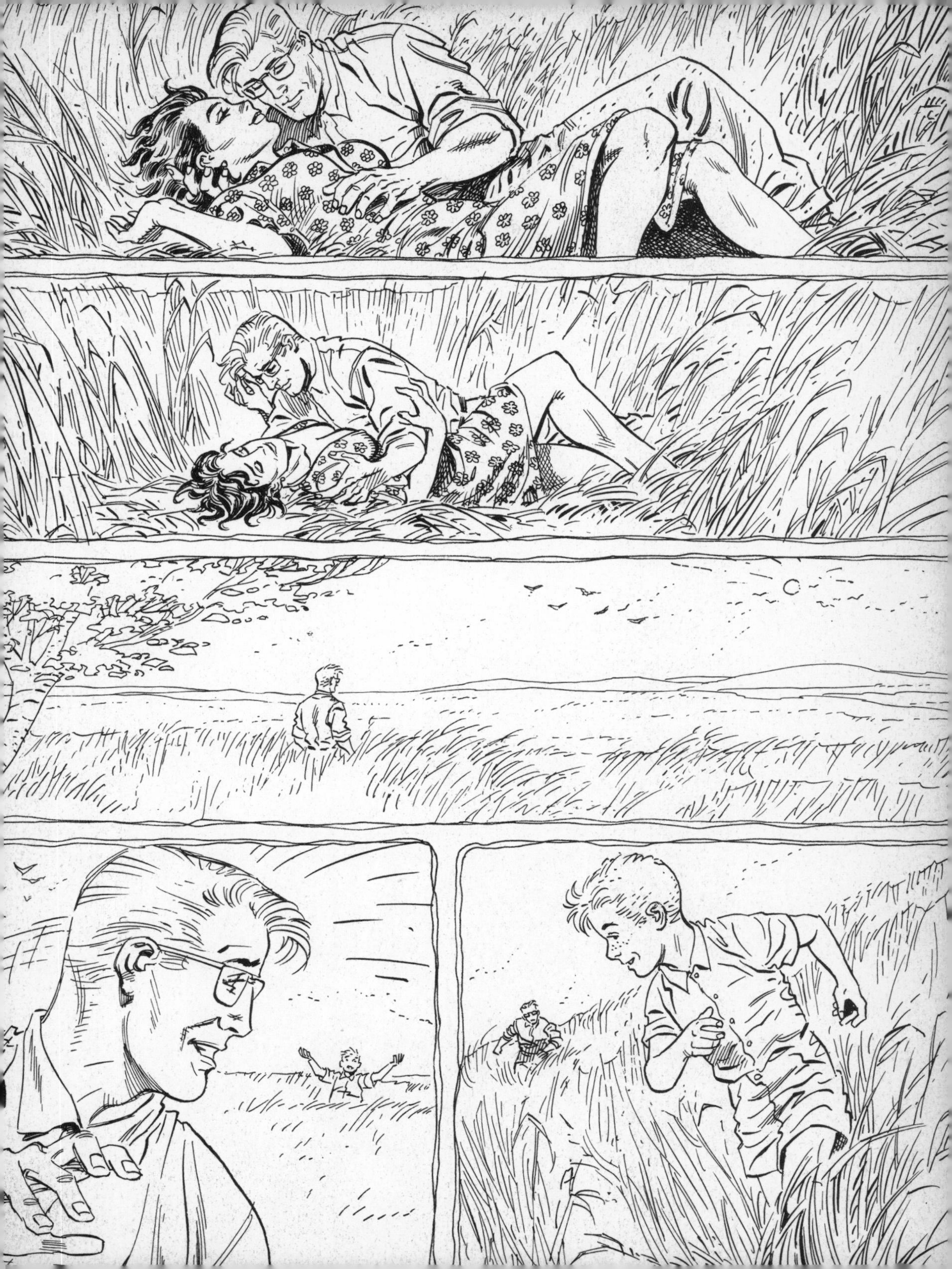

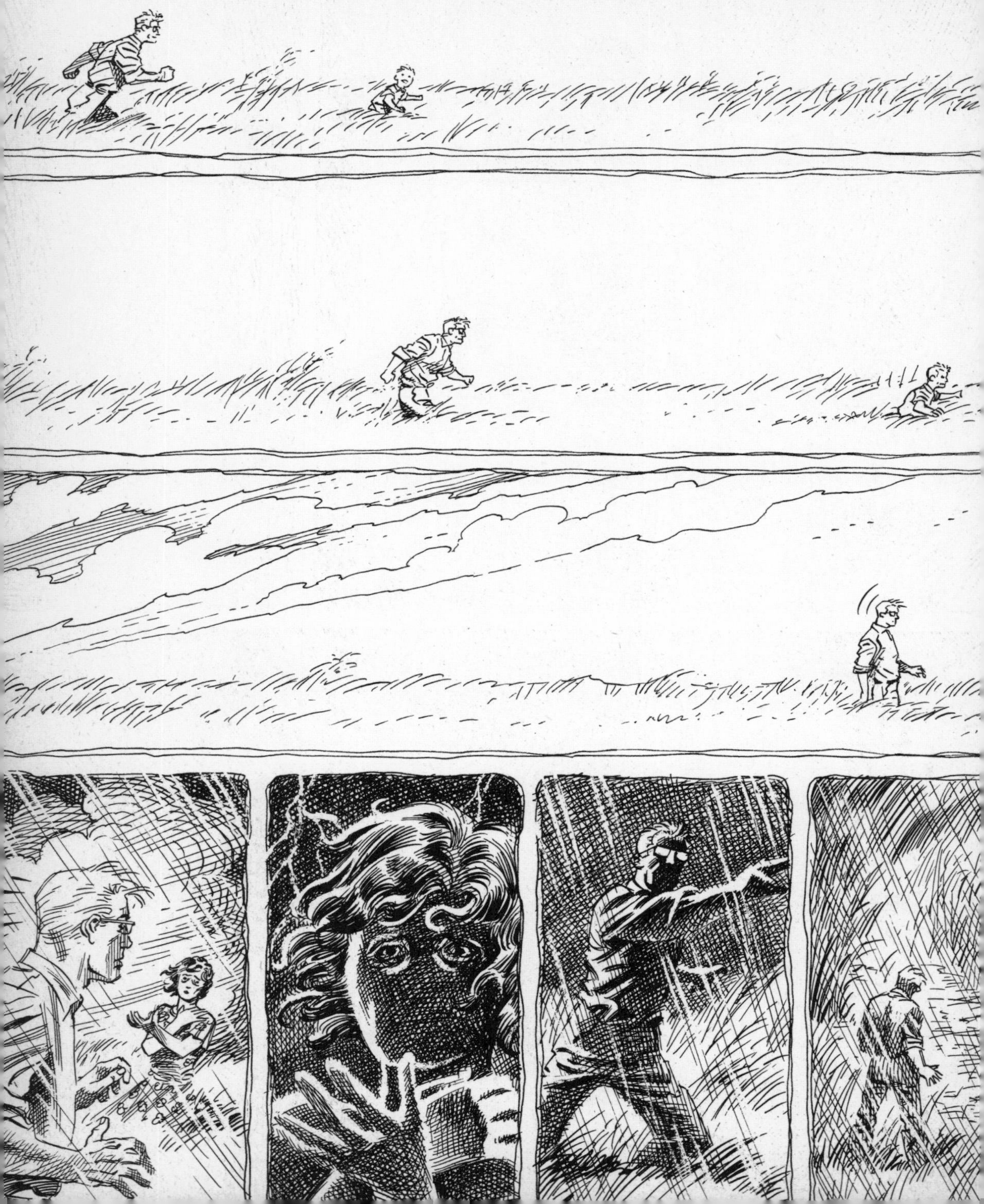

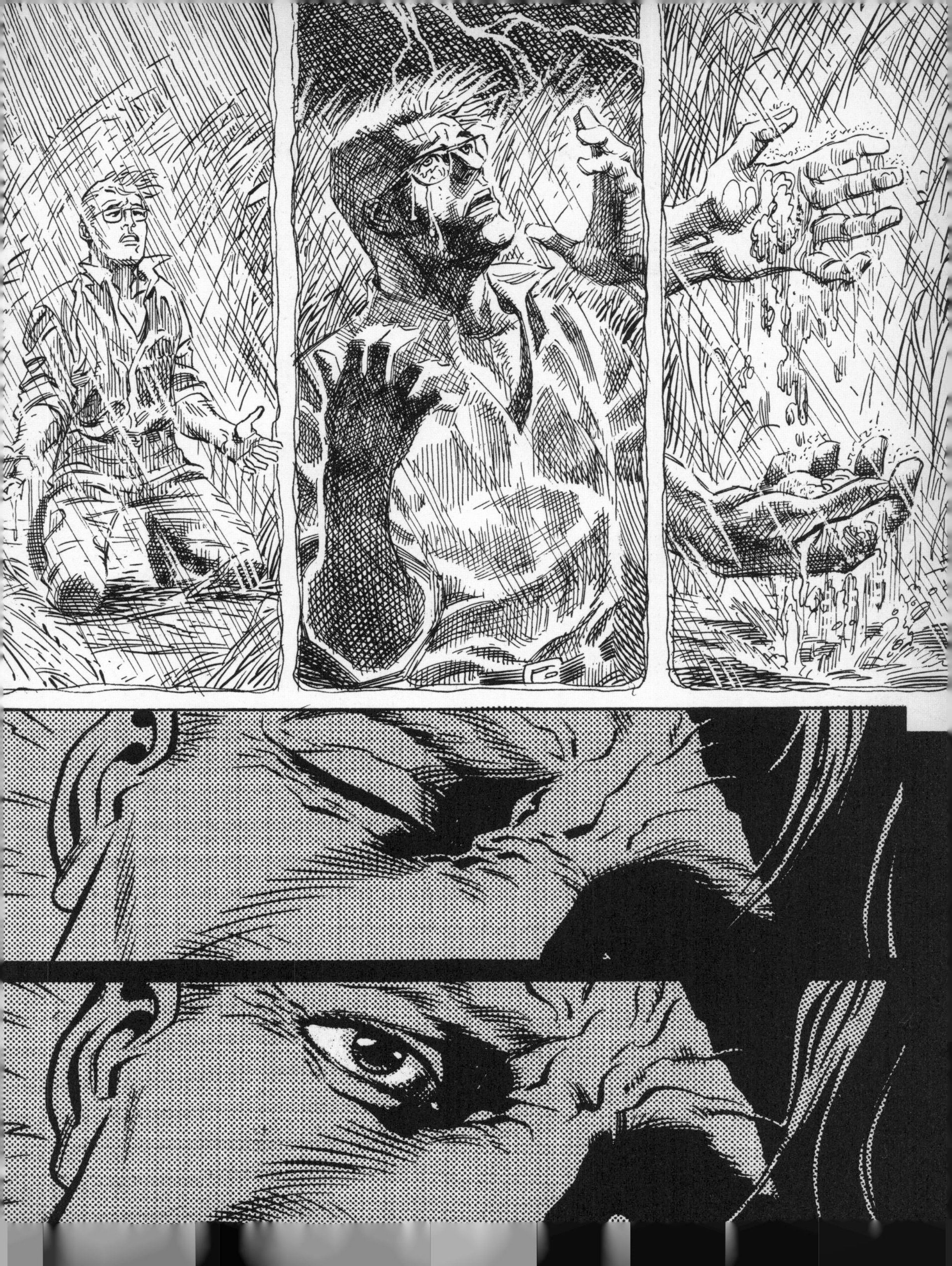

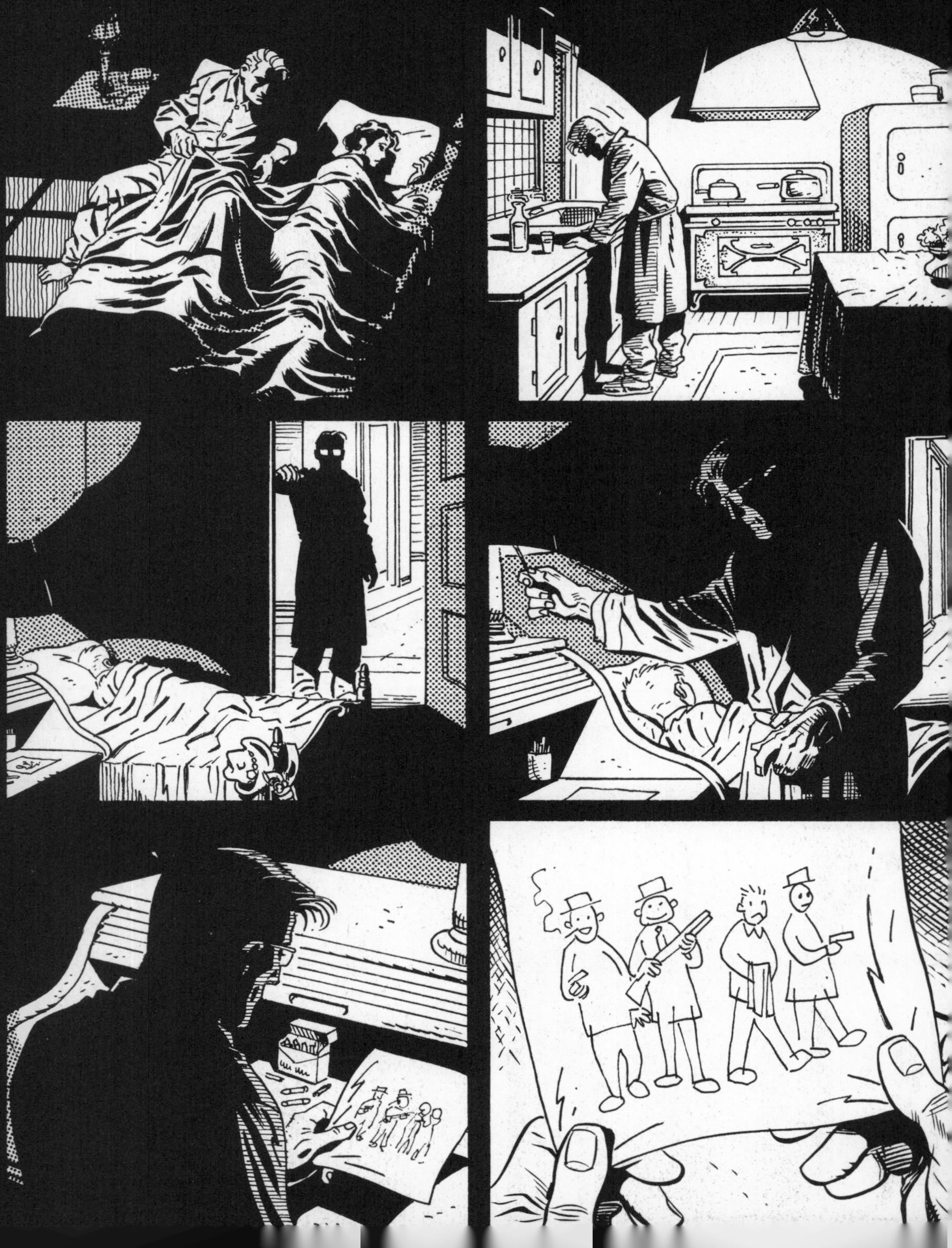

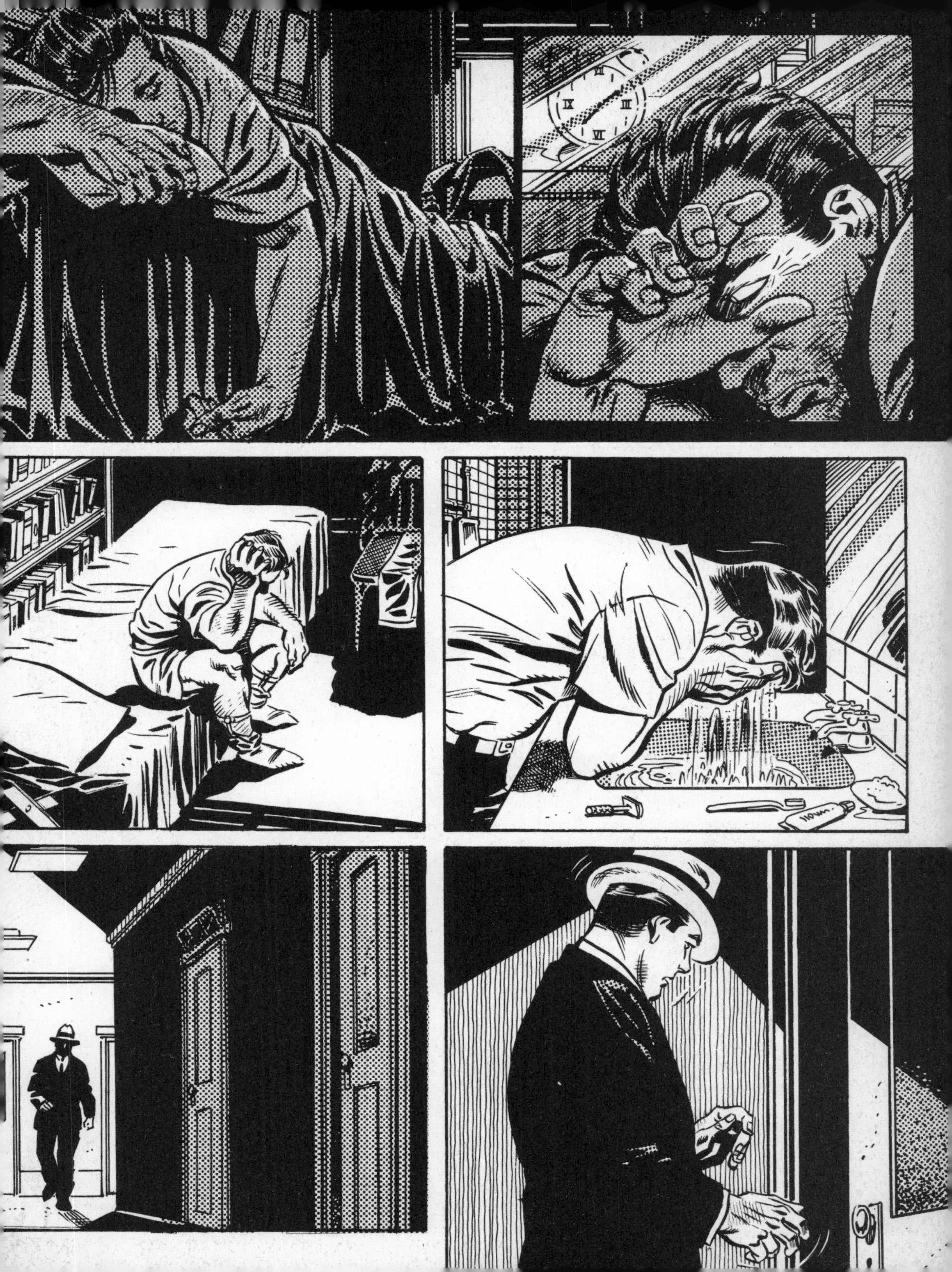

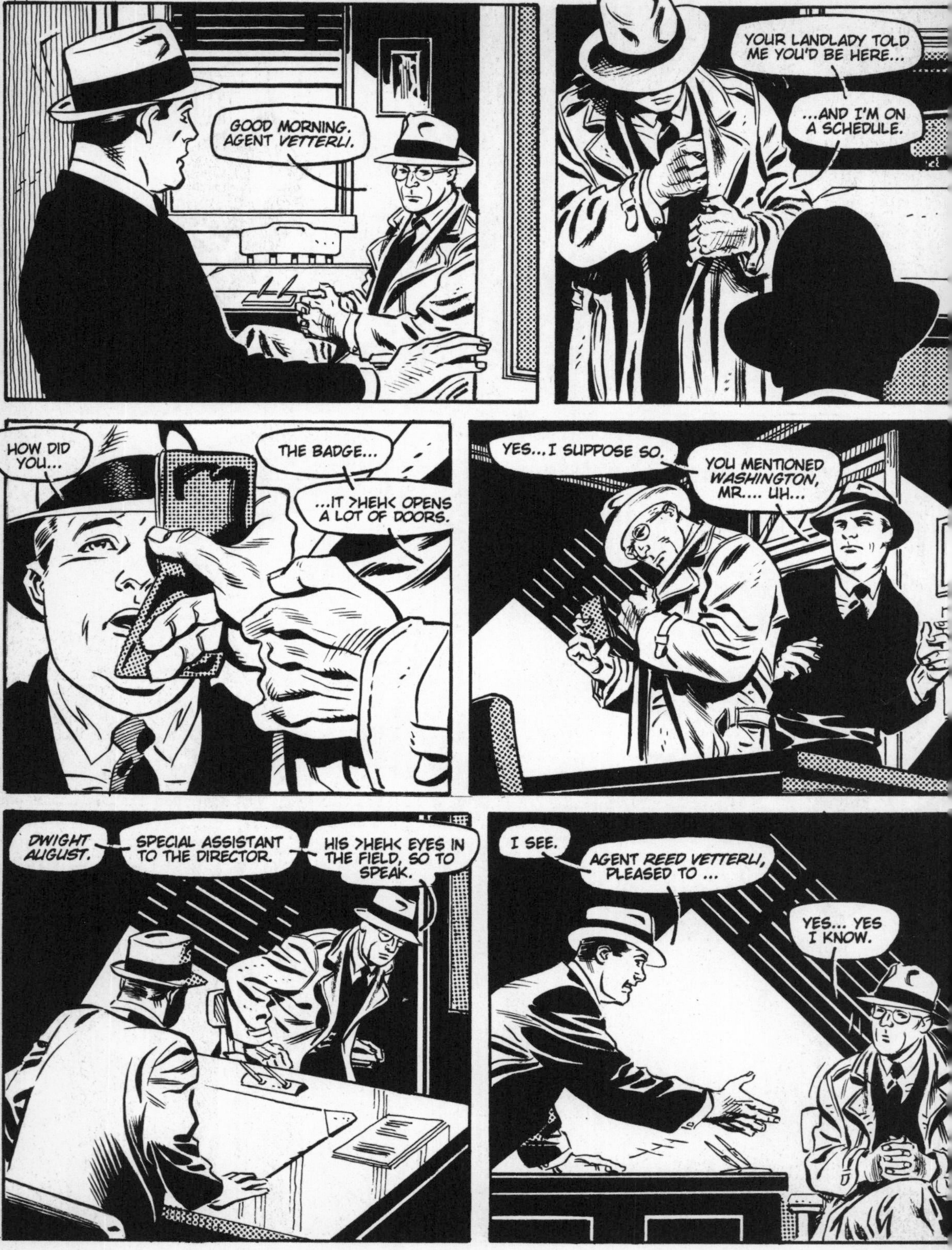
GOOD MORNING. AGENT VETTERLI.
YOUR LANDLADY TOLD ME YOU'D BE HERE...
...AND I'M ON A SCHEDULE.
HOW DID YOU...
THE BADGE...
...IT >HEH< OPENS A LOT OF DOORS.
YES...I SUPPOSE SO.
YOU MENTIONED WASHINGTON, MR.... UH...
DWIGHT AUGUST.
SPECIAL ASSISTANT TO THE DIRECTOR.
HIS >HEH< EYES IN THE FIELD, SO TO SPEAK.
I SEE.
AGENT REED VETTERLI, PLEASED TO ...
YES... YES I KNOW.

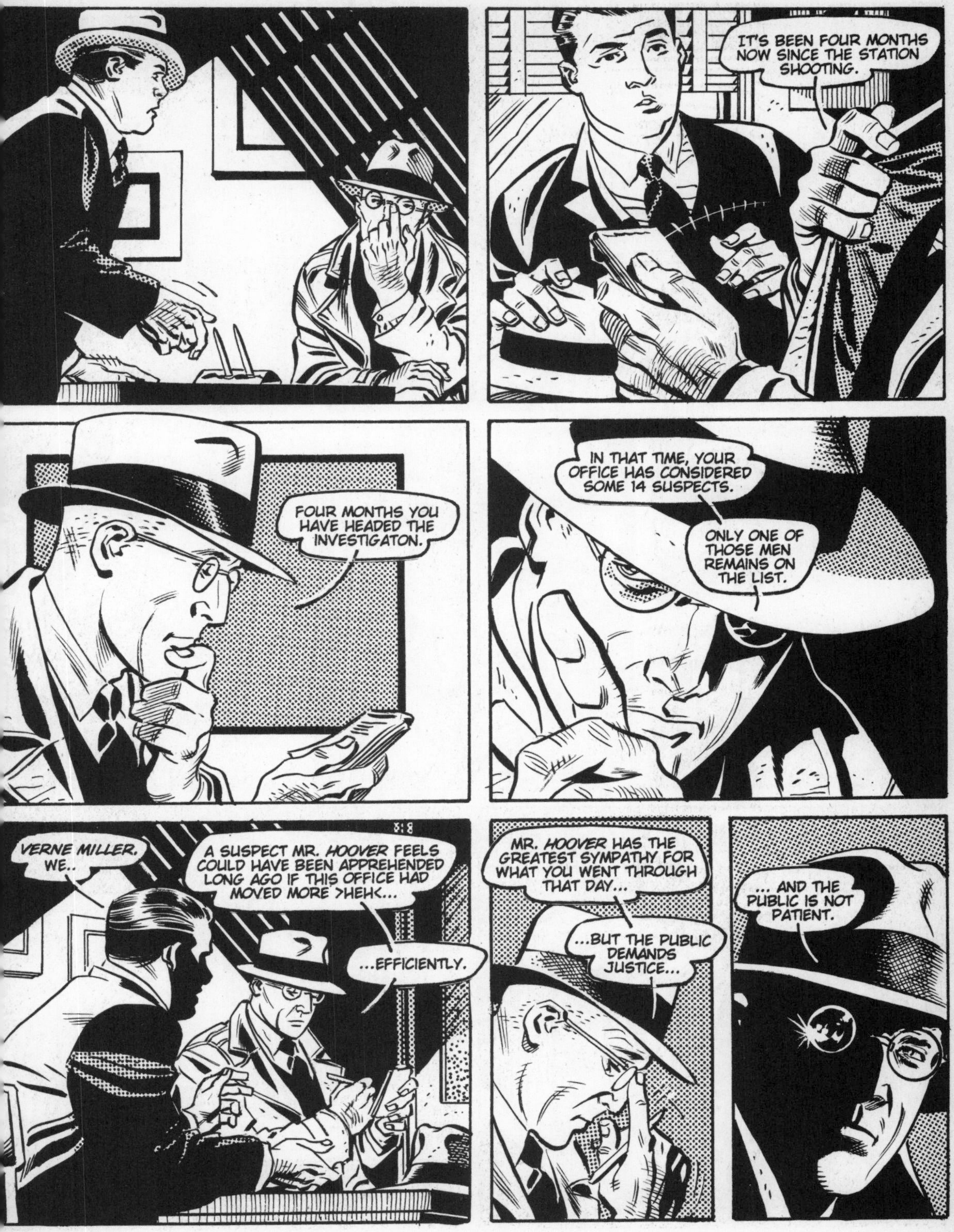
IT'S BEEN FOUR MONTHS NOW SINCE THE STATION SHOOTING.
FOUR MONTHS YOU HAVE HEADED THE INVESTIGATON.
IN THAT TIME, YOUR OFFICE HAS CONSIDERED SOME 14 SUSPECTS.
ONLY ONE OF THOSE MEN REMAINS ON THE LIST.
VERNE MILLER. WE..
A SUSPECT MR. HOOVER FEELS COULD HAVE BEEN APPREHENDED LONG AGO IF THIS OFFICE HAD MOVED MORE >HEH<...
...EFFICIENTLY.
MR. HOOVER HAS THE GREATEST SYMPATHY FOR WHAT YOU WENT THROUGH THAT DAY...
...BUT THE PUBLIC DEMANDS JUSTICE...
... AND THE PUBLIC IS NOT PATIENT.

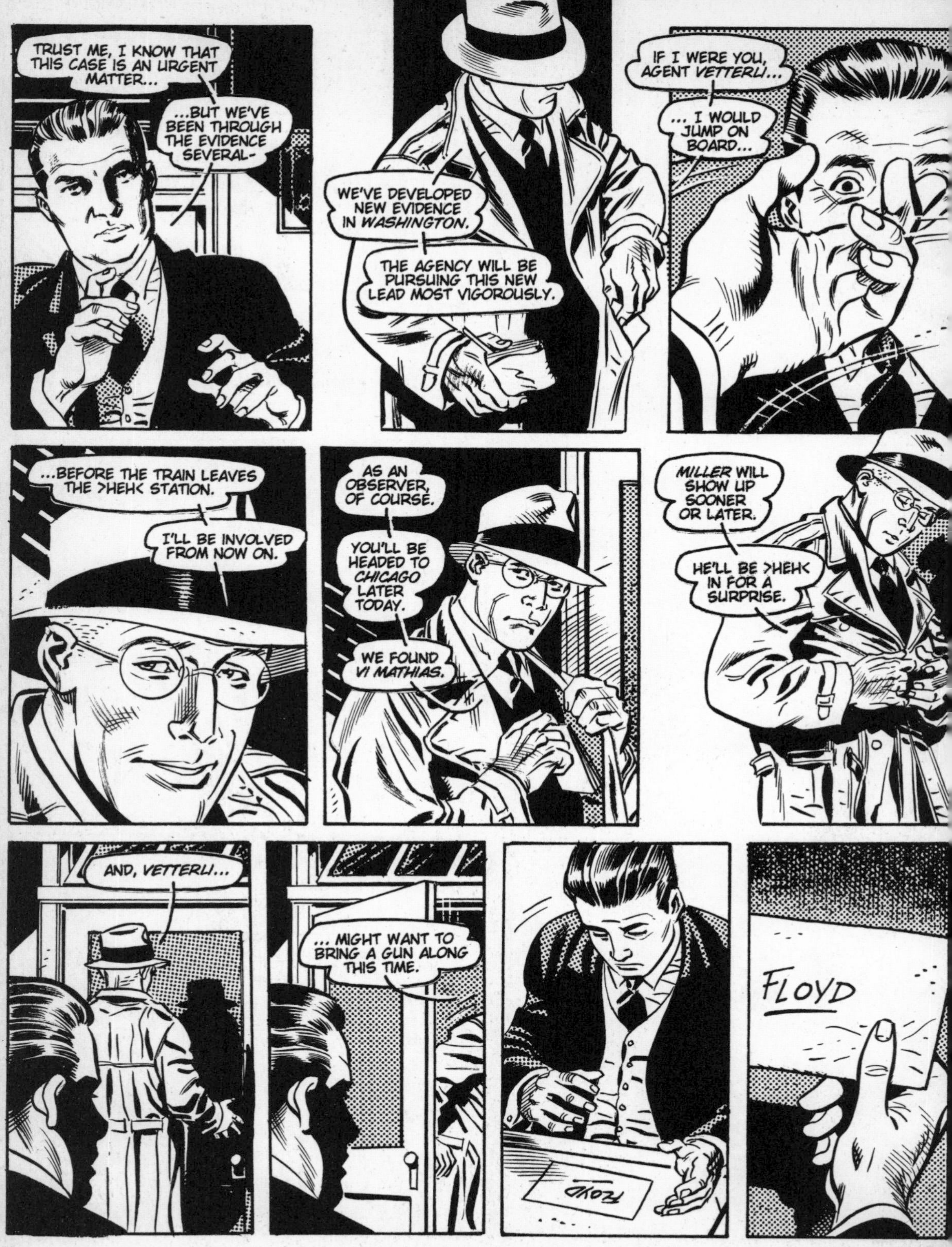
TRUST ME, I KNOW THAT THIS CASE IS AN URGENT MATTER...
...BUT WE'VE BEEN THROUGH THE EVIDENCE SEVERAL-
WE'VE DEVELOPED NEW EVIDENCE IN WASHINGTON.
THE AGENCY WILL BE PURSUING THIS NEW LEAD MOST VIGOROUSLY.
IF I WERE YOU, AGENT VETTERLI...
... I WOULD JUMP ON BOARD...
...BEFORE THE TRAIN LEAVES THE >HEH< STATION.
I'LL BE INVOLVED FROM NOW ON.
AS AN OBSERVER, OF COURSE.
YOU'LL BE HEADED TO CHICAGO LATER TODAY.
WE FOUND VI MATHIAS.
MILLER WILL SHOW UP SOONER OR LATER.
HE'LL BE >HEH< IN FOR A SURPRISE.
AND, VETTERLI...
... MIGHT WANT TO BRING A GUN ALONG THIS TIME.
FLOYD
FLOYD

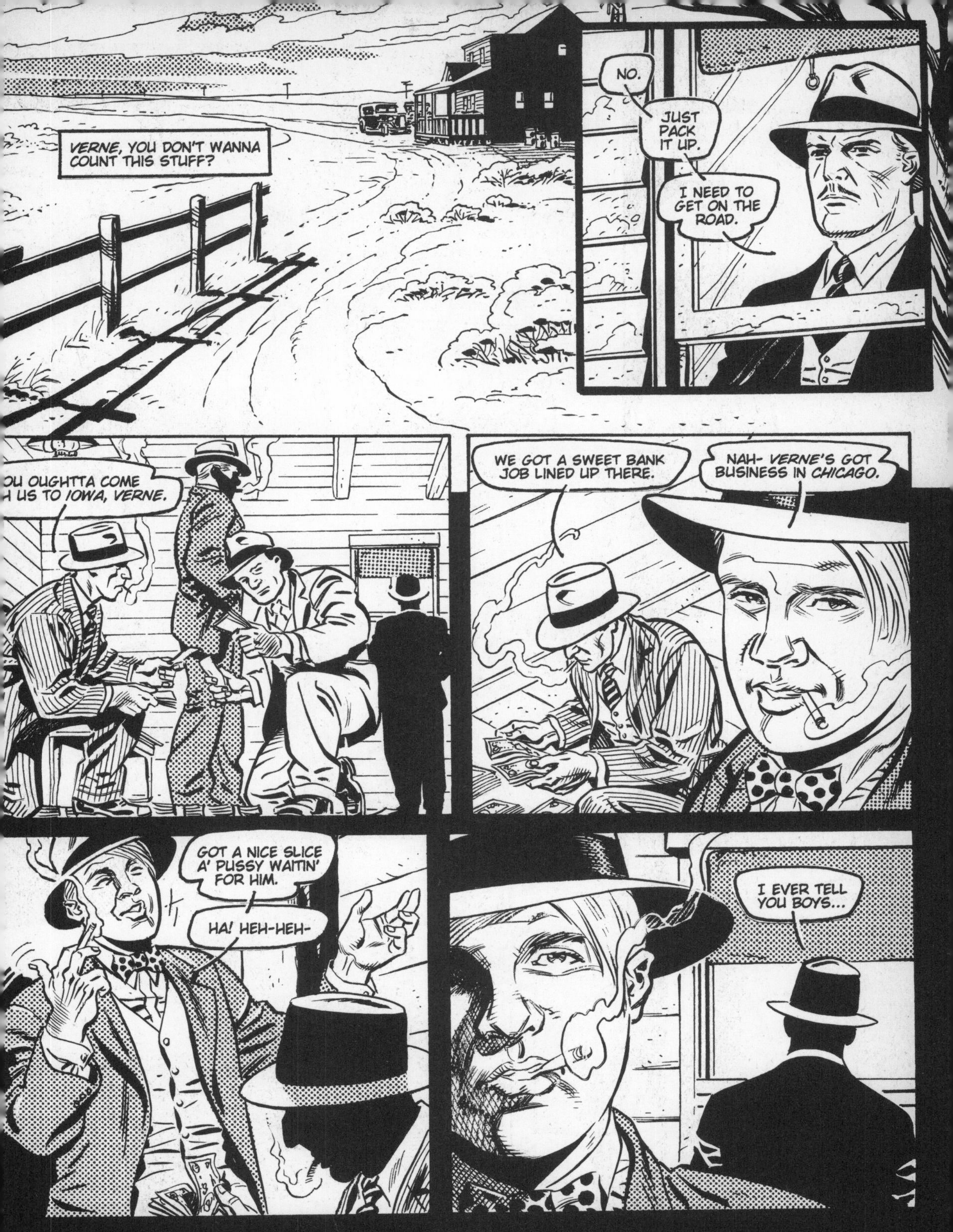
VERNE, YOU DON'T WANNA COUNT THIS STUFF?
NO.
JUST PACK IT UP.
I NEED TO GET ON THE ROAD.
OU OUGHTTA COME H US TO IOWA, VERNE.
WE GOT A SWEET BANK JOB LINED UP THERE.
NAH- VERNE'S GOT BUSINESS IN CHICAGO.
GOT A NICE SLICE A' PUSSY WAITIN' FOR HIM.
HA! HEH-HEH-
I EVER TELL YOU BOYS...

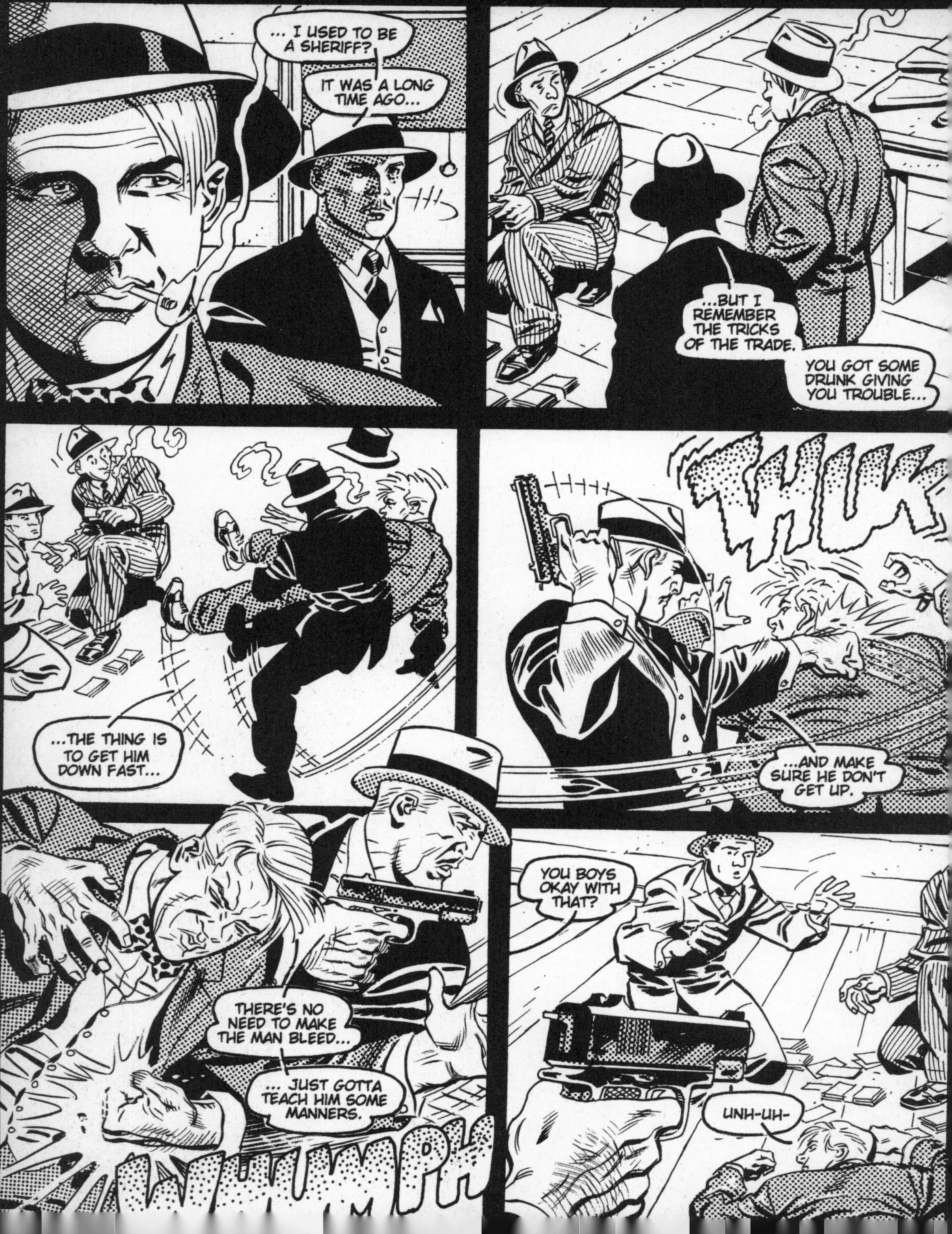

... I USED TO BE A SHERIFF?
IT WAS A LONG TIME AGO...
...BUT I REMEMBER THE TRICKS OF THE TRADE.
YOU GOT SOME DRUNK GIVING YOU TROUBLE...
...THE THING IS TO GET HIM DOWN FAST...
...AND MAKE SURE HE DON'T GET UP.
THERE'S NO NEED TO MAKE THE MAN BLEED...
... JUST GOTTA TEACH HIM SOME MANNERS.
YOU BOYS OKAY WITH THAT?
UNH-UH-

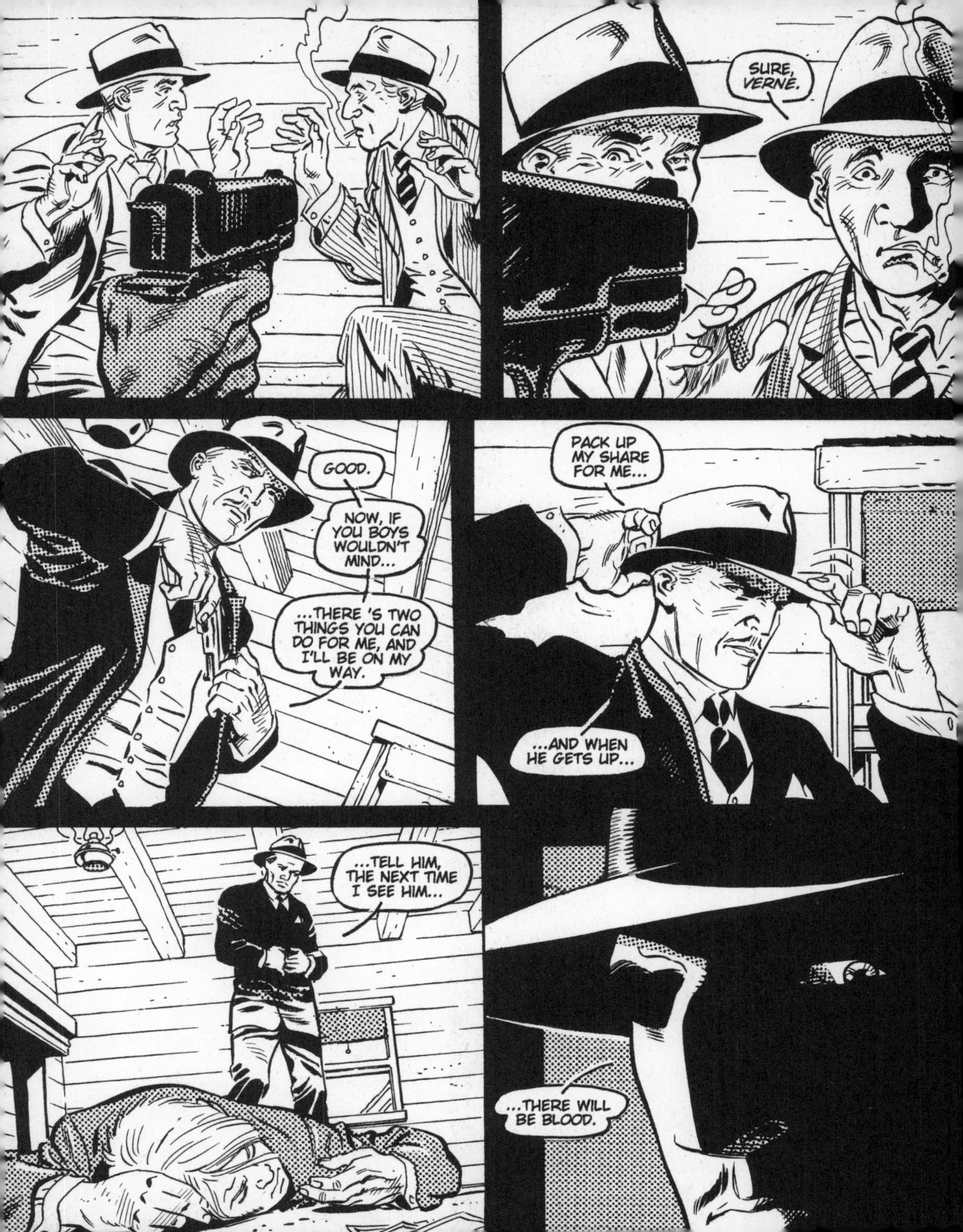

SURE, VERNE.
GOOD.
NOW, IF YOU BOYS WOULDN'T MIND...
...THERE'S TWO THINGS YOU CAN DO FOR ME, AND I'LL BE ON MY WAY.
PACK UP MY SHARE FOR ME...
...AND WHEN HE GETS UP...
...TELL HIM, THE NEXT TIME I SEE HIM...
...THERE WILL BE BLOOD.

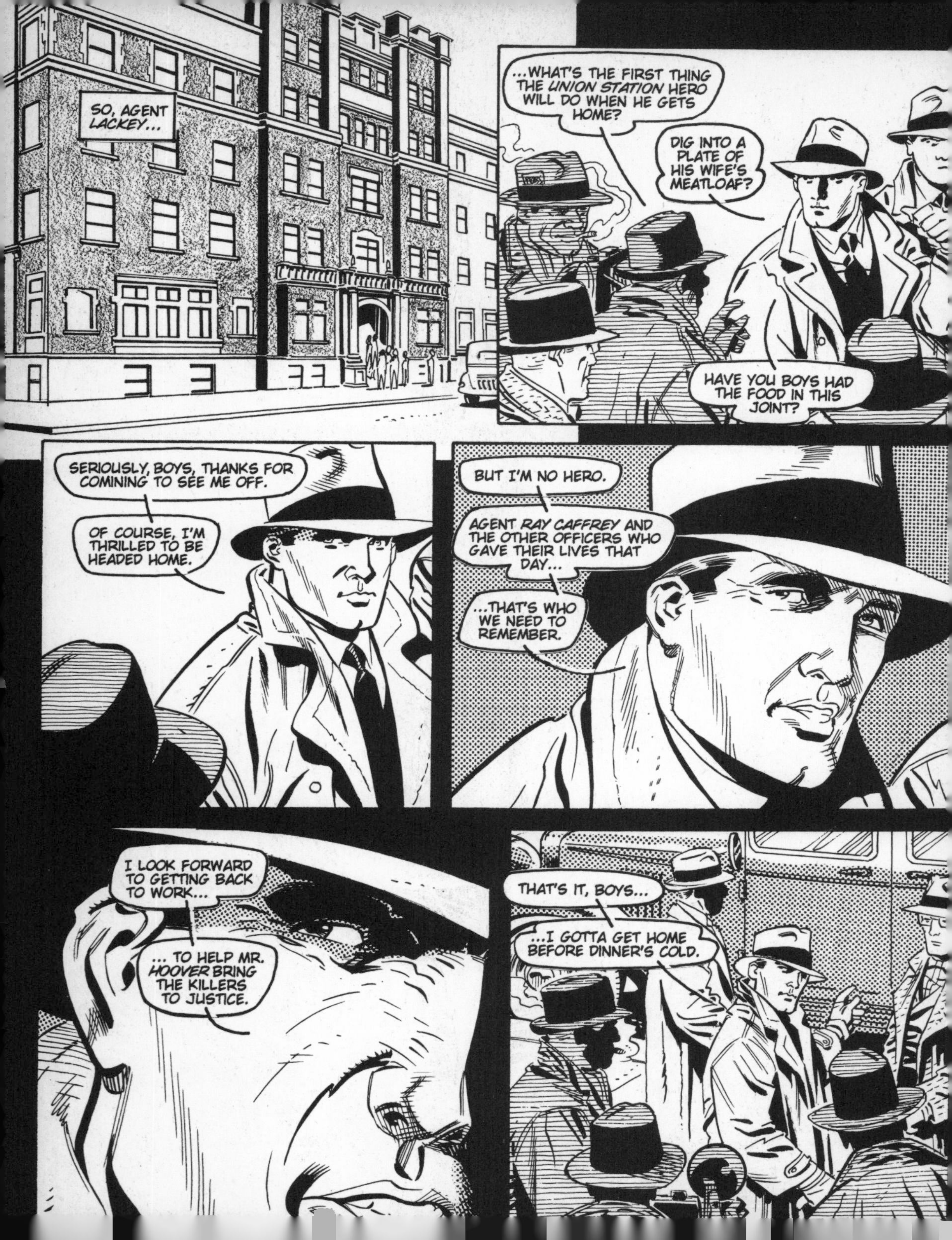
SO, AGENT LACKEY...
...WHAT'S THE FIRST THING THE UNION STATION HERO WILL DO WHEN HE GETS HOME?
DIG INTO A PLATE OF HIS WIFE'S MEATLOAF?
HAVE YOU BOYS HAD THE FOOD IN THIS JOINT?
SERIOUSLY, BOYS, THANKS FOR COMINING TO SEE ME OFF.
OF COURSE, I'M THRILLED TO BE HEADED HOME.
BUT I'M NO HERO.
AGENT RAY CAFFREY AND THE OTHER OFFICERS WHO GAVE THEIR LIVES THAT DAY...
...THAT'S WHO WE NEED TO REMEMBER.
I LOOK FORWARD TO GETTING BACK TO WORK...
... TO HELP MR. HOOVER BRING THE KILLERS TO JUSTICE.
THAT'S IT, BOYS...
...I GOTTA GET HOME BEFORE DINNER'S COLD.

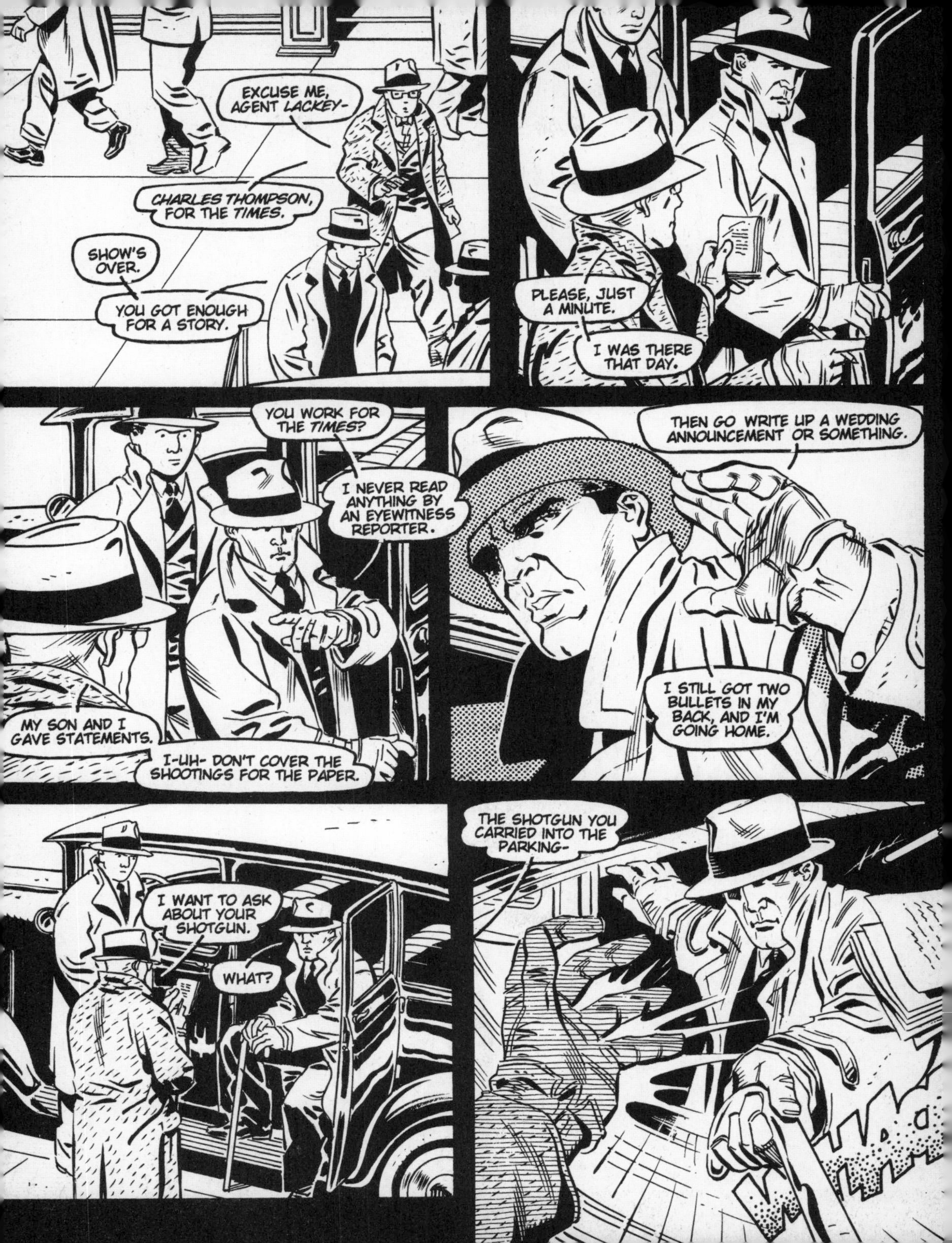
EXCUSE ME, AGENT LACKEY-
CHARLES THOMPSON, FOR THE TIMES.
SHOW'S OVER.
YOU GOT ENOUGH FOR A STORY.
PLEASE, JUST A MINUTE.
I WAS THERE THAT DAY.
YOU WORK FOR THE TIMES?
I NEVER READ ANYTHING BY AN EYEWITNESS REPORTER.
MY SON AND I GAVE STATEMENTS.
I-UH- DON'T COVER THE SHOOTINGS FOR THE PAPER.
THEN GO WRITE UP A WEDDING ANNOUNCEMENT OR SOMETHING.
I STILL GOT TWO BULLETS IN MY BACK, AND I'M GOING HOME.
I WANT TO ASK ABOUT YOUR SHOTGUN.
WHAT?
THE SHOTGUN YOU CARRIED INTO THE PARKING-

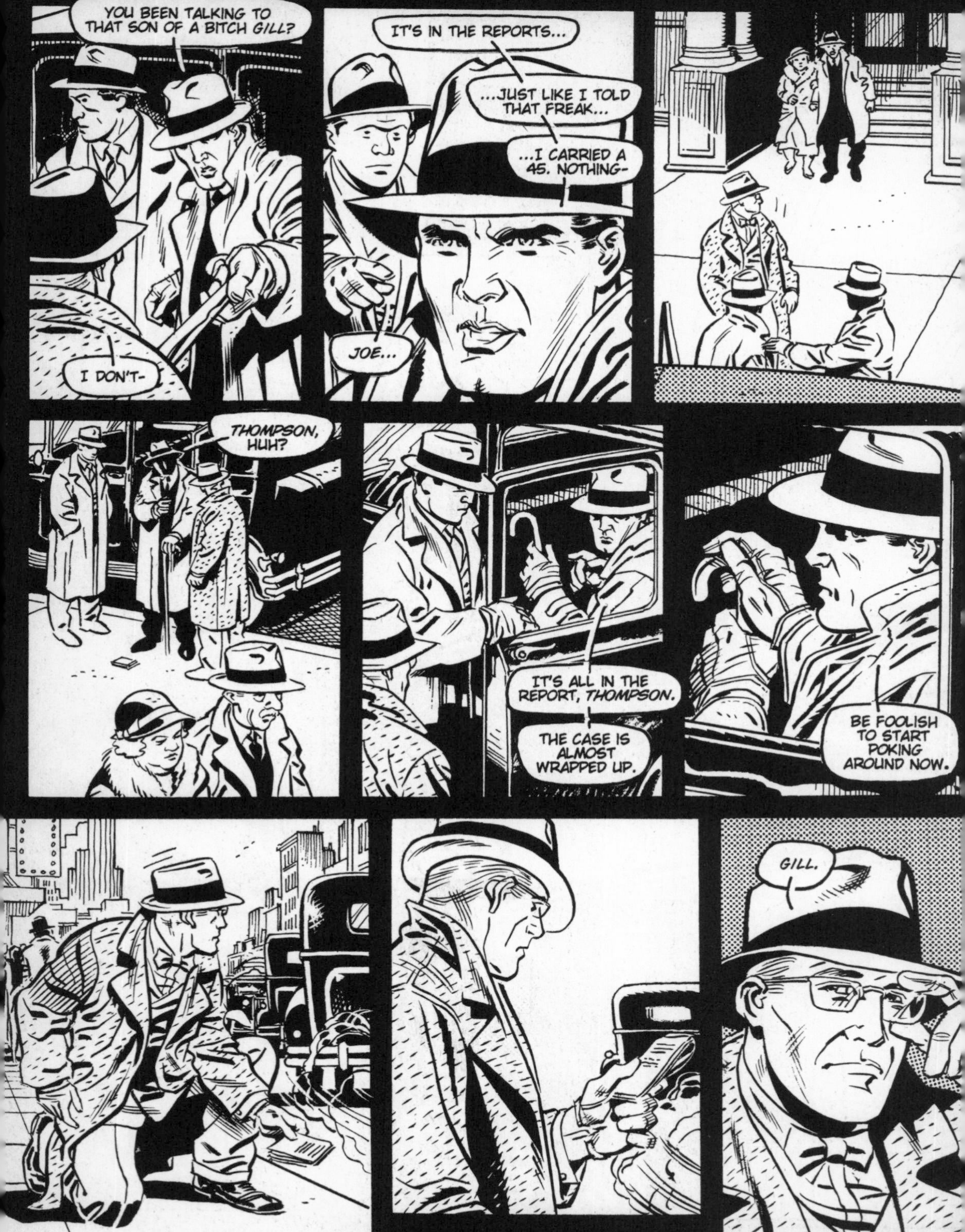
YOU BEEN TALKING TO THAT SON OF A BITCH GILL?
I DON'T-
IT'S IN THE REPORTS...
...JUST LIKE I TOLD THAT FREAK...
...I CARRIED A 45. NOTHING-
JOE...
THOMPSON, HUH?
IT'S ALL IN THE REPORT, THOMPSON.
THE CASE IS ALMOST WRAPPED UP.
BE FOOLISH TO START POKING AROUND NOW.
GILL.

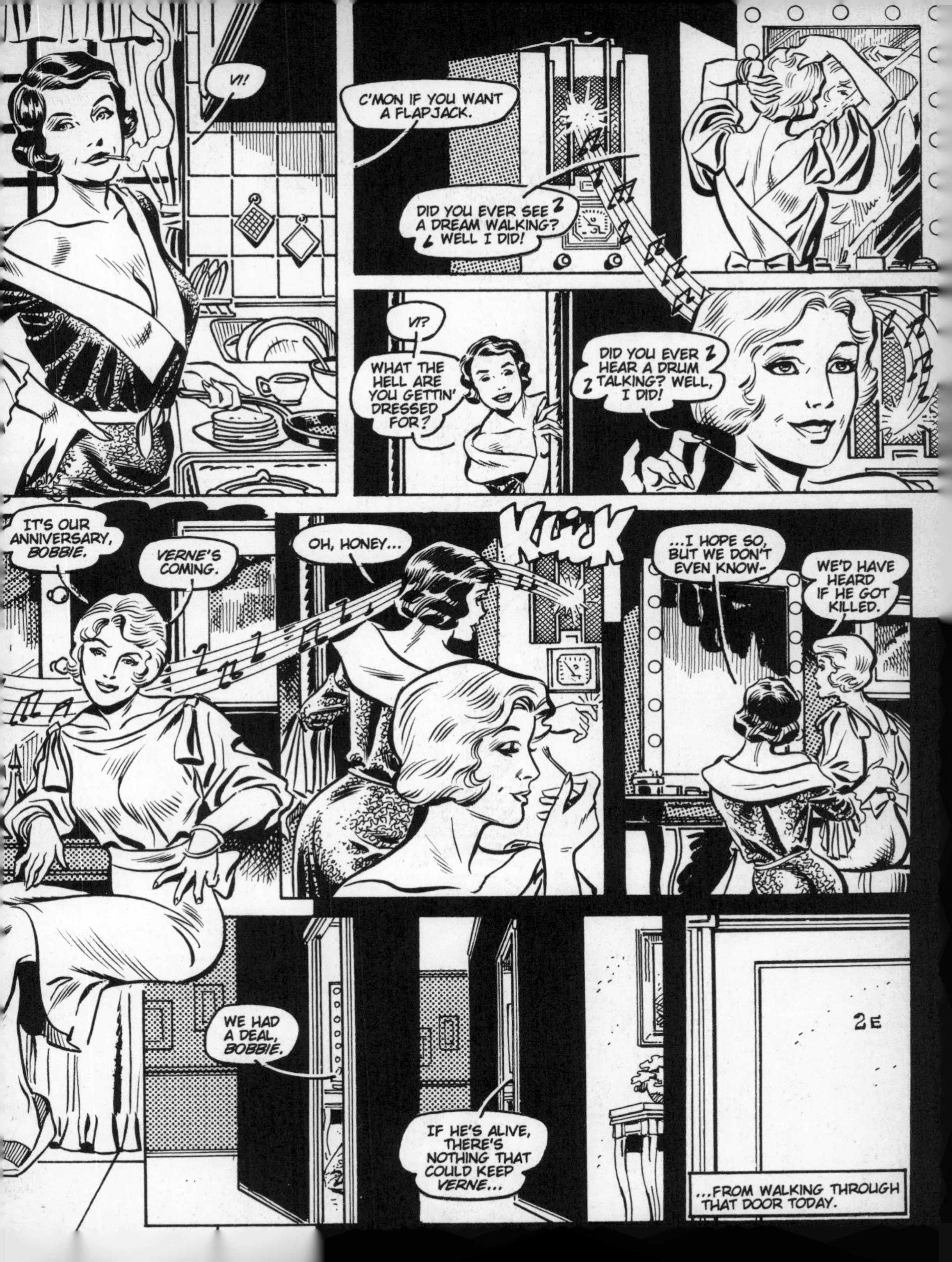
VI!
C'MON IF YOU WANT A FLAPJACK.
DID YOU EVER SEE A DREAM WALKING? WELL I DID!
VI?
WHAT THE HELL ARE YOU GETTIN' DRESSED FOR?
DID YOU EVER HEAR A DRUM TALKING? WELL, I DID!
IT'S OUR ANNIVERSARY, BOBBIE.
VERNE'S COMING.
OH, HONEY...
KLICK
...I HOPE SO, BUT WE DON'T EVEN KNOW-
WE'D HAVE HEARD IF HE GOT KILLED.
WE HAD A DEAL, BOBBIE.
IF HE'S ALIVE, THERE'S NOTHING THAT COULD KEEP VERNE...
2E
...FROM WALKING THROUGH THAT DOOR TODAY.

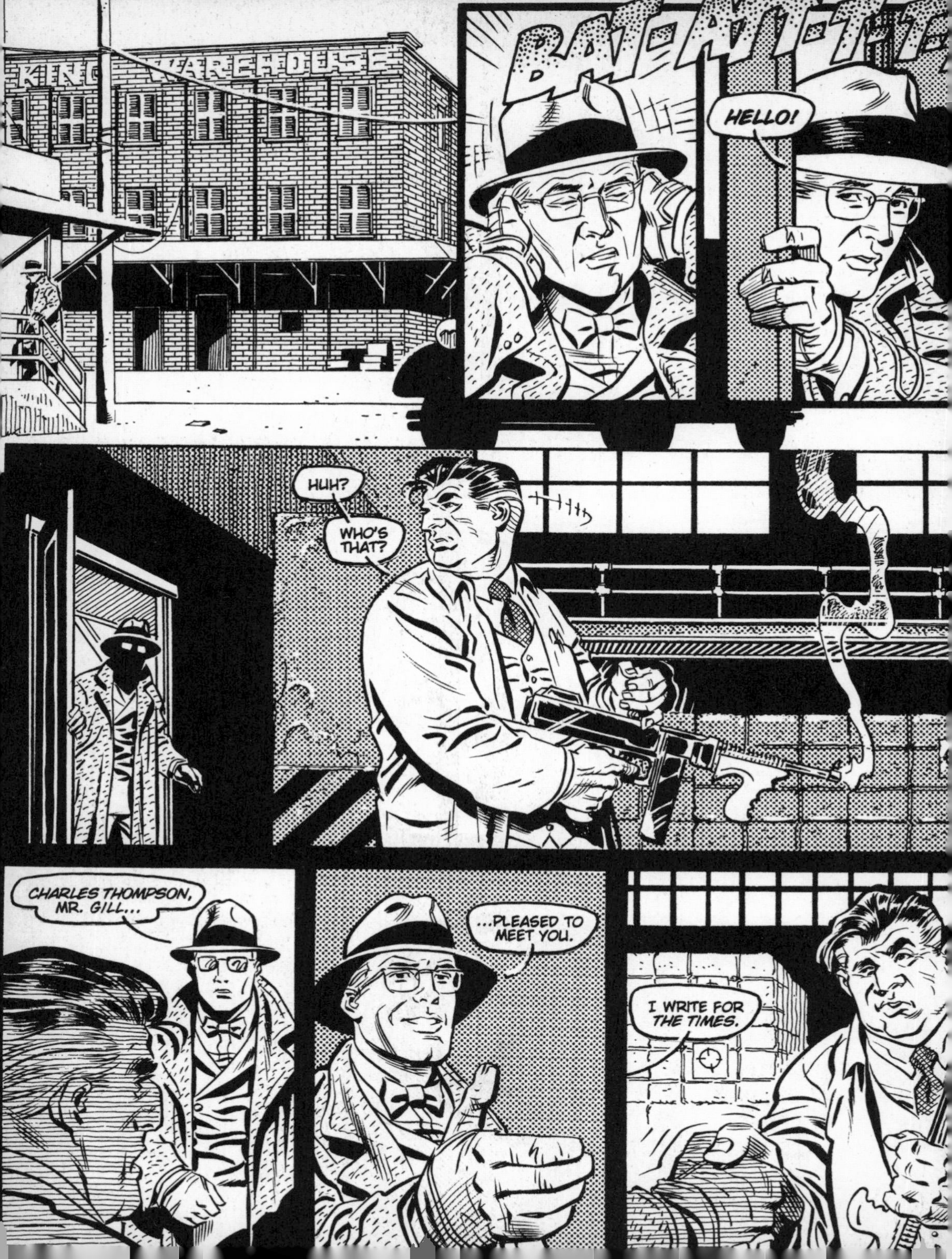
KING WAREHOUSE
BAT-AT-AT-AT
HELLO!
HUH?
WHO'S THAT?
CHARLES THOMPSON, MR. GILL...
...PLEASED TO MEET YOU.
I WRITE FOR THE TIMES.

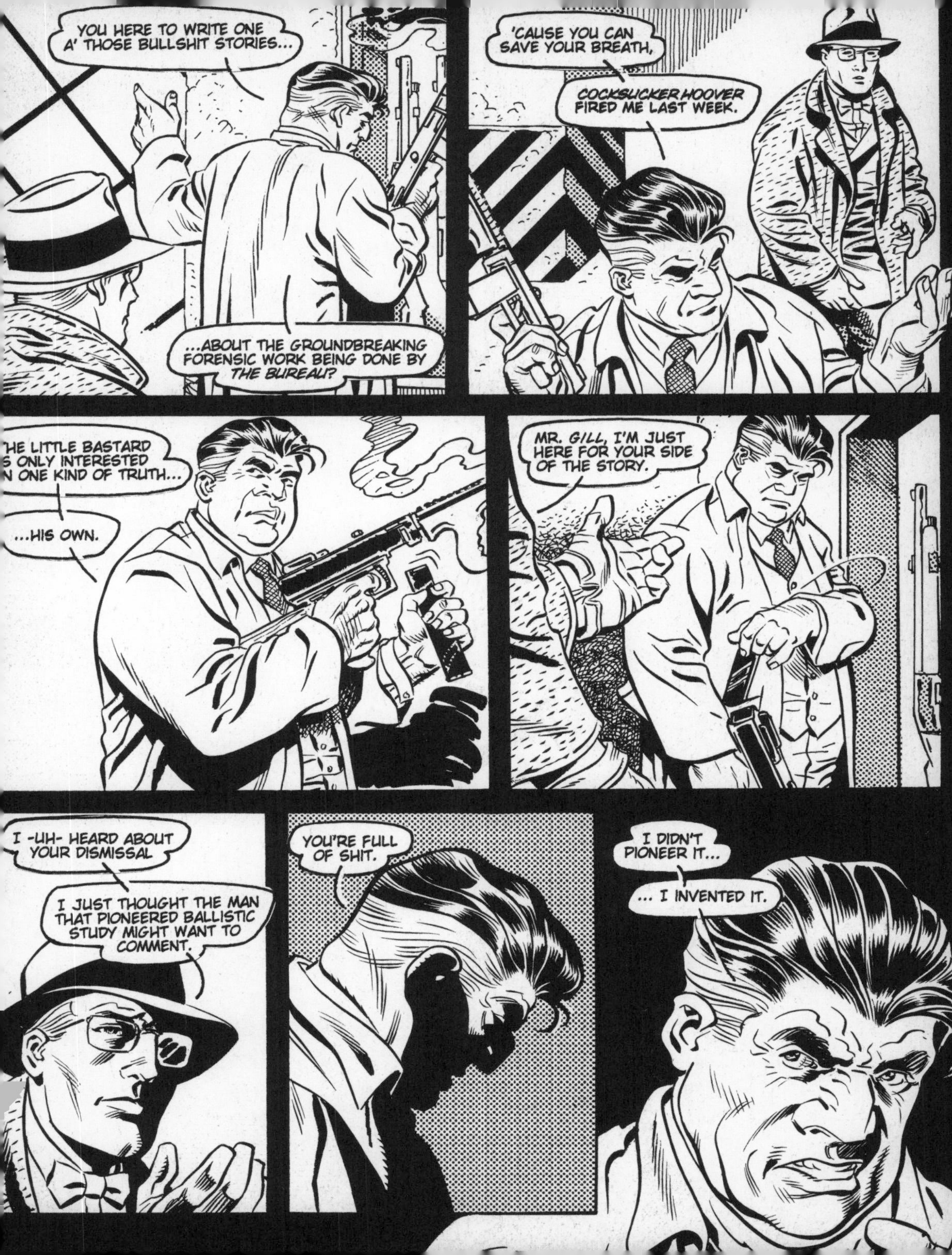
YOU HERE TO WRITE ONE A' THOSE BULLSHIT STORIES...
...ABOUT THE GROUNDBREAKING FORENSIC WORK BEING DONE BY THE BUREAU?
'CAUSE YOU CAN SAVE YOUR BREATH,
COCKSUCKER HOOVER FIRED ME LAST WEEK.
HE LITTLE BASTARD S ONLY INTERESTED N ONE KIND OF TRUTH...
...HIS OWN.
MR. GILL, I'M JUST HERE FOR YOUR SIDE OF THE STORY.
I -UH- HEARD ABOUT YOUR DISMISSAL
I JUST THOUGHT THE MAN THAT PIONEERED BALLISTIC STUDY MIGHT WANT TO COMMENT.
YOU'RE FULL OF SHIT.
I DIDN'T PIONEER IT...
... I INVENTED IT.

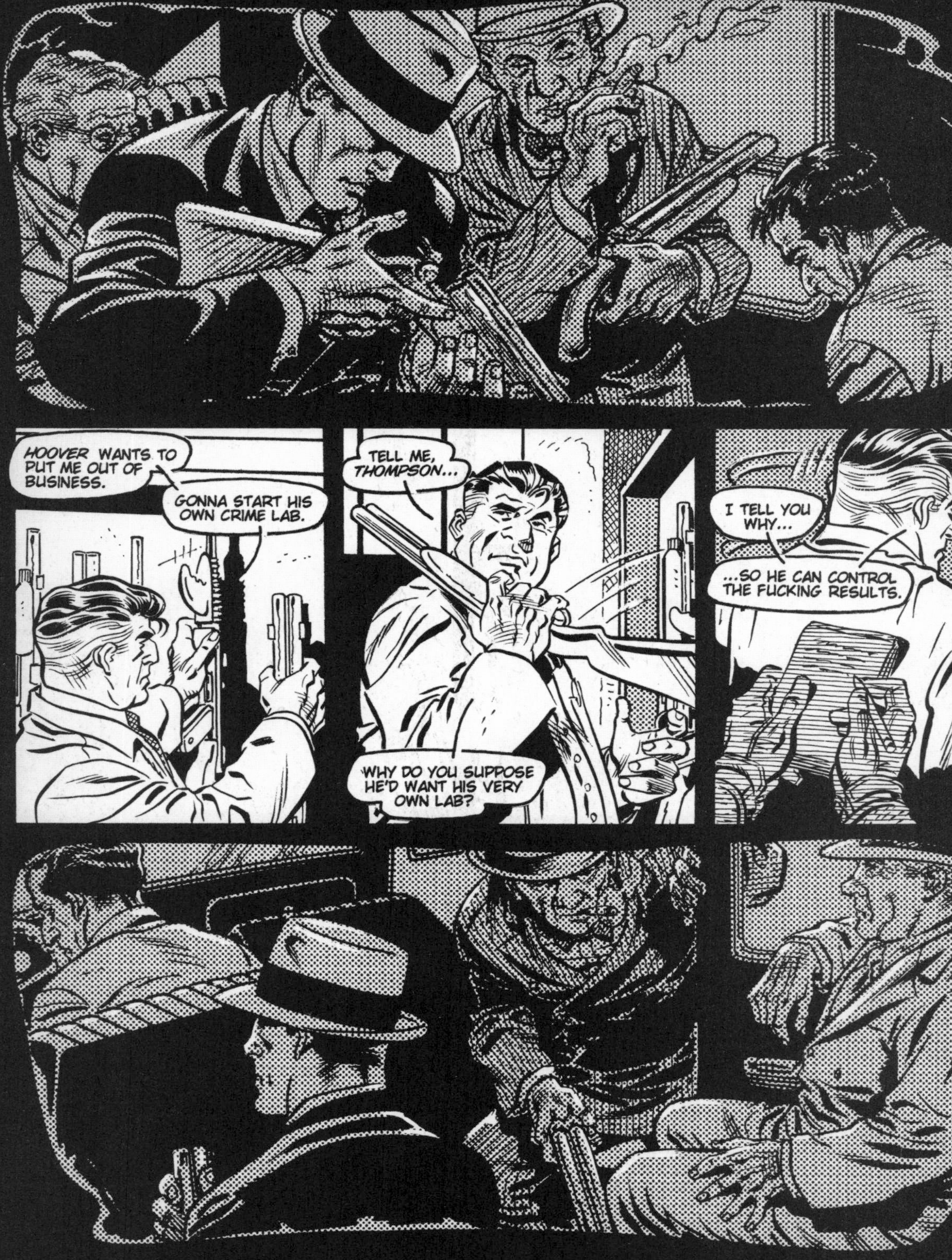
HOOVER WANTS TO PUT ME OUT OF BUSINESS.
GONNA START HIS OWN CRIME LAB.
TELL ME, THOMPSON...
WHY DO YOU SUPPOSE HE'D WANT HIS VERY OWN LAB?
I TELL YOU WHY...
...SO HE CAN CONTROL THE FUCKING RESULTS.

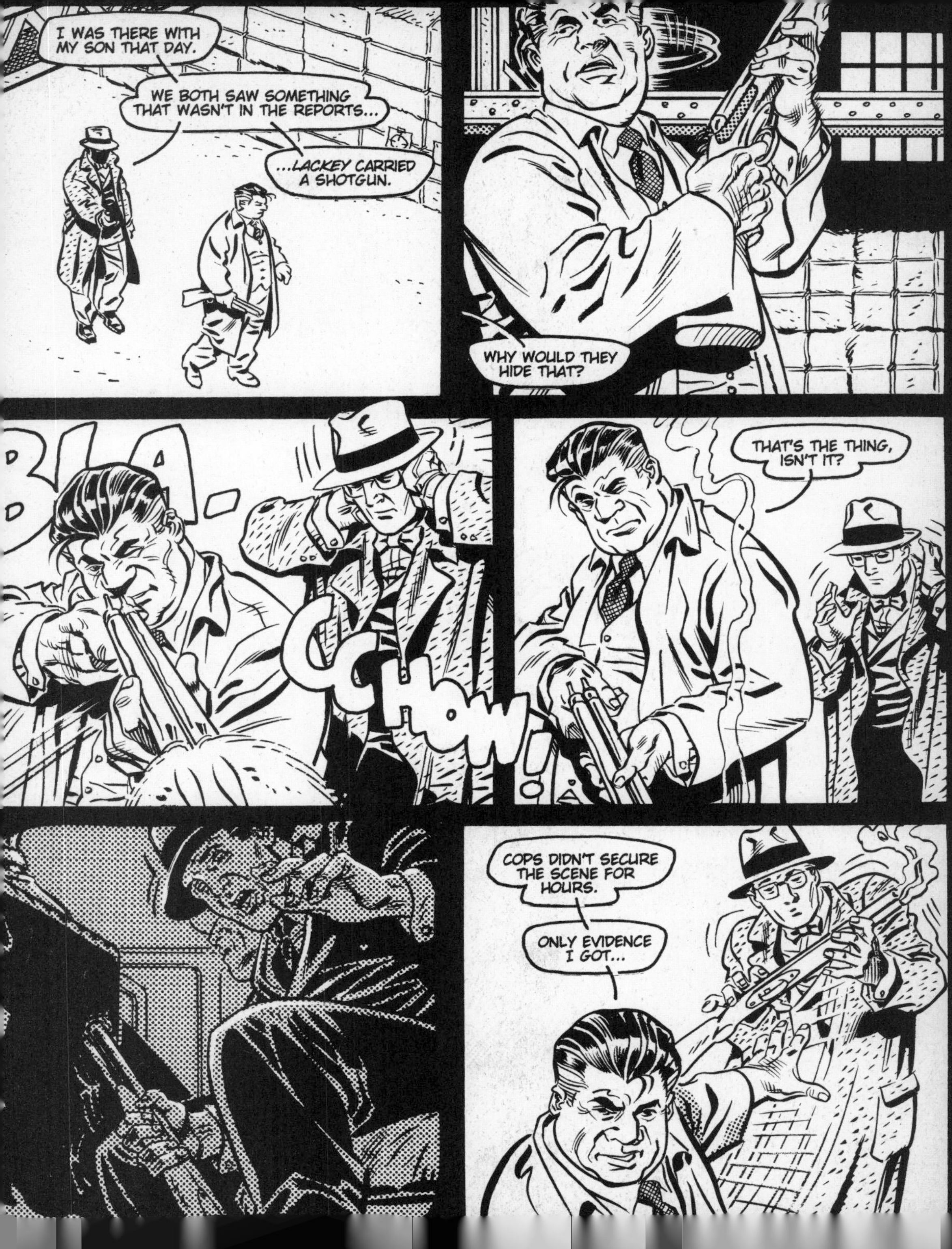
I WAS THERE WITH MY SON THAT DAY.
WE BOTH SAW SOMETHING THAT WASN'T IN THE REPORTS...
...LACKEY CARRIED A SHOTGUN.
WHY WOULD THEY HIDE THAT?
CHOW!
THAT'S THE THING, ISN'T IT?
COPS DIDN'T SECURE THE SCENE FOR HOURS.
ONLY EVIDENCE I GOT...

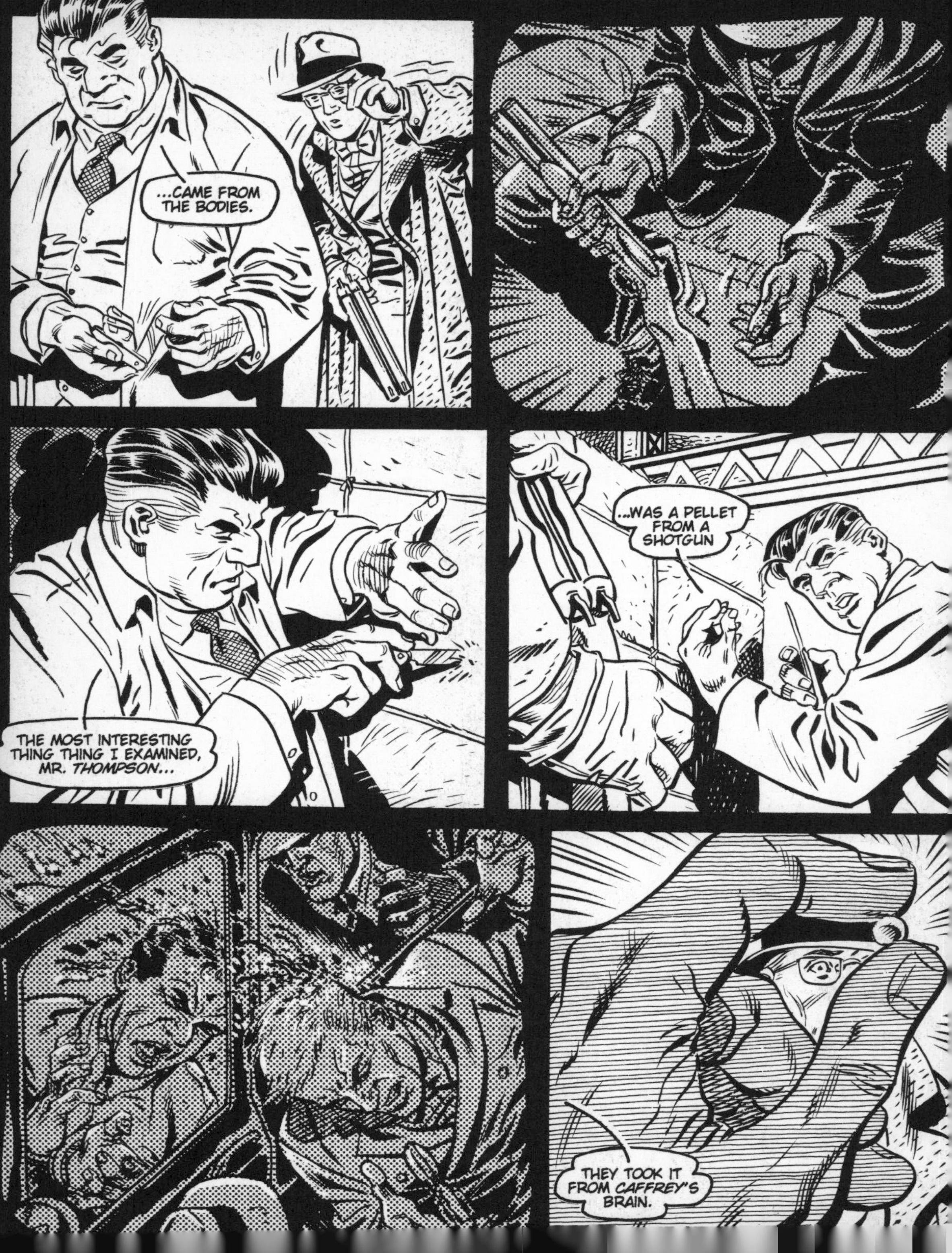
...CAME FROM THE BODIES.
THE MOST INTERESTING THING THING I EXAMINED, MR. THOMPSON...
...WAS A PELLET FROM A SHOTGUN
THEY TOOK IT FROM CAFFREY'S BRAIN.

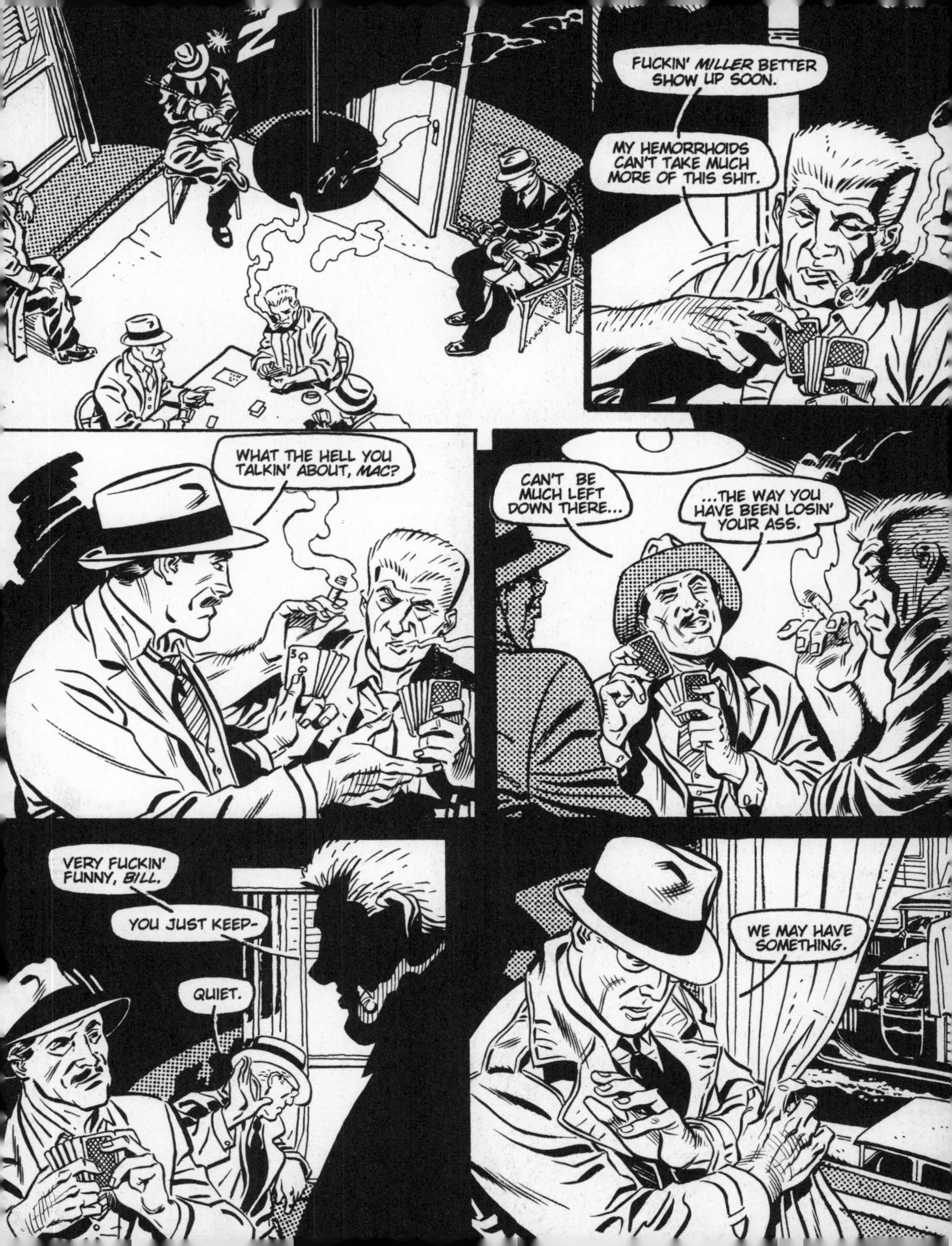
FUCKIN' MILLER BETTER SHOW UP SOON.
MY HEMORRHOIDS CAN'T TAKE MUCH MORE OF THIS SHIT.
WHAT THE HELL YOU TALKIN' ABOUT, MAC?
CAN'T BE MUCH LEFT DOWN THERE...
...THE WAY YOU HAVE BEEN LOSIN' YOUR ASS.
VERY FUCKIN' FUNNY, BILL.
YOU JUST KEEP-
QUIET.
WE MAY HAVE SOMETHING.

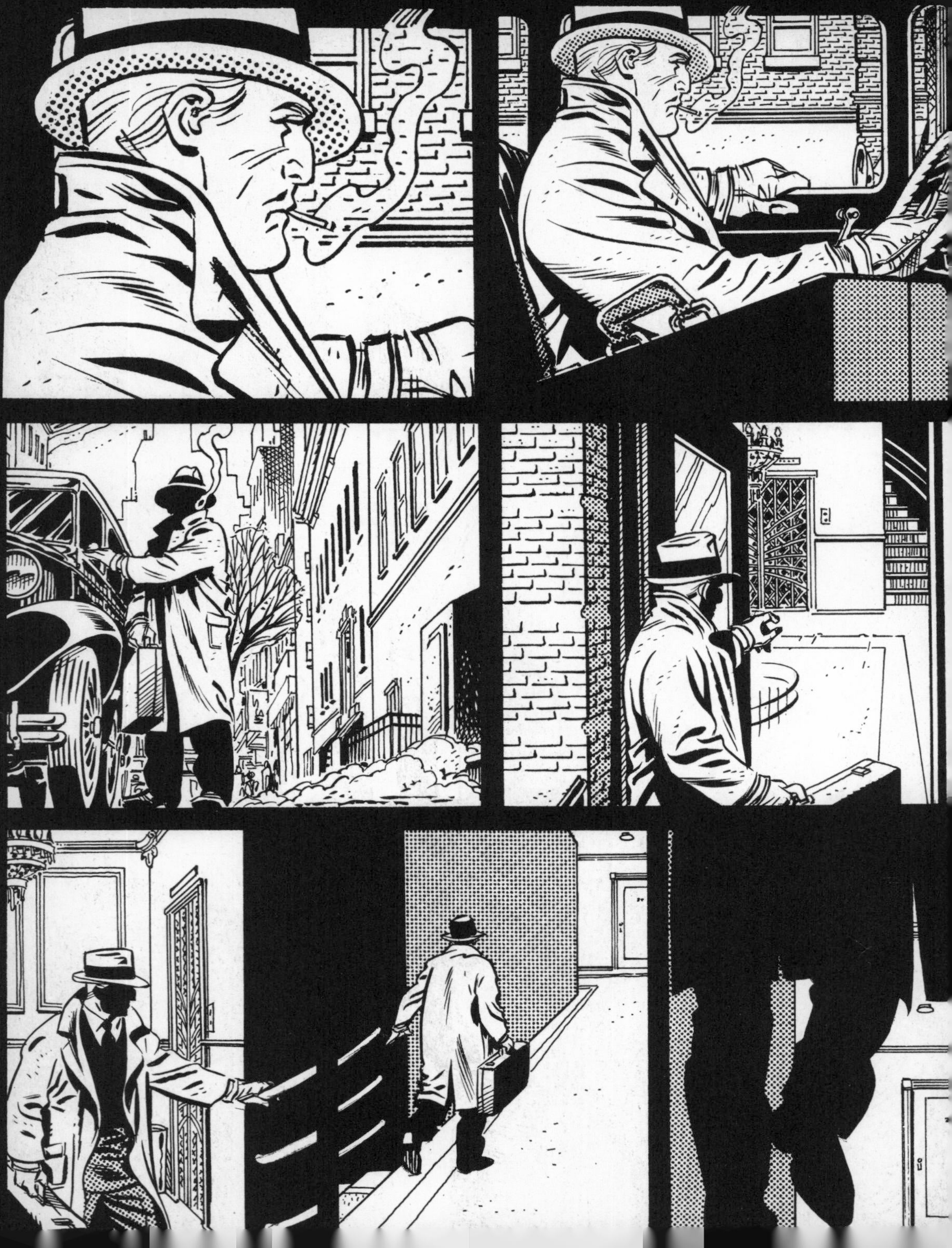

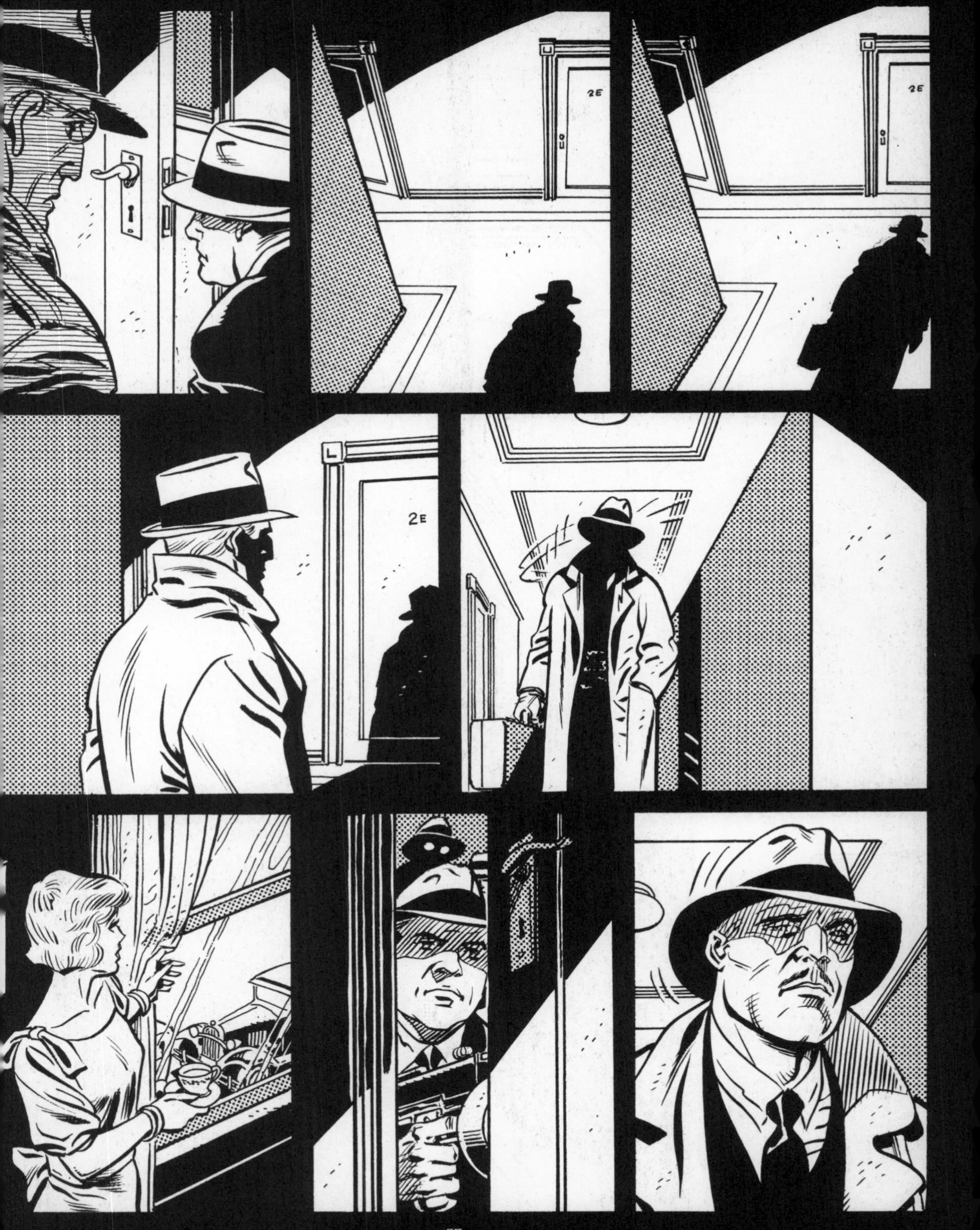
2E
2E
2E

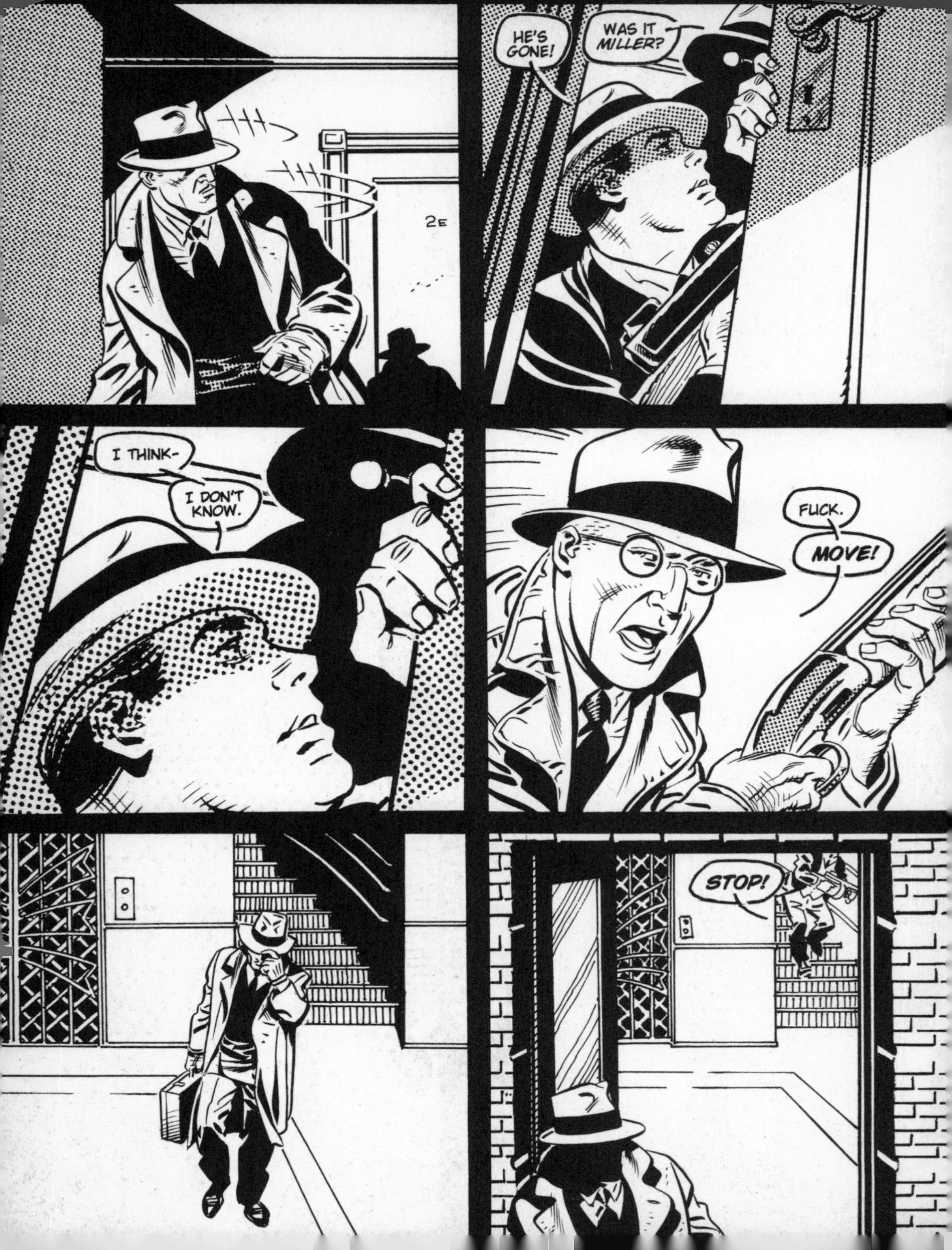

2E
HE'S GONE!
WAS IT MILLER?
I THINK-
I DON'T KNOW.
FUCK.
MOVE!
STOP!

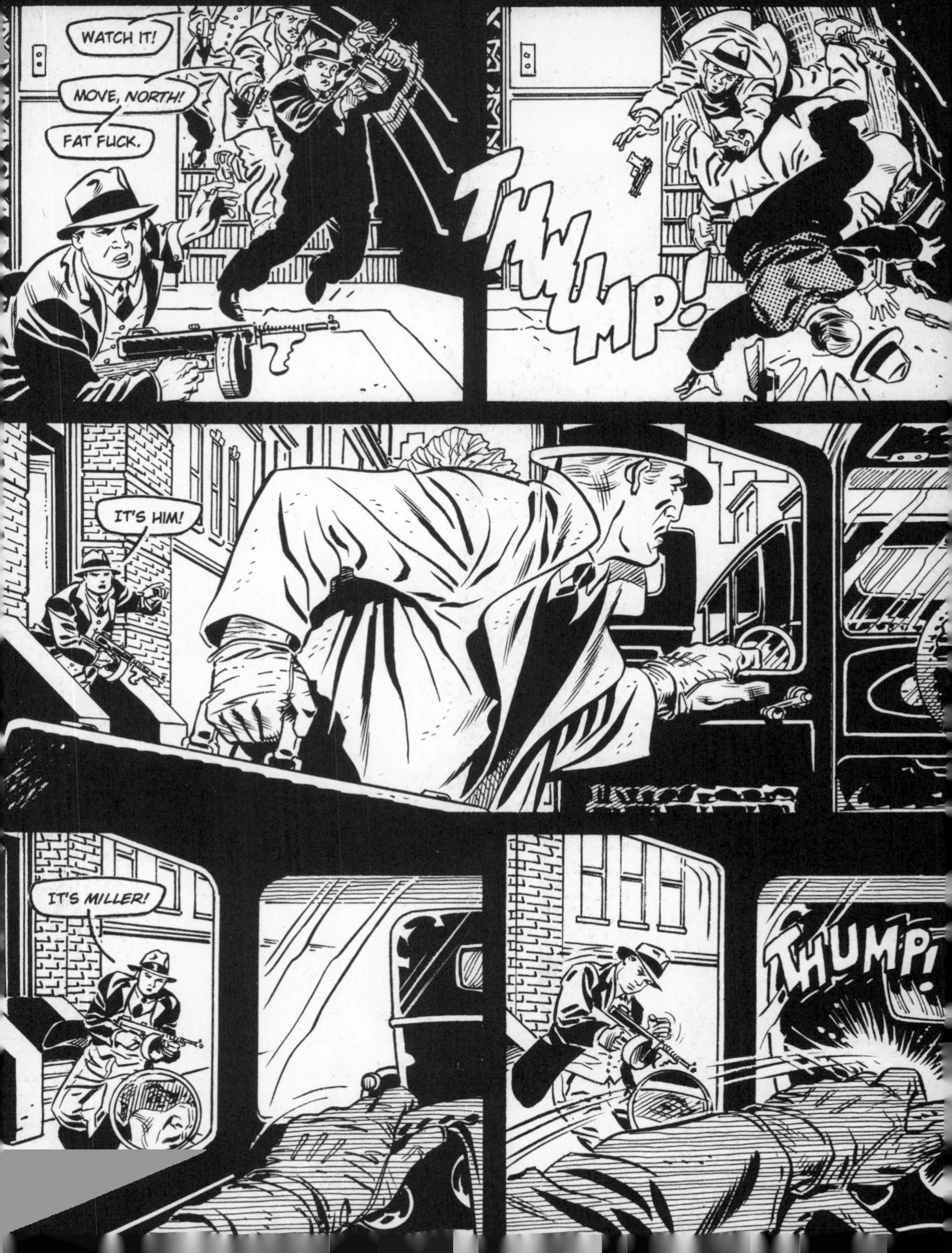
WATCH IT!
MOVE, NORTH!
FAT FUCK.
THUMP!
IT'S HIM!
IT'S MILLER!
THUMP!

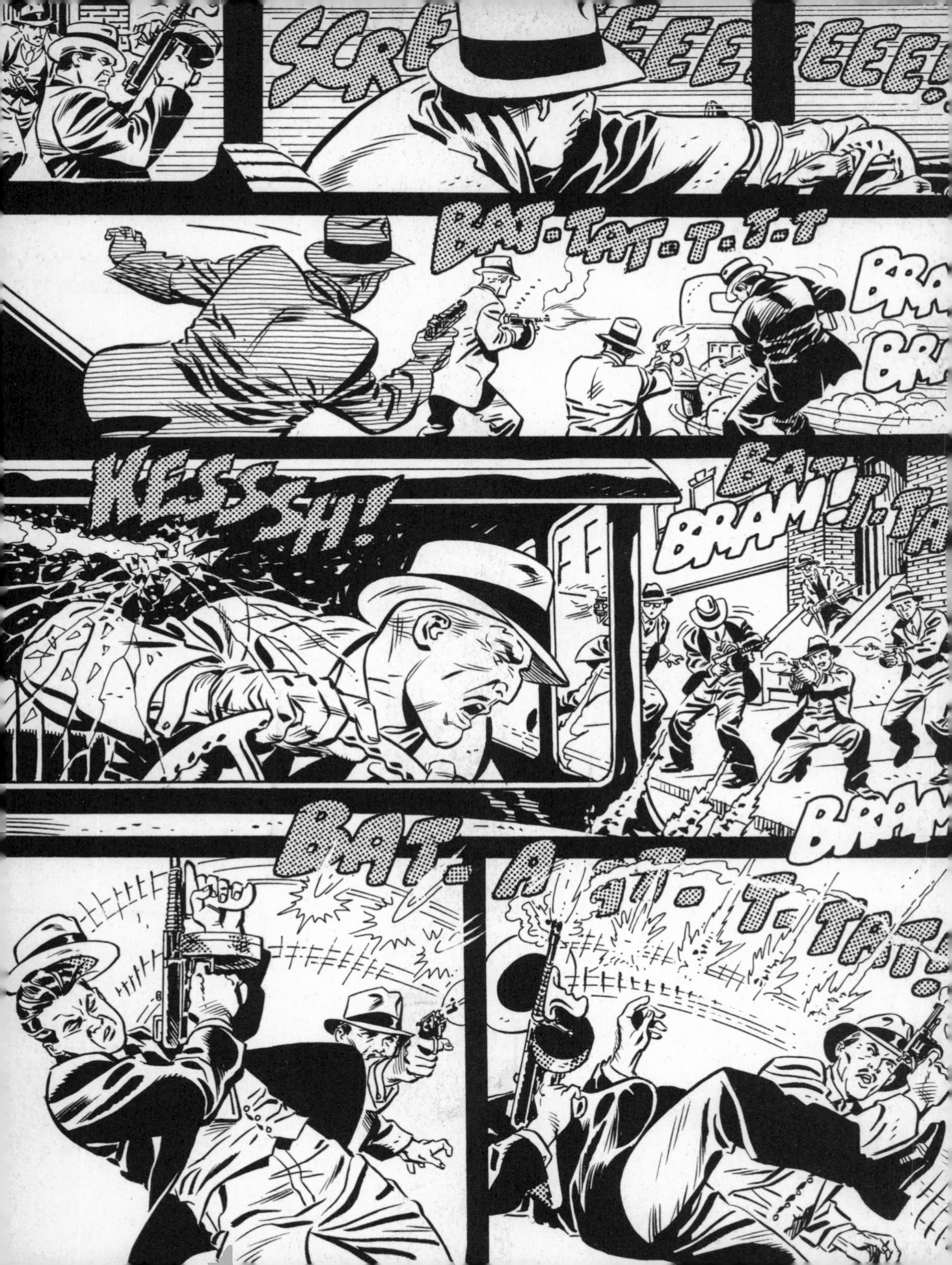
BAT-TAT-T-T-T
BRAM!
BAT-A-TAT-T-TAT!

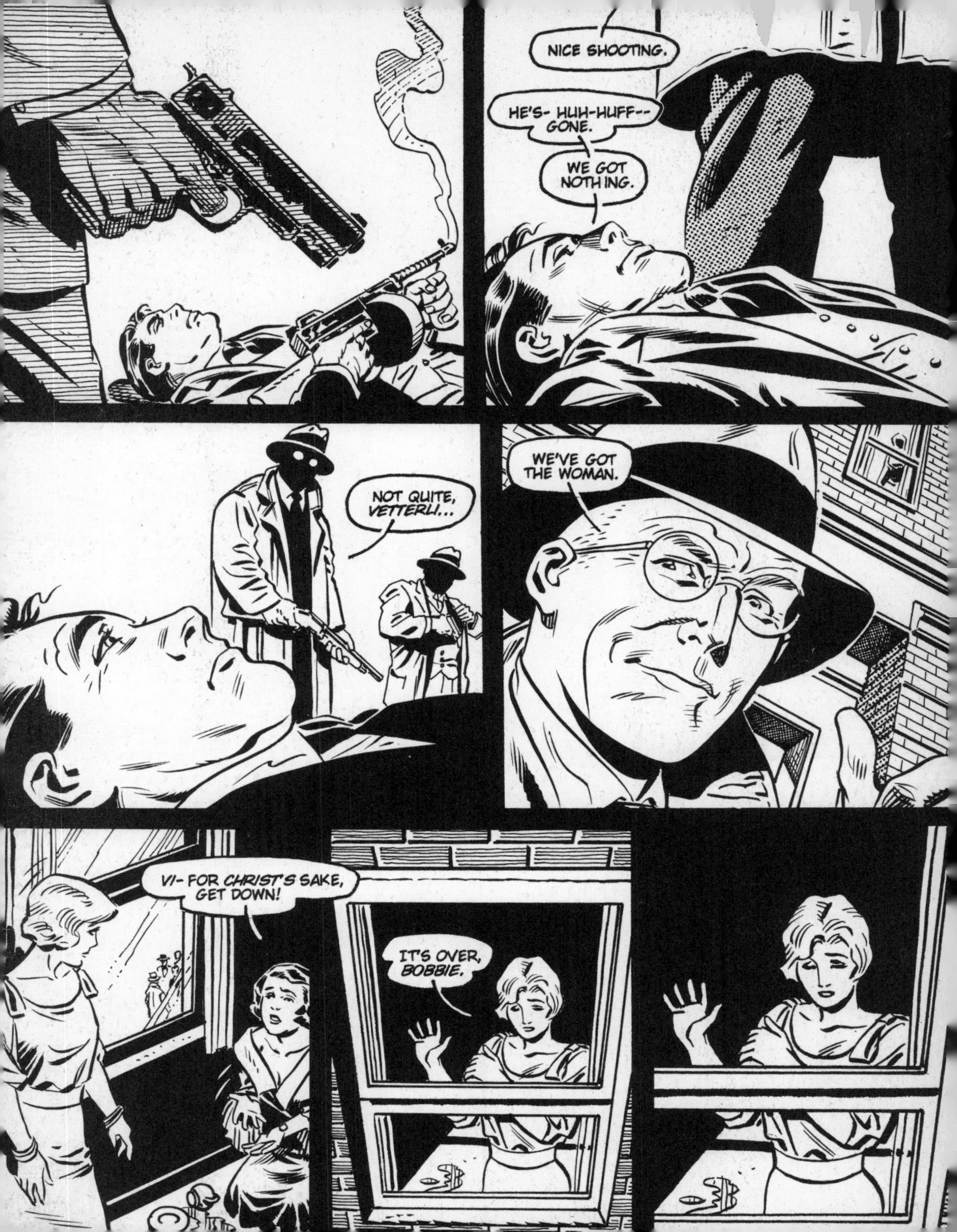

NICE SHOOTING.
HE'S- HUH-HUFF-- GONE.
WE GOT NOTHING.
NOT QUITE, VETTERLI...
WE'VE GOT THE WOMAN.
VI- FOR CHRIST'S SAKE, GET DOWN!
IT'S OVER, BOBBIE.

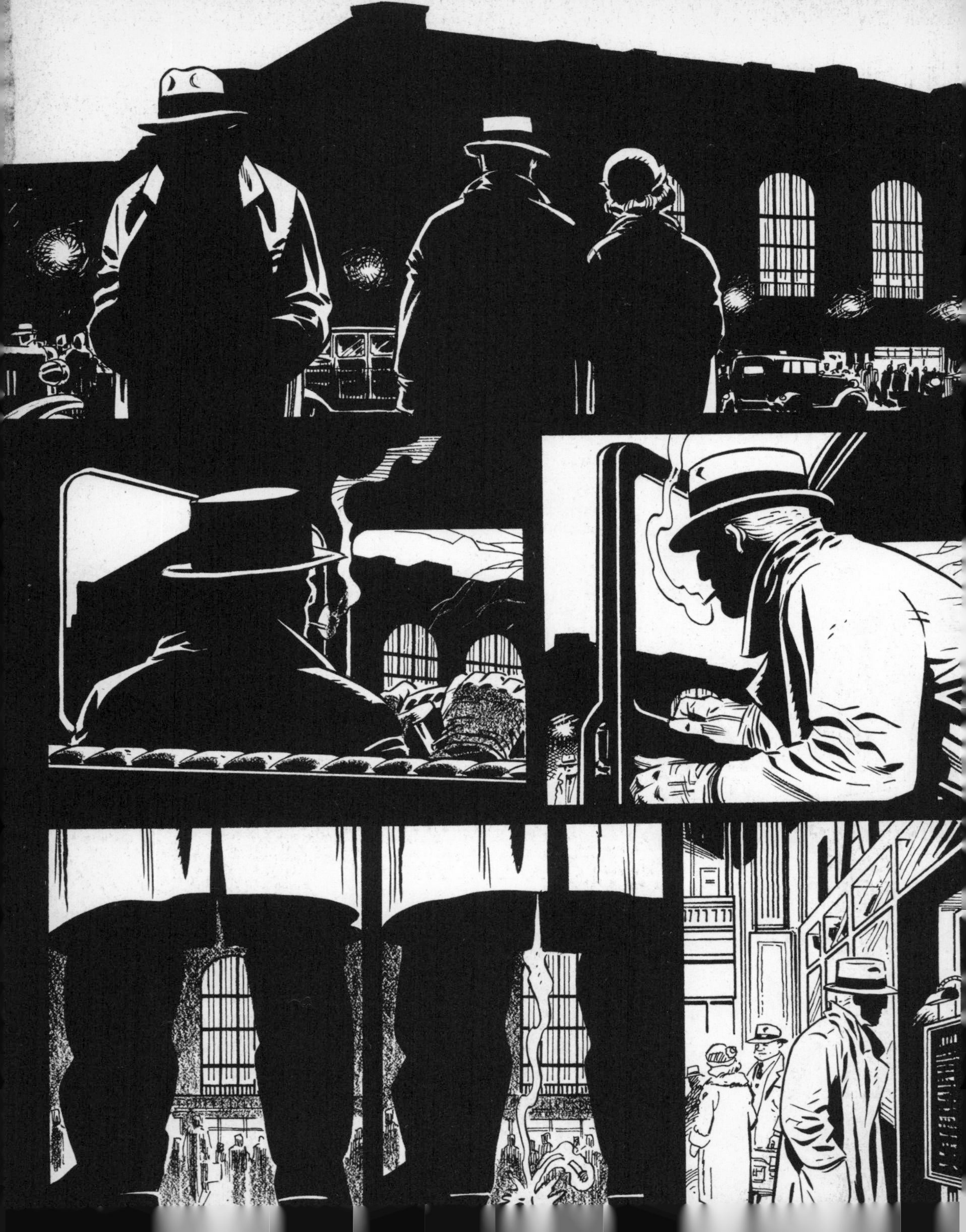

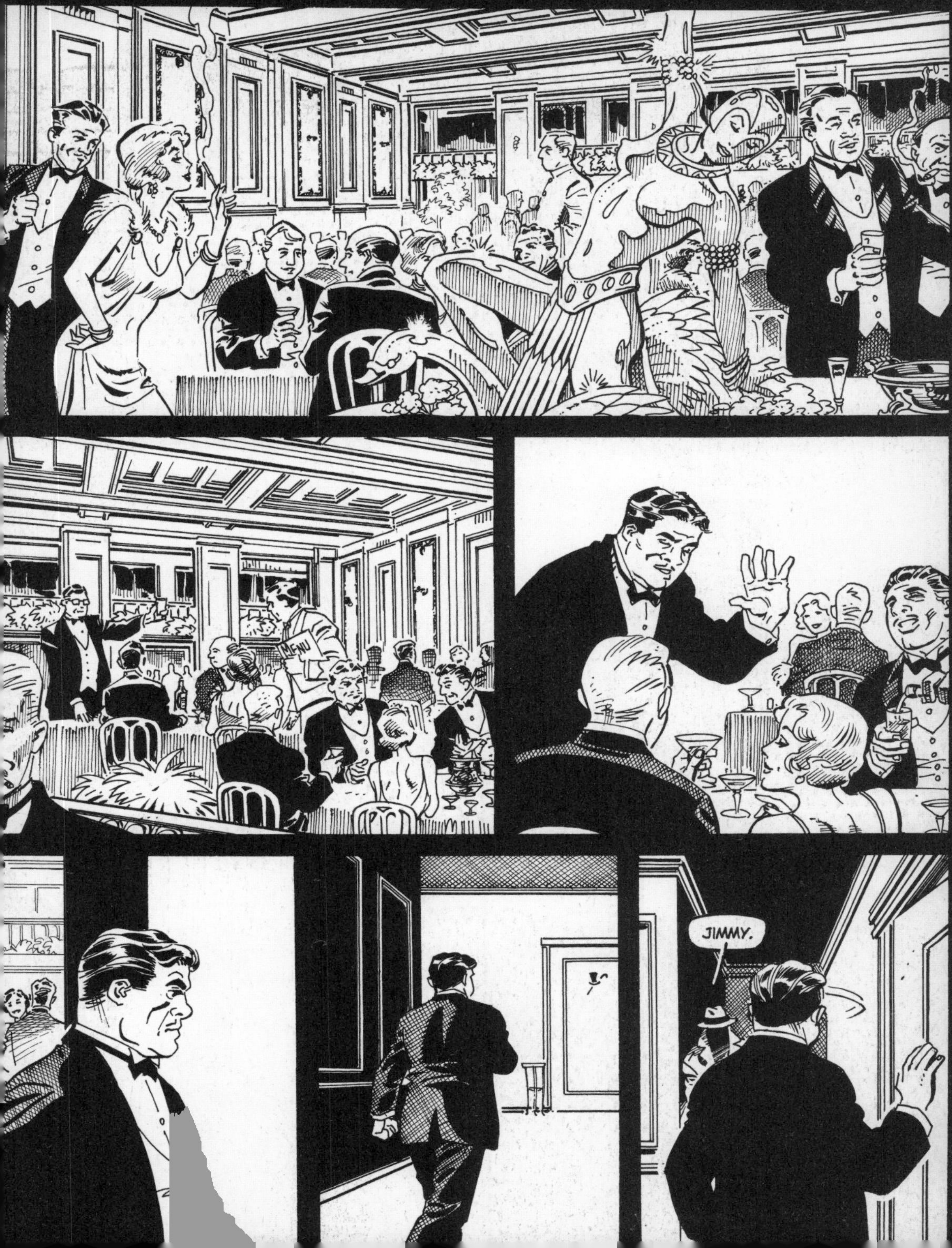
JIMMY.

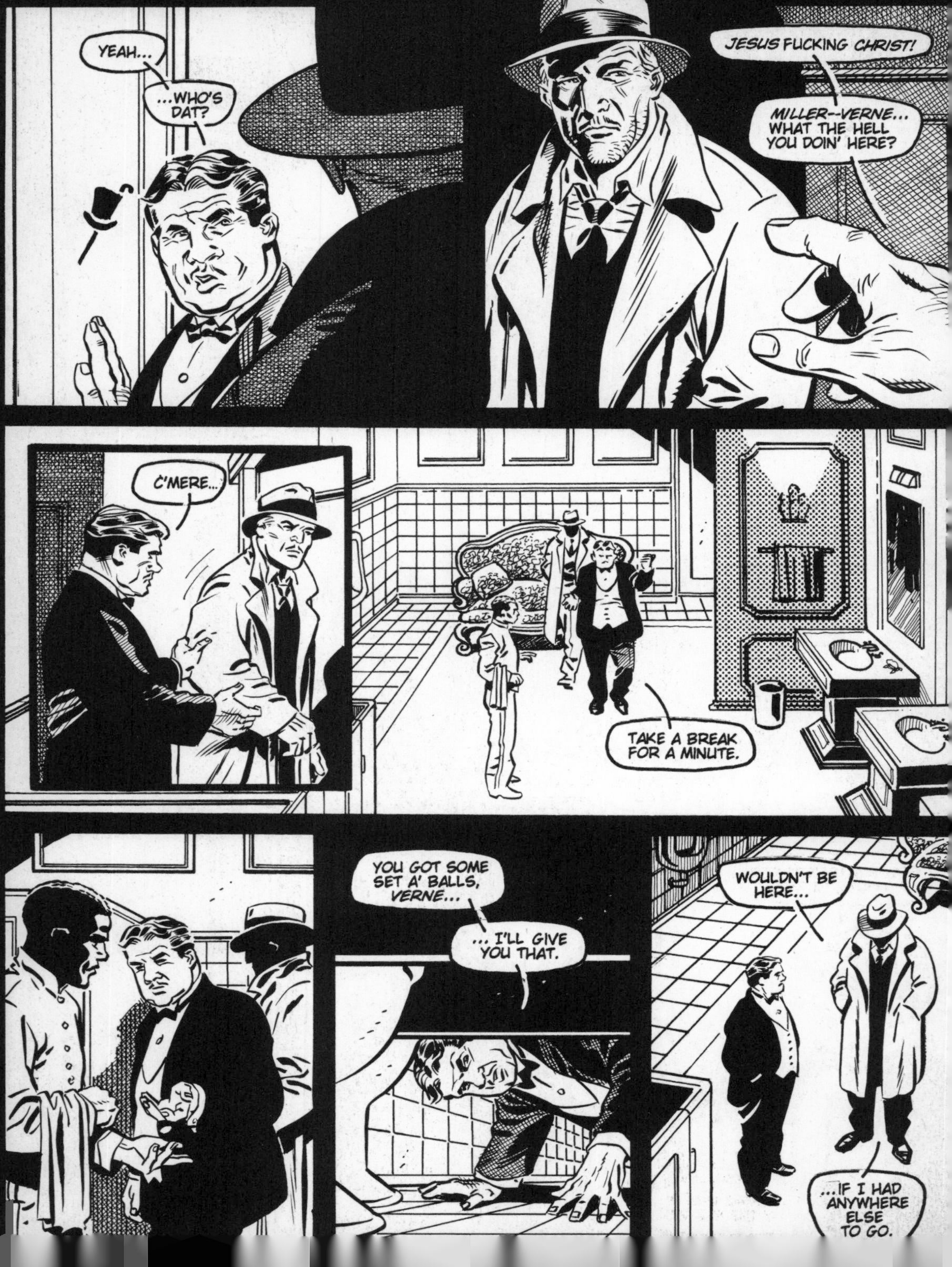
YEAH...
...WHO'S DAT?
JESUS FUCKING CHRIST!
MILLER--VERNE... WHAT THE HELL YOU DOIN' HERE?
C'MERE...
TAKE A BREAK FOR A MINUTE.
YOU GOT SOME SET A' BALLS, VERNE...
... I'LL GIVE YOU THAT.
WOULDN'T BE HERE...
...IF I HAD ANYWHERE ELSE TO GO.

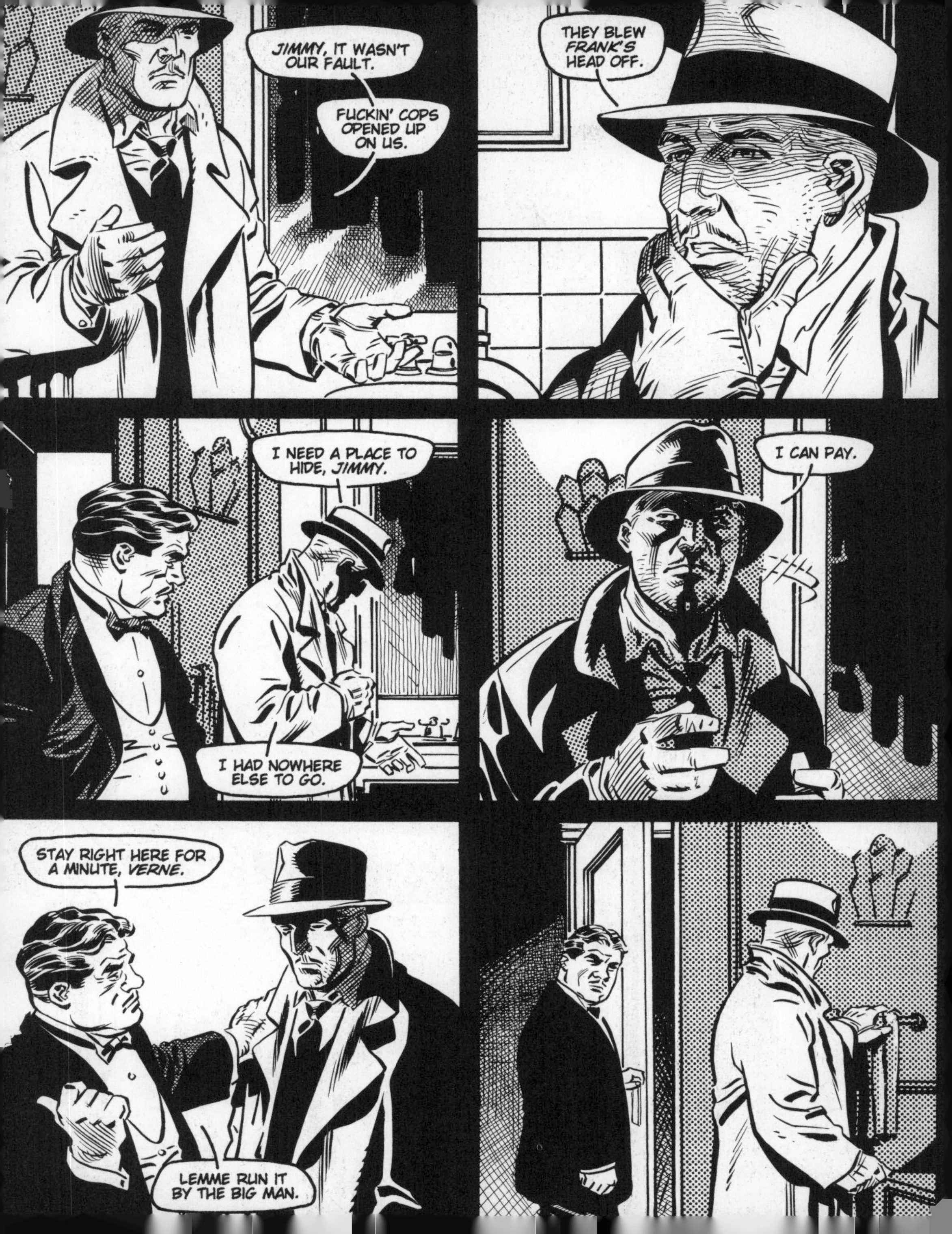

JIMMY, IT WASN'T OUR FAULT.
FUCKIN' COPS OPENED UP ON US.
THEY BLEW FRANK'S HEAD OFF.
I NEED A PLACE TO HIDE, JIMMY.
I HAD NOWHERE ELSE TO GO.
I CAN PAY.
STAY RIGHT HERE FOR A MINUTE, VERNE.
LEMME RUN IT BY THE BIG MAN.

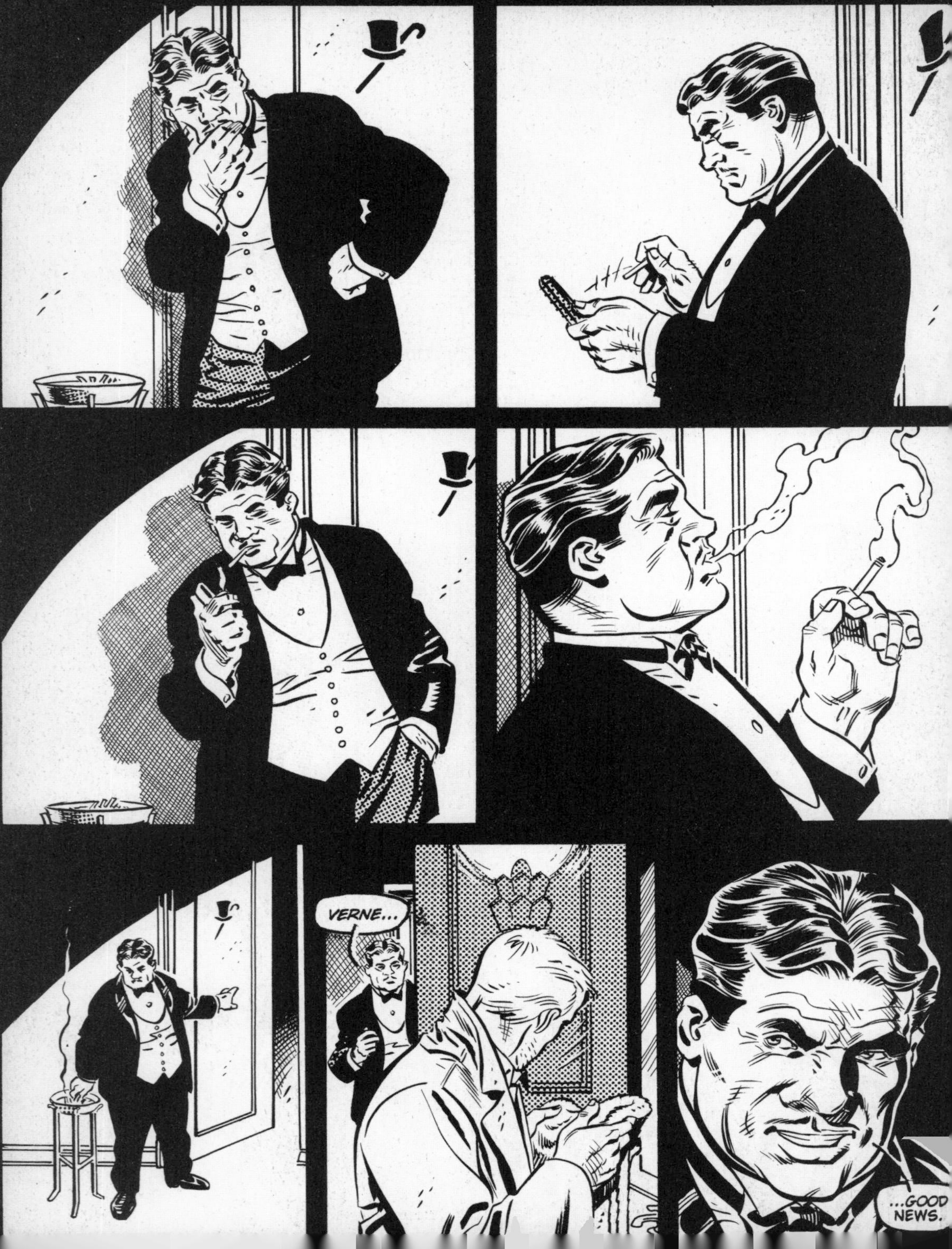
VERNE...
...GOOD NEWS.

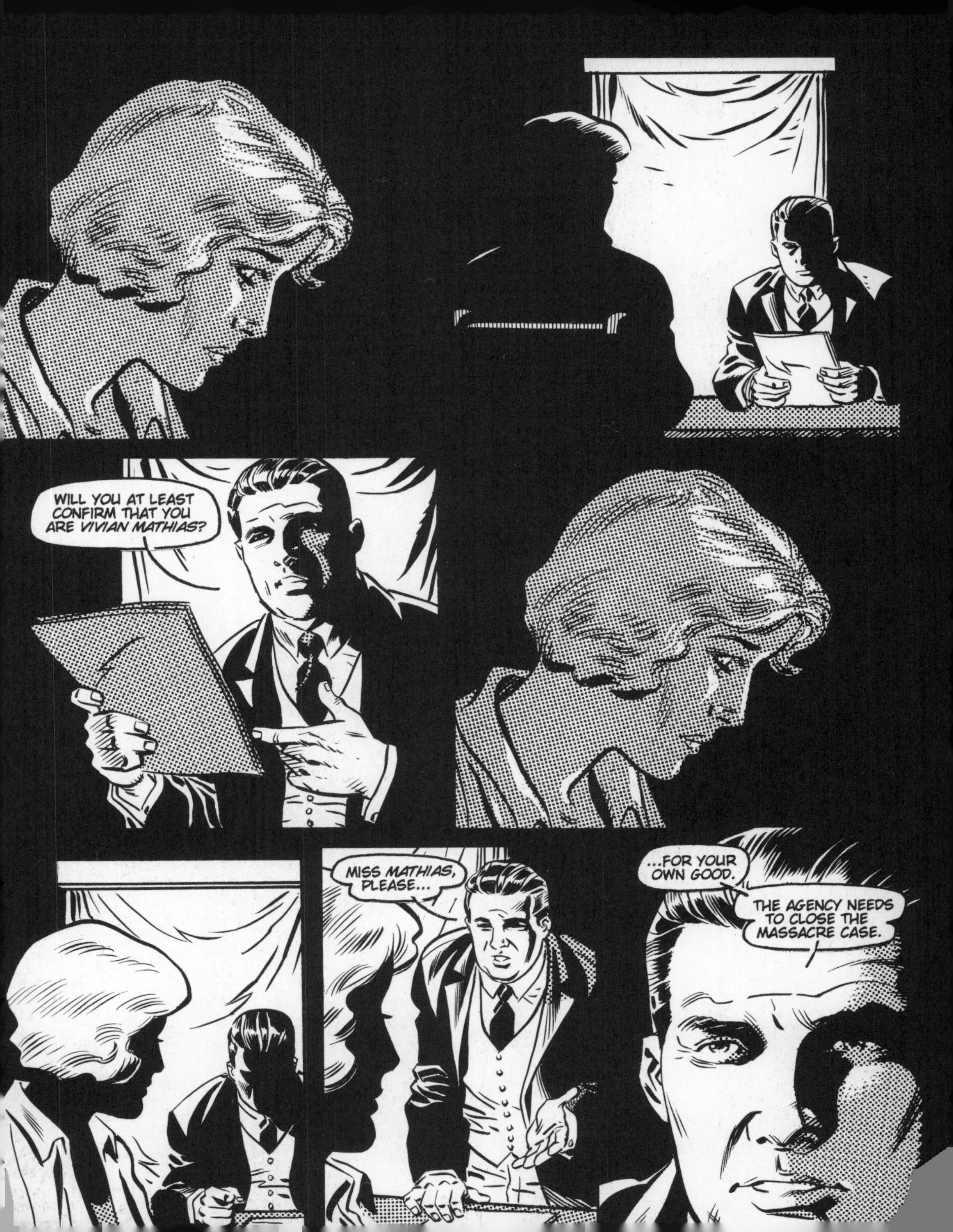
WILL YOU AT LEAST CONFIRM THAT YOU ARE VIVIAN MATHIAS?
MISS MATHIAS, PLEASE...
...FOR YOUR OWN GOOD.
THE AGENCY NEEDS TO CLOSE THE MASSACRE CASE.

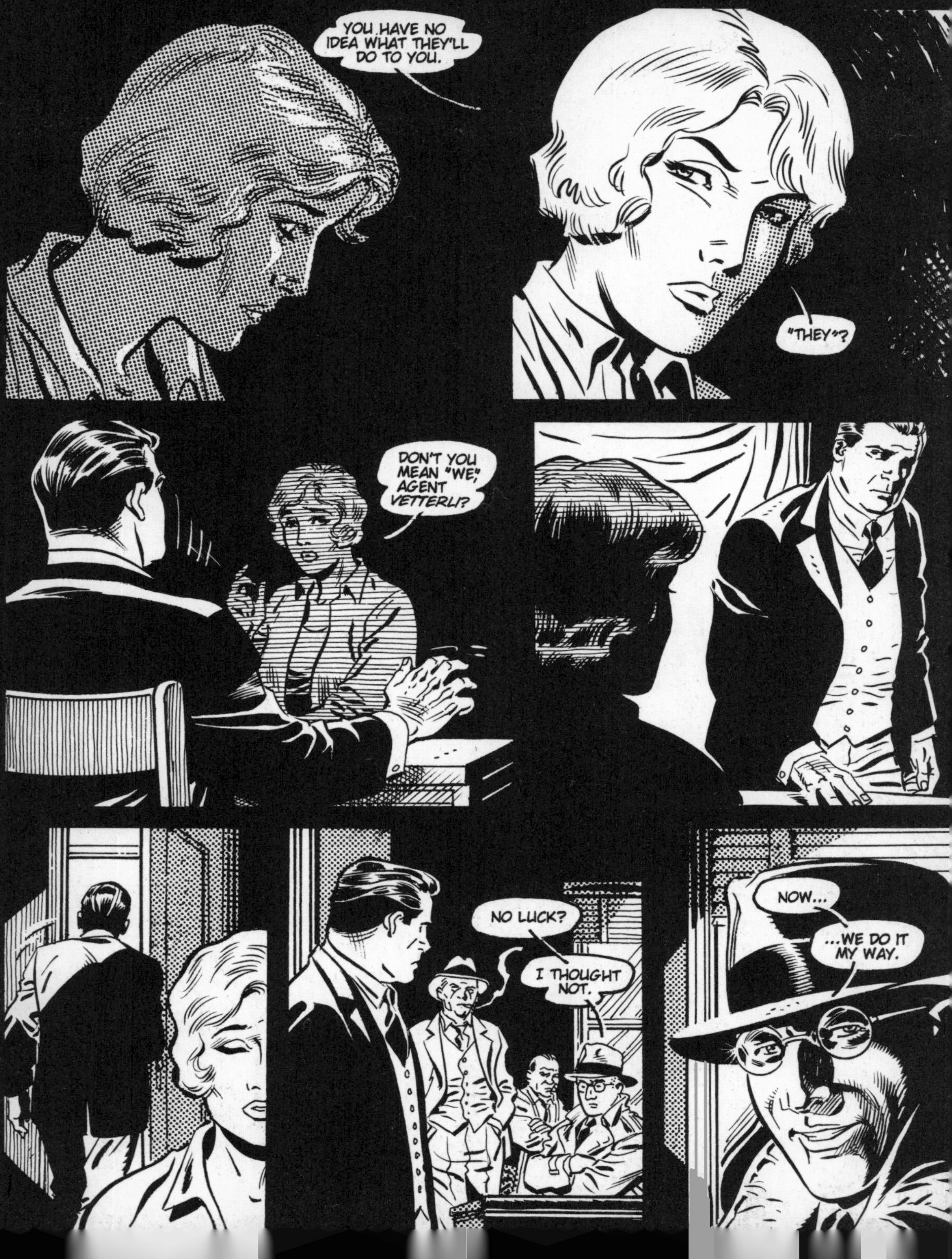
YOU HAVE NO IDEA WHAT THEY'LL DO TO YOU.
"THEY"?
DON'T YOU MEAN "WE," AGENT VETTERLI?
NO LUCK?
I THOUGHT NOT.
NOW...
...WE DO IT MY WAY.

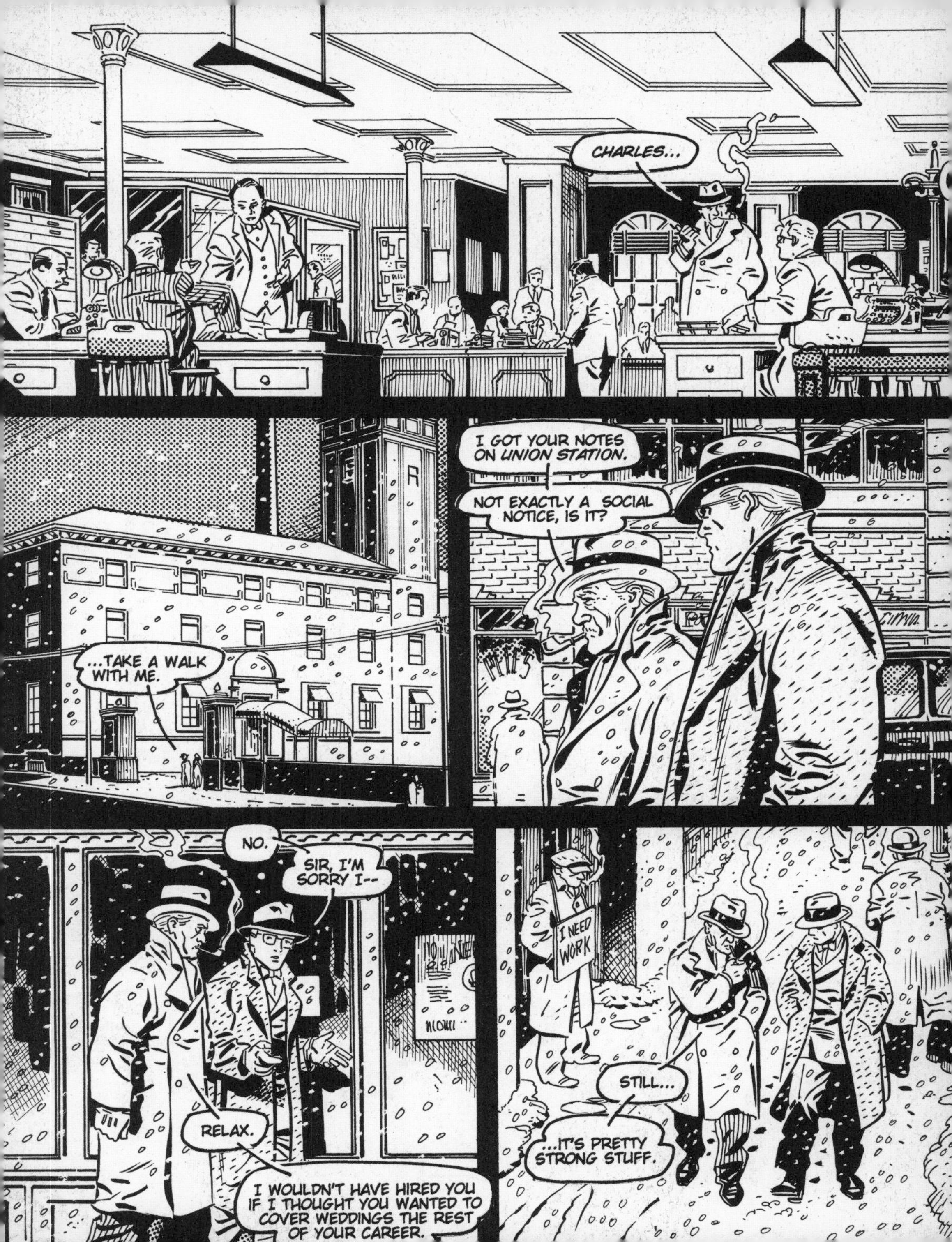
CHARLES...
...TAKE A WALK WITH ME.
I GOT YOUR NOTES ON UNION STATION.
NOT EXACTLY A SOCIAL NOTICE, IS IT?
NO.
SIR, I'M SORRY I--
RELAX.
I WOULDN'T HAVE HIRED YOU IF I THOUGHT YOU WANTED TO COVER WEDDINGS THE REST OF YOUR CAREER.
I NEED WORK
STILL...
...IT'S PRETTY STRONG STUFF.

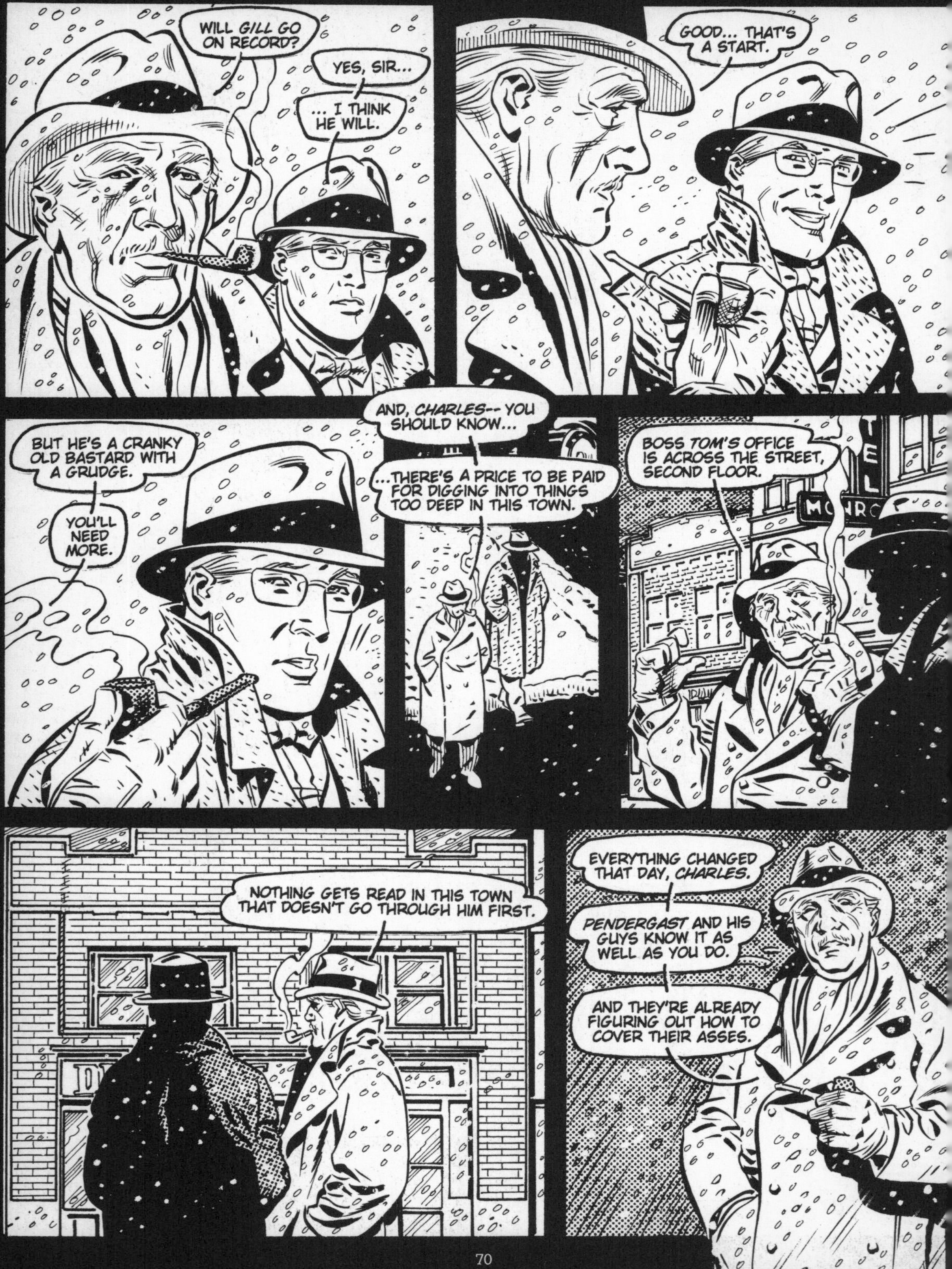

WILL GILL GO ON RECORD?
YES, SIR...
... I THINK HE WILL.
GOOD... THAT'S A START.
BUT HE'S A CRANKY OLD BASTARD WITH A GRUDGE.
YOU'LL NEED MORE.
AND, CHARLES-- YOU SHOULD KNOW...
...THERE'S A PRICE TO BE PAID FOR DIGGING INTO THINGS TOO DEEP IN THIS TOWN.
BOSS TOM'S OFFICE IS ACROSS THE STREET, SECOND FLOOR.
NOTHING GETS READ IN THIS TOWN THAT DOESN'T GO THROUGH HIM FIRST.
EVERYTHING CHANGED THAT DAY, CHARLES.
PENDERGAST AND HIS GUYS KNOW IT AS WELL AS YOU DO.
AND THEY'RE ALREADY FIGURING OUT HOW TO COVER THEIR ASSES.

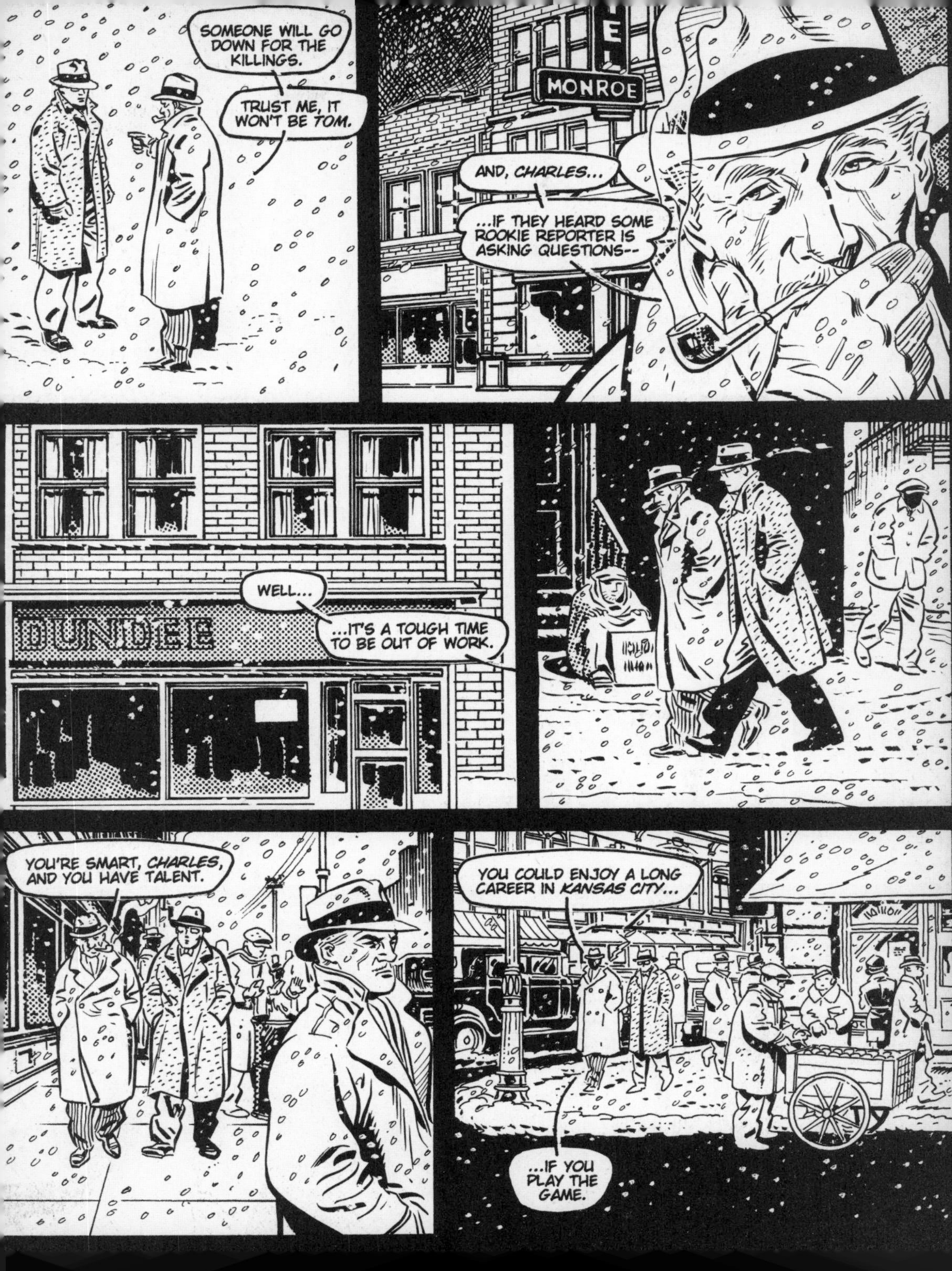
SOMEONE WILL GO DOWN FOR THE KILLINGS.
TRUST ME, IT WON'T BE TOM.
MONROE
AND, CHARLES...
...IF THEY HEARD SOME ROOKIE REPORTER IS ASKING QUESTIONS--
DUNDEE
WELL...
...IT'S A TOUGH TIME TO BE OUT OF WORK.
YOU'RE SMART, CHARLES, AND YOU HAVE TALENT.
YOU COULD ENJOY A LONG CAREER IN KANSAS CITY...
...IF YOU PLAY THE GAME.

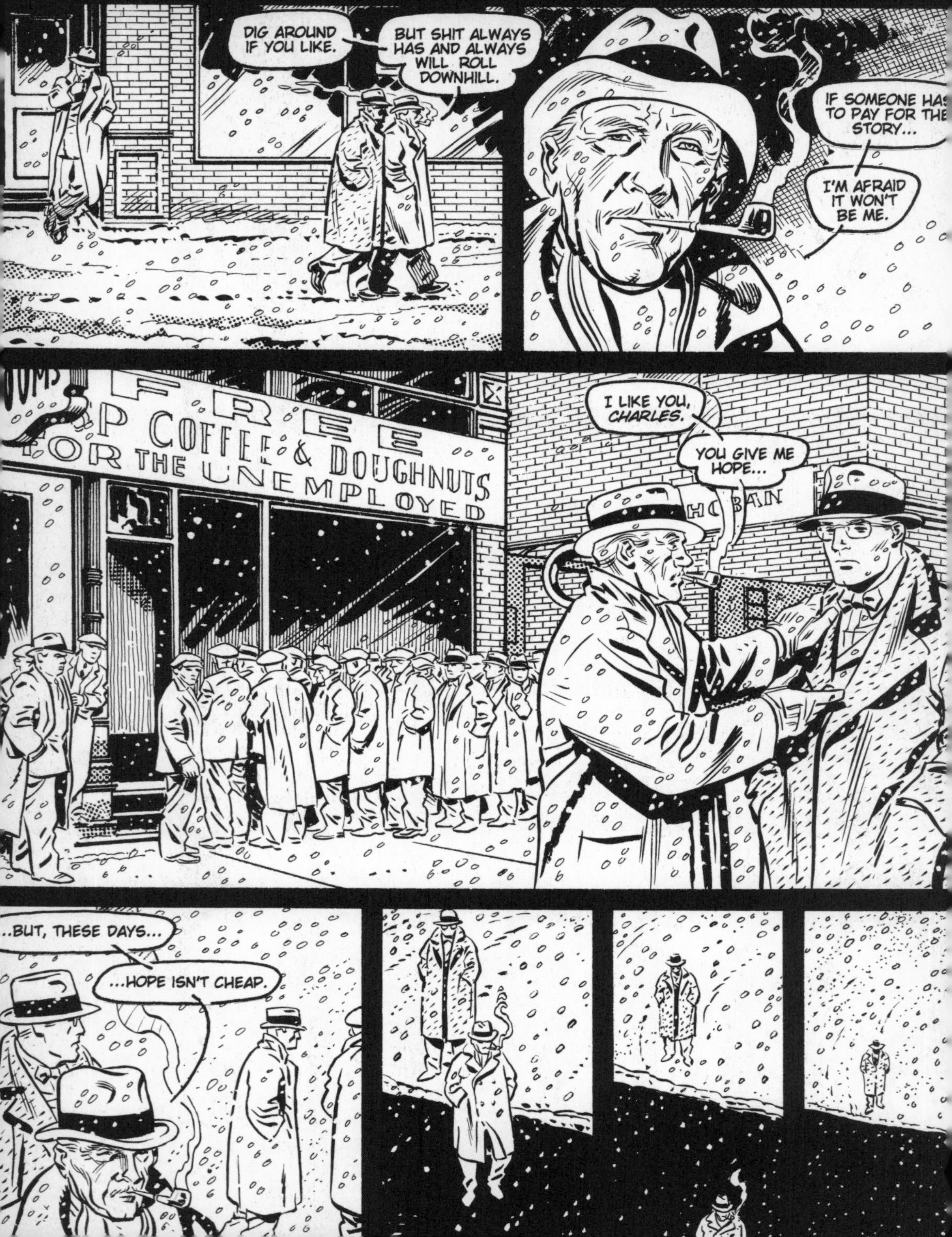

DIG AROUND IF YOU LIKE.
BUT SHIT ALWAYS HAS AND ALWAYS WILL ROLL DOWNHILL.
IF SOMEONE HAS TO PAY FOR THE STORY...
I'M AFRAID IT WON'T BE ME.
FREE COFFEE & DOUGHNUTS FOR THE UNEMPLOYED
I LIKE YOU, CHARLES.
YOU GIVE ME HOPE...
...BUT, THESE DAYS...
...HOPE ISN'T CHEAP.

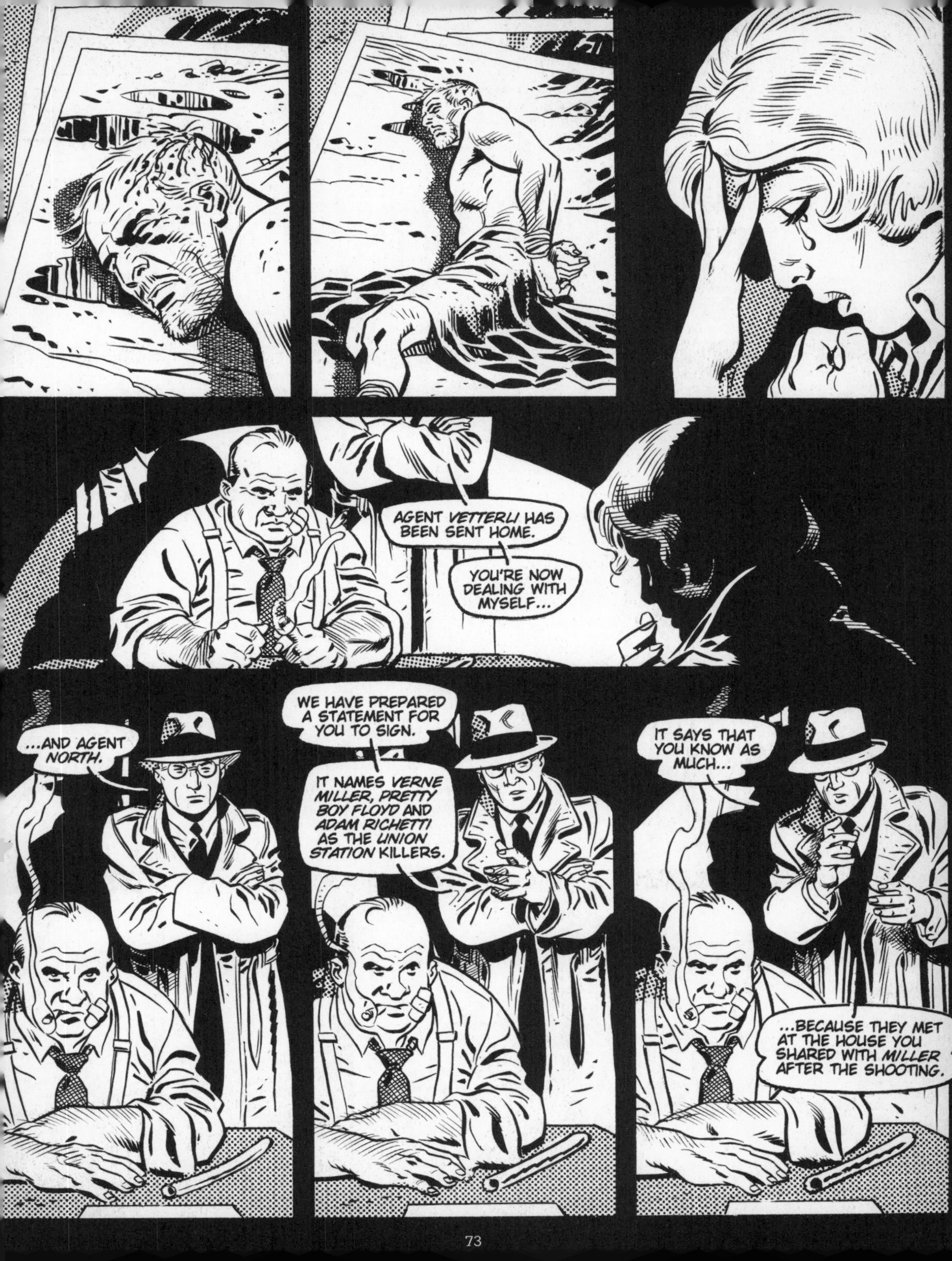

AGENT VETTERLI HAS BEEN SENT HOME.
YOU'RE NOW DEALING WITH MYSELF...
...AND AGENT NORTH.
WE HAVE PREPARED A STATEMENT FOR YOU TO SIGN.
IT NAMES VERNE MILLER, PRETTY BOY FLOYD AND ADAM RICHETTI AS THE UNION STATION KILLERS.
IT SAYS THAT YOU KNOW AS MUCH...
...BECAUSE THEY MET AT THE HOUSE YOU SHARED WITH MILLER AFTER THE SHOOTING.

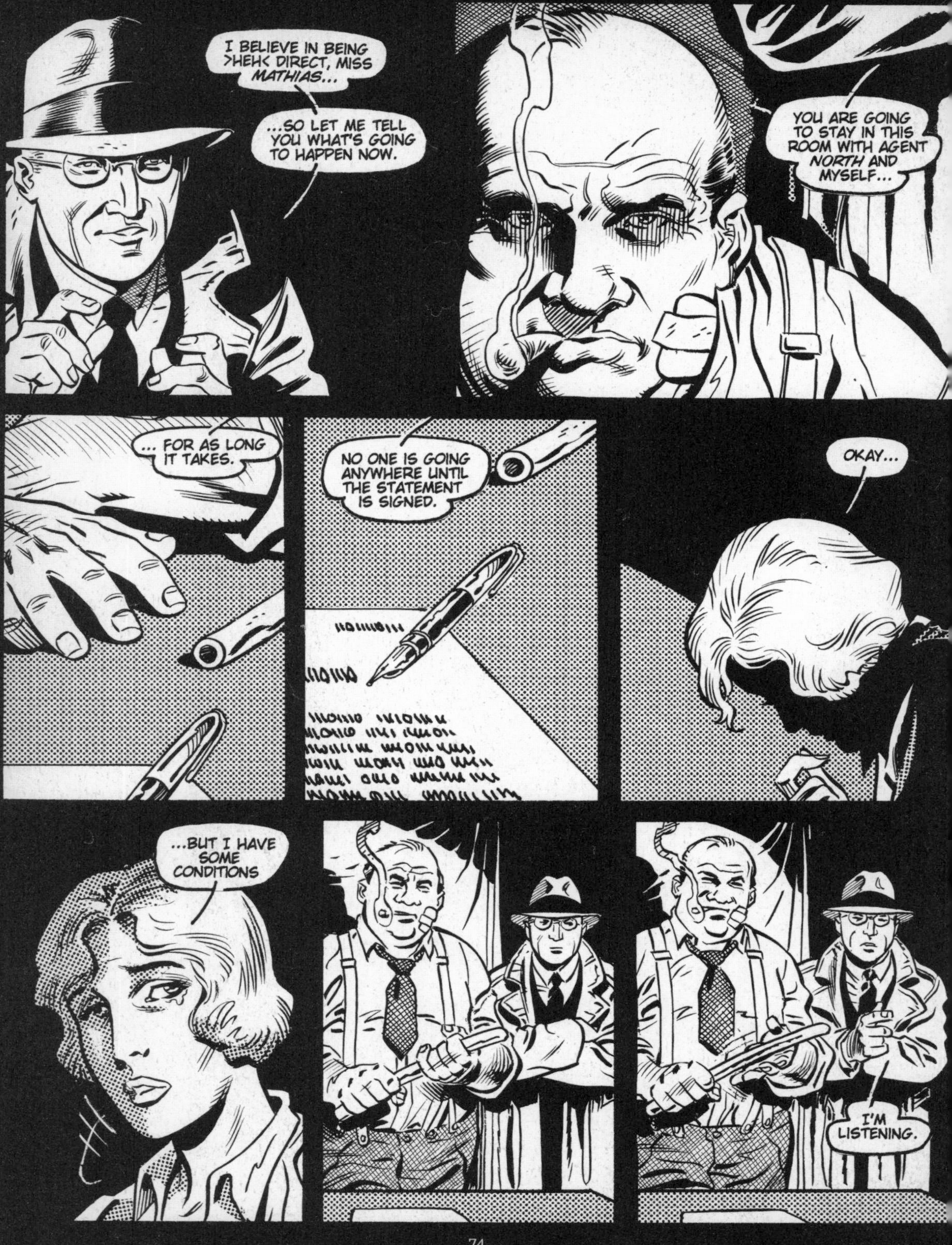
I BELIEVE IN BEING >HEH< DIRECT, MISS MATHIAS...
...SO LET ME TELL YOU WHAT'S GOING TO HAPPEN NOW.
YOU ARE GOING TO STAY IN THIS ROOM WITH AGENT NORTH AND MYSELF...
... FOR AS LONG IT TAKES.
NO ONE IS GOING ANYWHERE UNTIL THE STATEMENT IS SIGNED.
OKAY...
...BUT I HAVE SOME CONDITIONS
I'M LISTENING.

ACT III

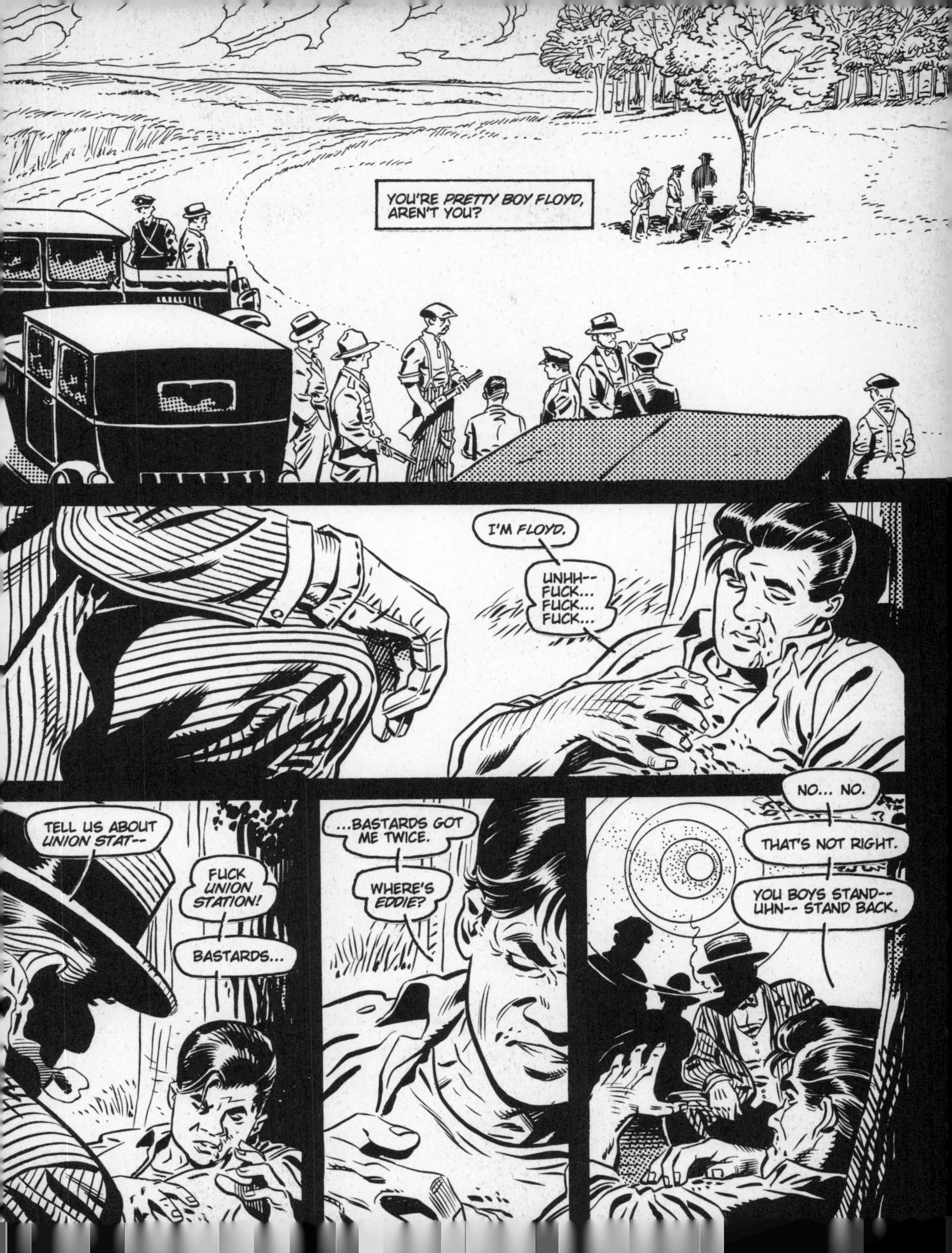

YOU'RE PRETTY BOY FLOYD, AREN'T YOU?
I'M FLOYD.
UNHH-- FUCK... FUCK... FUCK...
TELL US ABOUT UNION STAT--
FUCK UNION STATION!
BASTARDS...
...BASTARDS GOT ME TWICE.
WHERE'S EDDIE?
NO... NO.
THAT'S NOT RIGHT.
YOU BOYS STAND-- UHN-- STAND BACK.

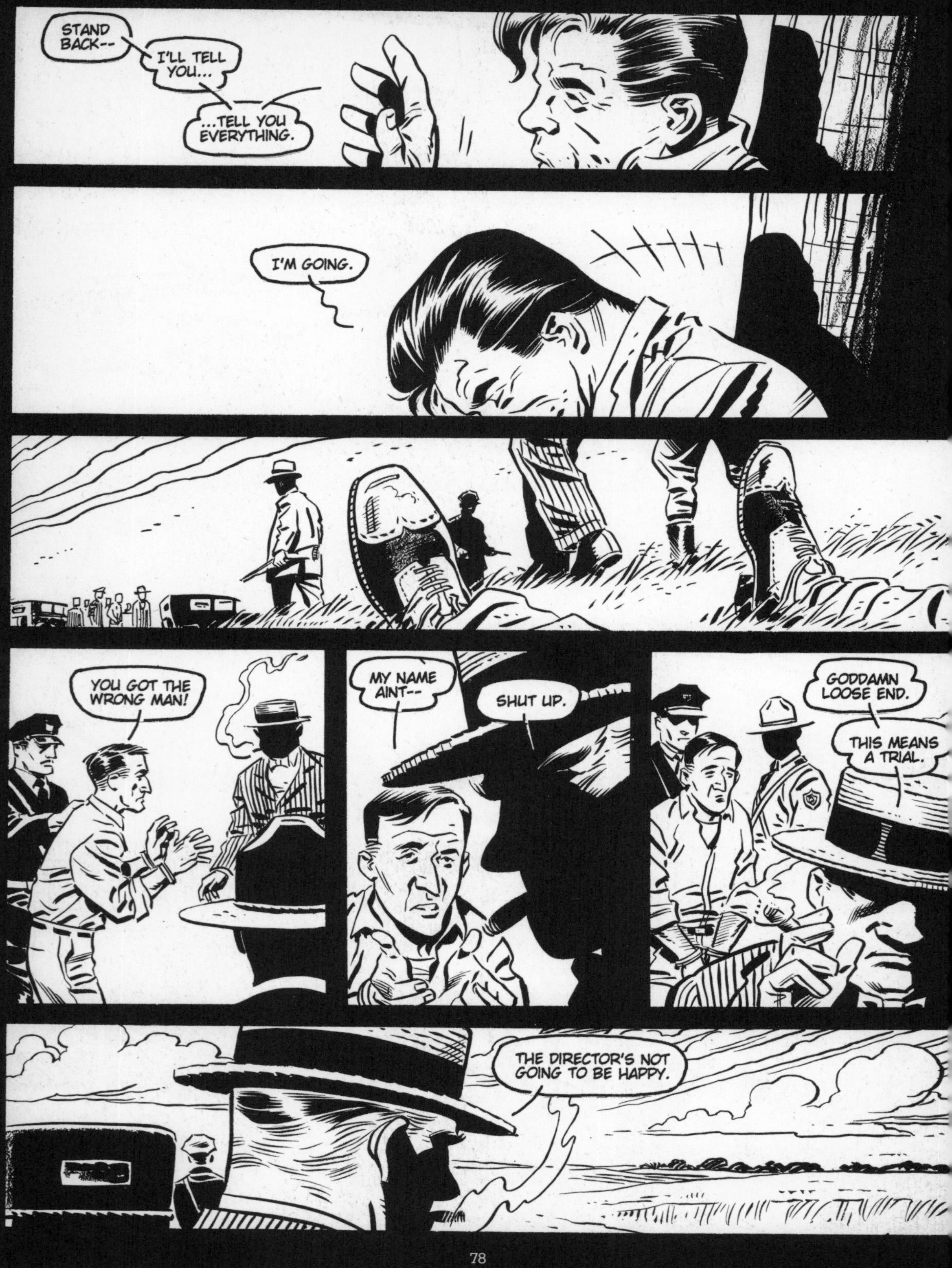
STAND BACK--
I'LL TELL YOU...
...TELL YOU EVERYTHING.
I'M GOING.
YOU GOT THE WRONG MAN!
MY NAME AINT--
SHUT UP.
GODDAMN LOOSE END.
THIS MEANS A TRIAL.
THE DIRECTOR'S NOT GOING TO BE HAPPY.

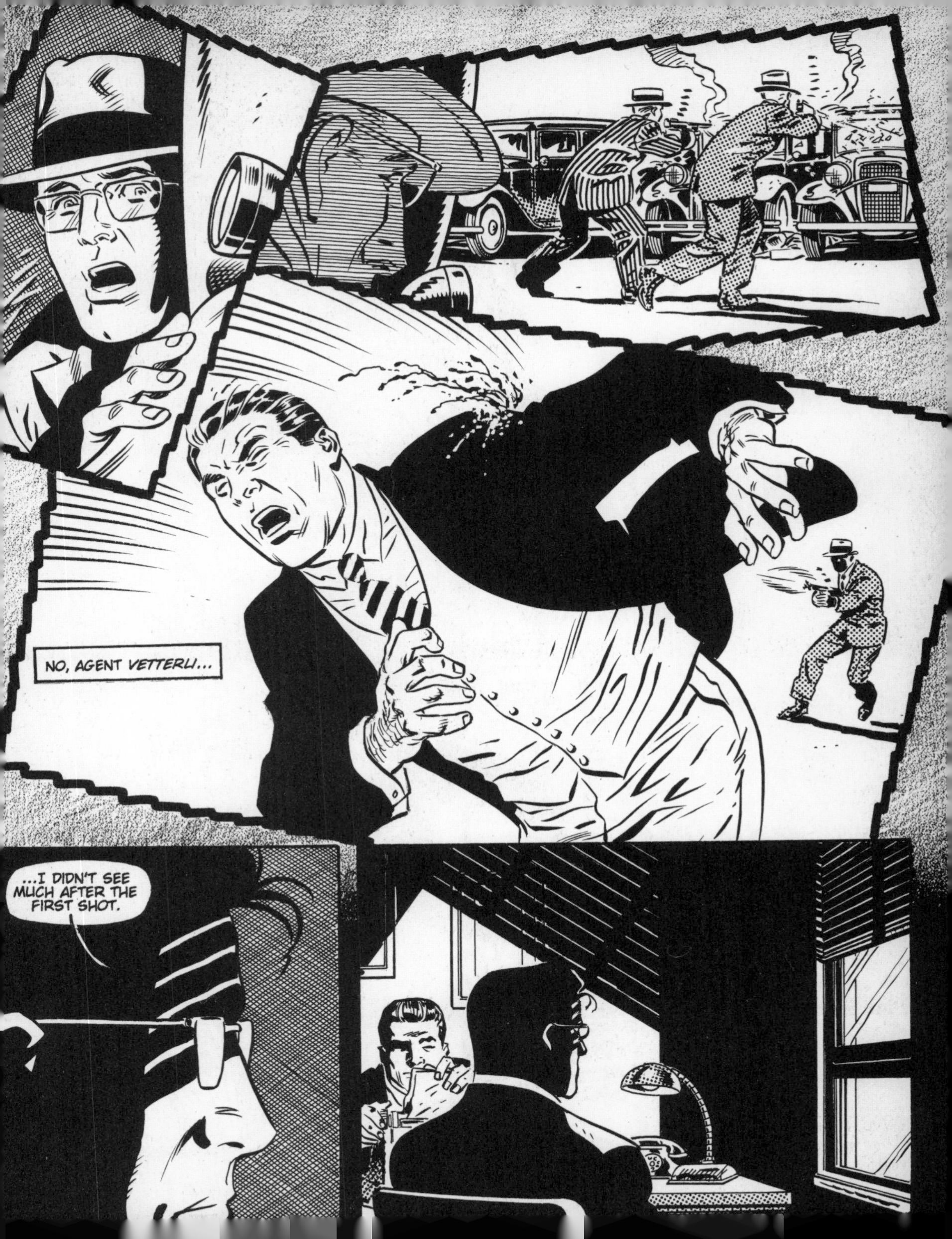
NO, AGENT VETTERLI...
...I DIDN'T SEE MUCH AFTER THE FIRST SHOT.

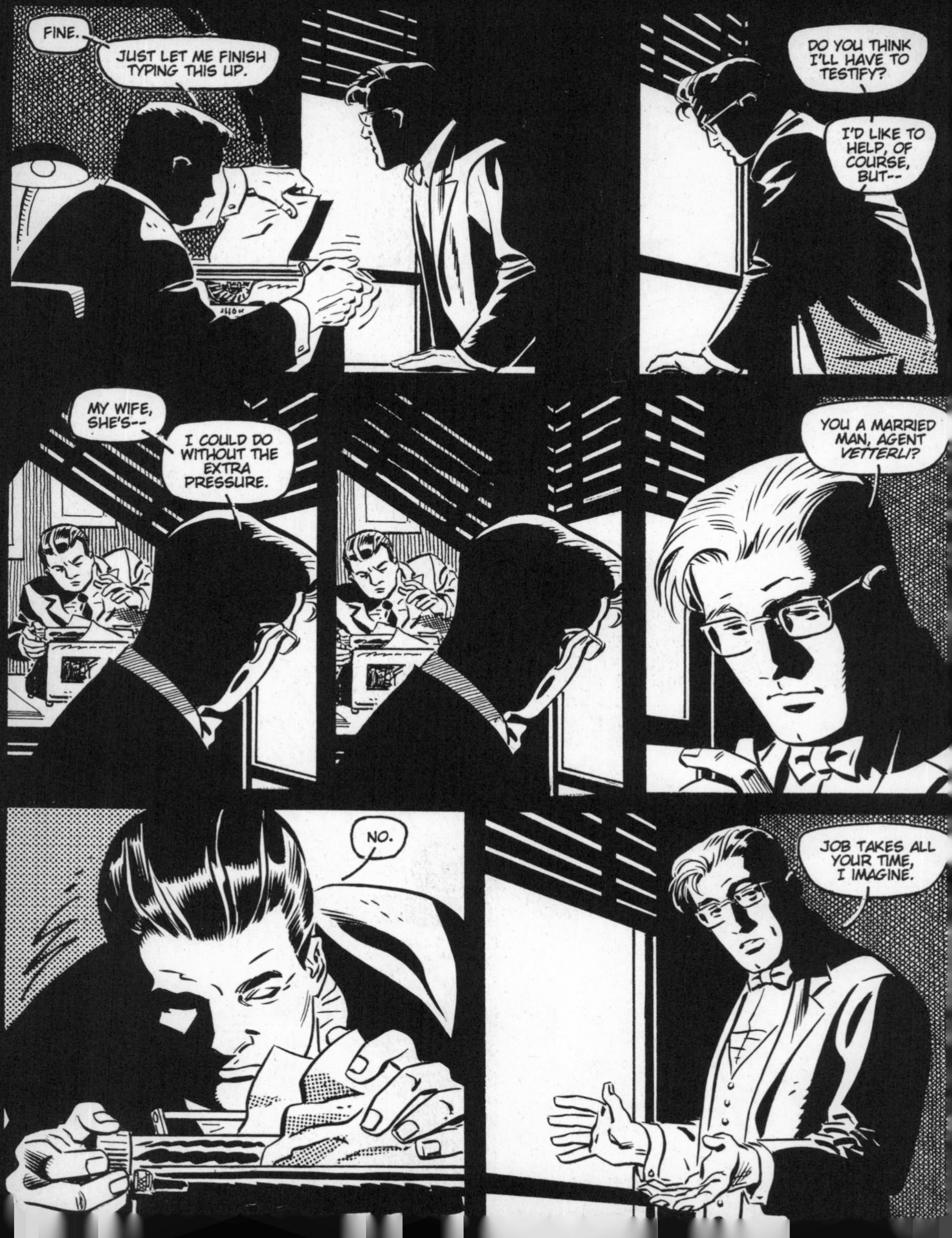
FINE.
JUST LET ME FINISH TYPING THIS UP.
DO YOU THINK I'LL HAVE TO TESTIFY?
I'D LIKE TO HELP, OF COURSE, BUT--
MY WIFE, SHE'S--
I COULD DO WITHOUT THE EXTRA PRESSURE.
YOU A MARRIED MAN, AGENT *VETTERLI?*
NO.
JOB TAKES ALL YOUR TIME, I IMAGINE.

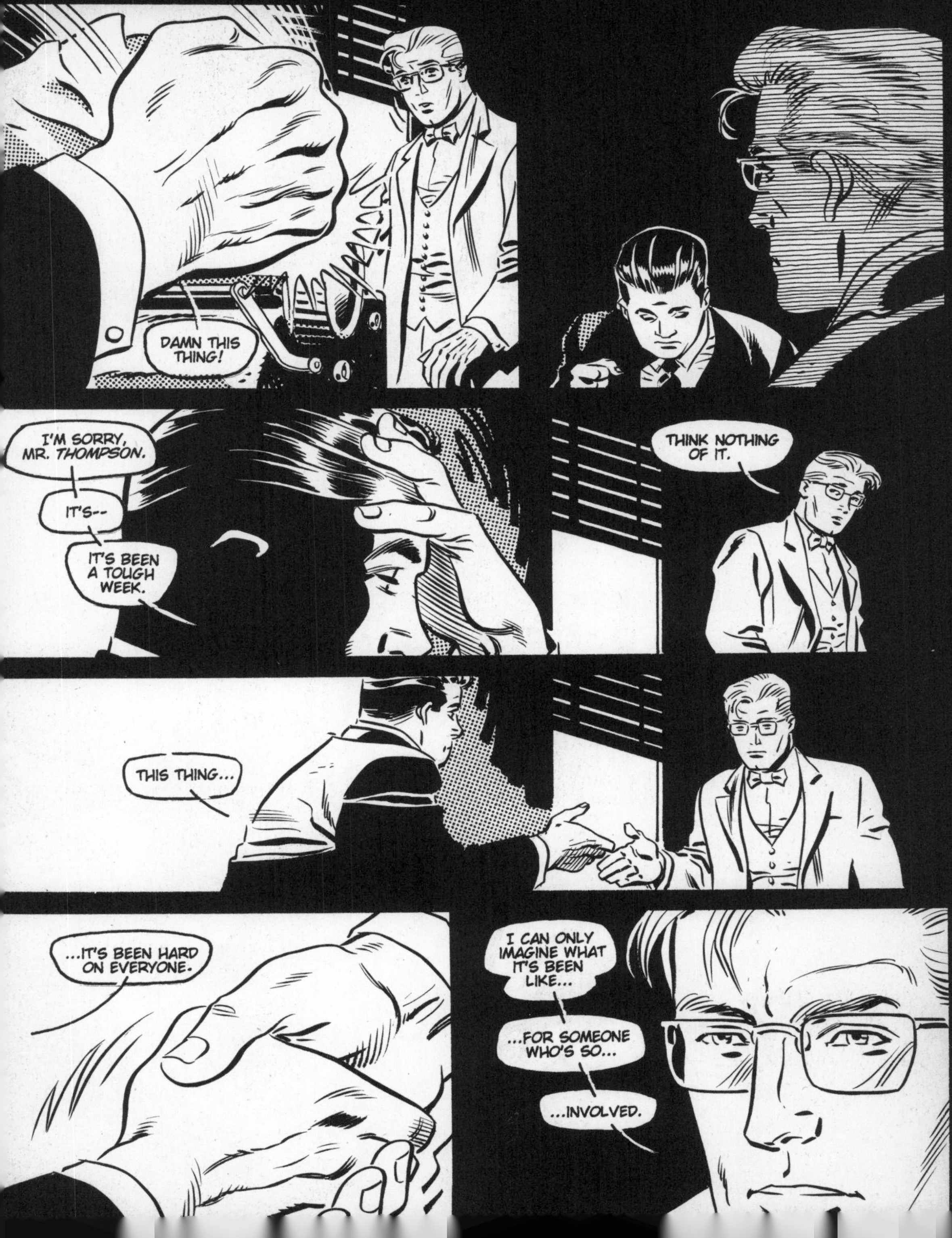
DAMN THIS THING!
I'M SORRY, MR. THOMPSON.
IT'S--
IT'S BEEN A TOUGH WEEK.
THINK NOTHING OF IT.
THIS THING...
...IT'S BEEN HARD ON EVERYONE.
I CAN ONLY IMAGINE WHAT IT'S BEEN LIKE...
...FOR SOMEONE WHO'S SO...
...INVOLVED.

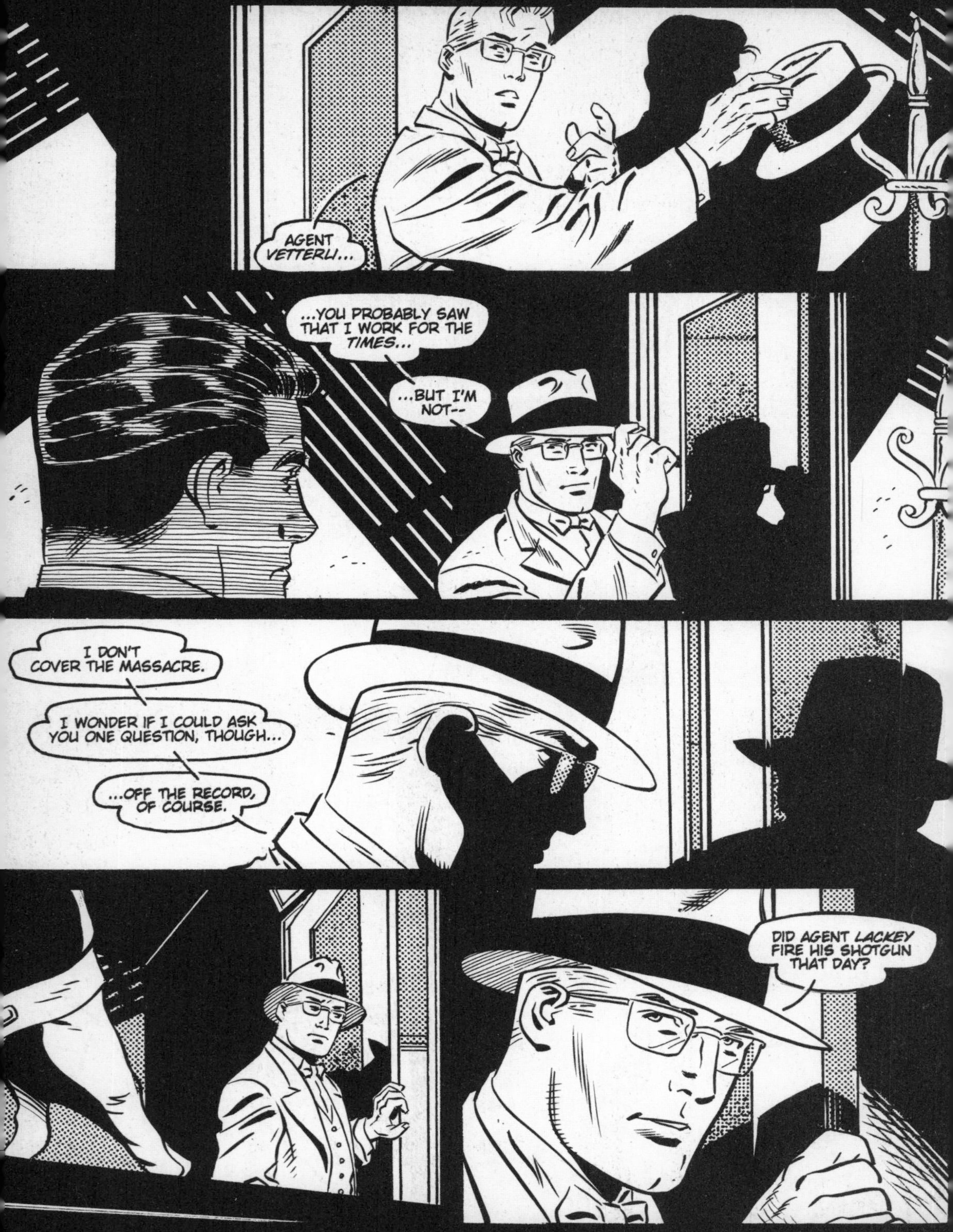
AGENT VETTERLI...
...YOU PROBABLY SAW THAT I WORK FOR THE TIMES...
...BUT I'M NOT--
I DON'T COVER THE MASSACRE.
I WONDER IF I COULD ASK YOU ONE QUESTION, THOUGH...
...OFF THE RECORD, OF COURSE.
DID AGENT LACKEY FIRE HIS SHOTGUN THAT DAY?

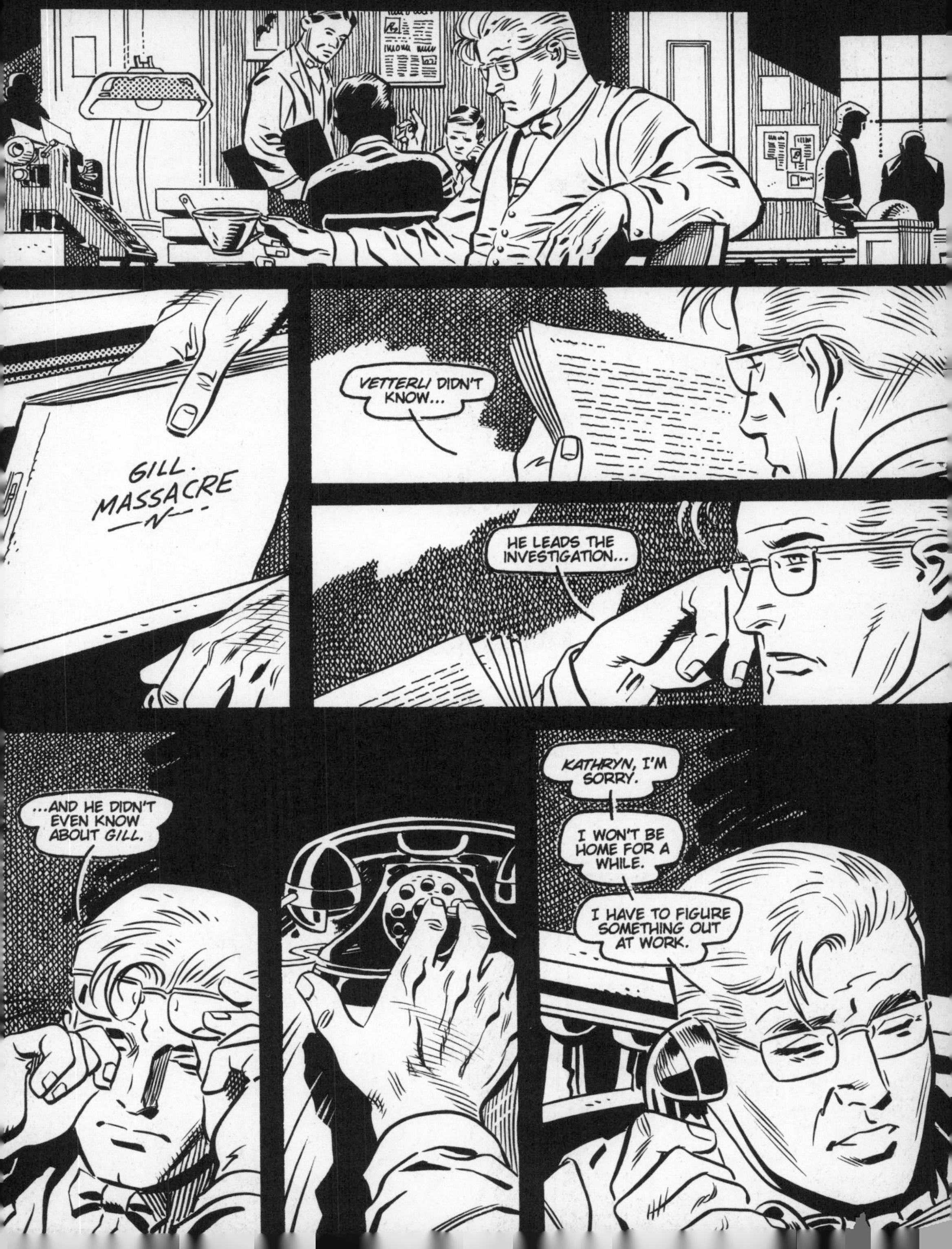
GILL.
MASSACRE
VETTERLI DIDN'T KNOW...
HE LEADS THE INVESTIGATION...
...AND HE DIDN'T EVEN KNOW ABOUT GILL.
KATHRYN, I'M SORRY.
I WON'T BE HOME FOR A WHILE.
I HAVE TO FIGURE SOMETHING OUT AT WORK.

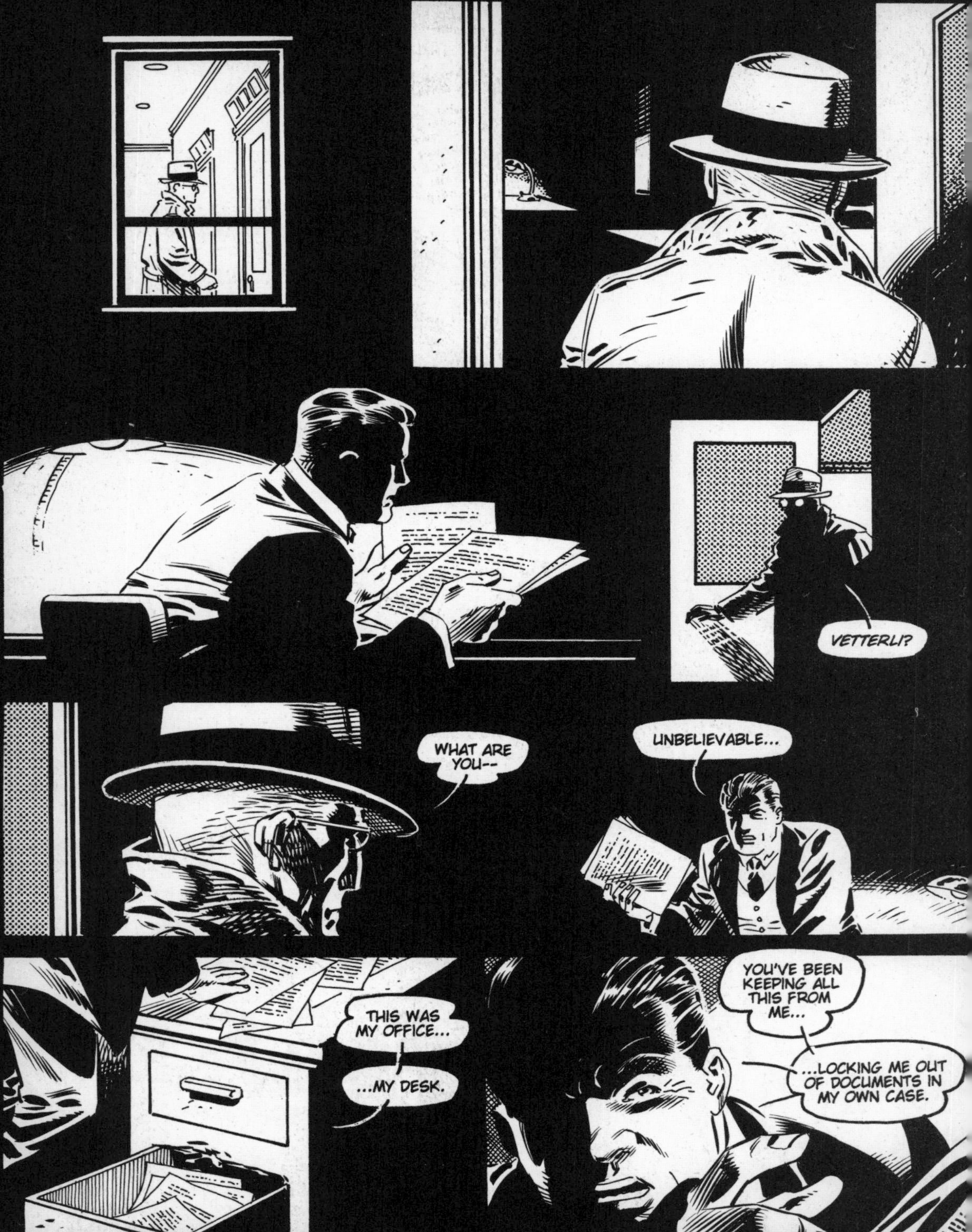
VETTERLI?
WHAT ARE YOU--
UNBELIEVABLE...
THIS WAS MY OFFICE...
...MY DESK.
YOU'VE BEEN KEEPING ALL THIS FROM ME...
...LOCKING ME OUT OF DOCUMENTS IN MY OWN CASE.

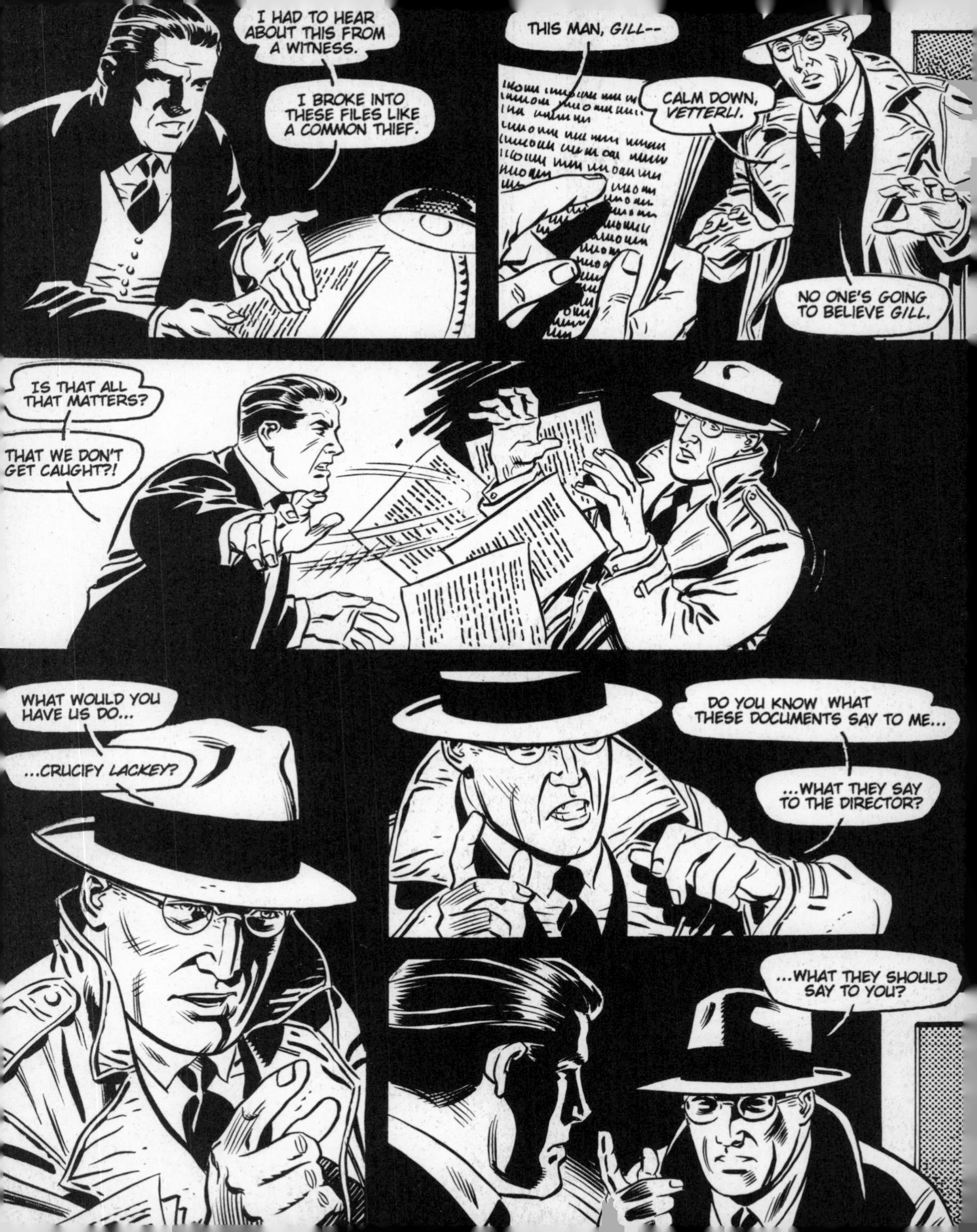

I HAD TO HEAR ABOUT THIS FROM A WITNESS.
I BROKE INTO THESE FILES LIKE A COMMON THIEF.
THIS MAN, *GILL*--
CALM DOWN, *VETTERLI*.
NO ONE'S GOING TO BELIEVE *GILL*.
IS THAT ALL THAT MATTERS?
THAT WE DON'T GET CAUGHT?!
WHAT WOULD YOU HAVE US DO...
...CRUCIFY *LACKEY*?
DO YOU KNOW WHAT THESE DOCUMENTS SAY TO ME...
...WHAT THEY SAY TO THE DIRECTOR?
...WHAT THEY SHOULD SAY TO YOU?

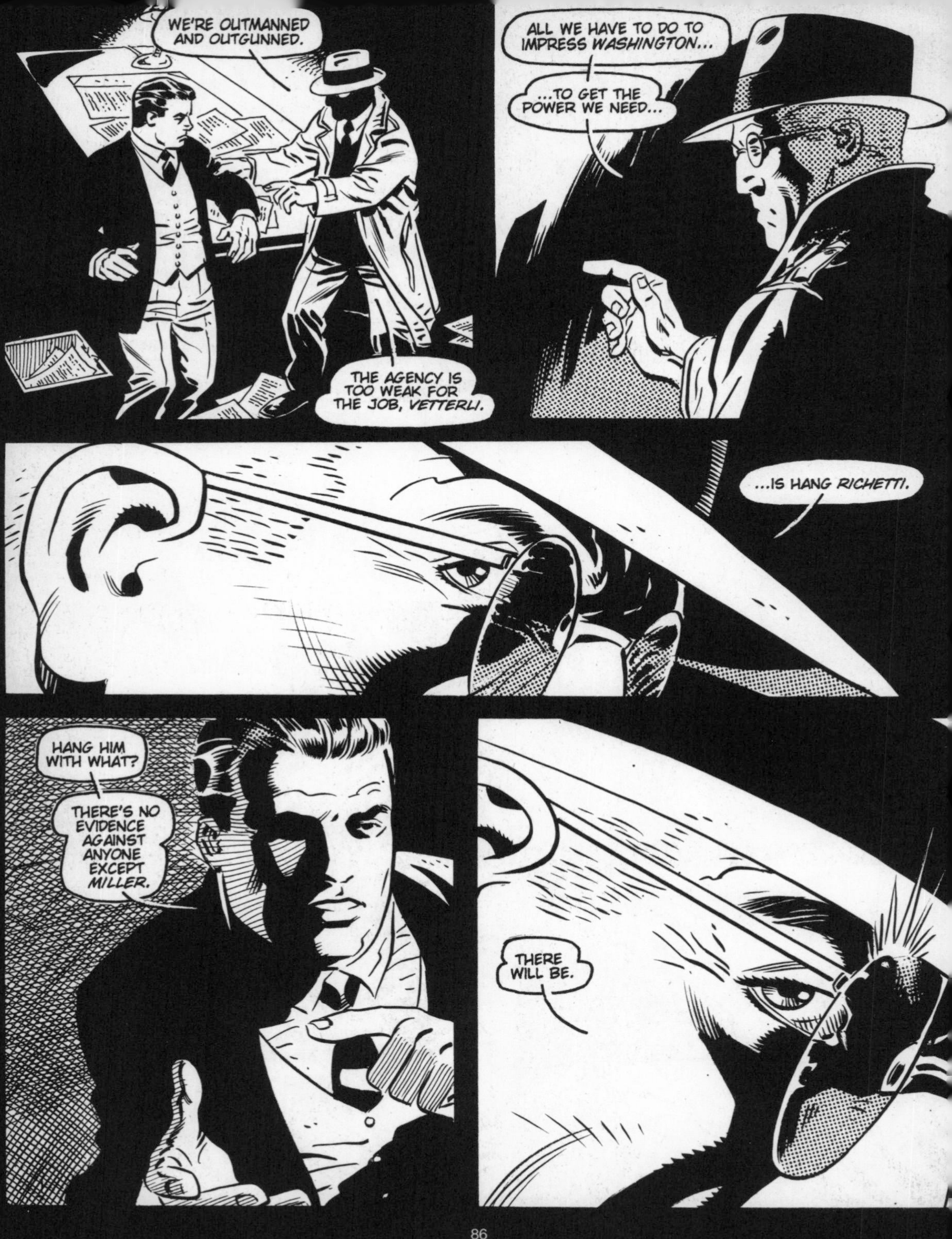

WE'RE OUTMANNED AND OUTGUNNED.
THE AGENCY IS TOO WEAK FOR THE JOB, VETTERLI.
ALL WE HAVE TO DO TO IMPRESS WASHINGTON...
...TO GET THE POWER WE NEED...
...IS HANG RICHETTI.
HANG HIM WITH WHAT?
THERE'S NO EVIDENCE AGAINST ANYONE EXCEPT MILLER.
THERE WILL BE.

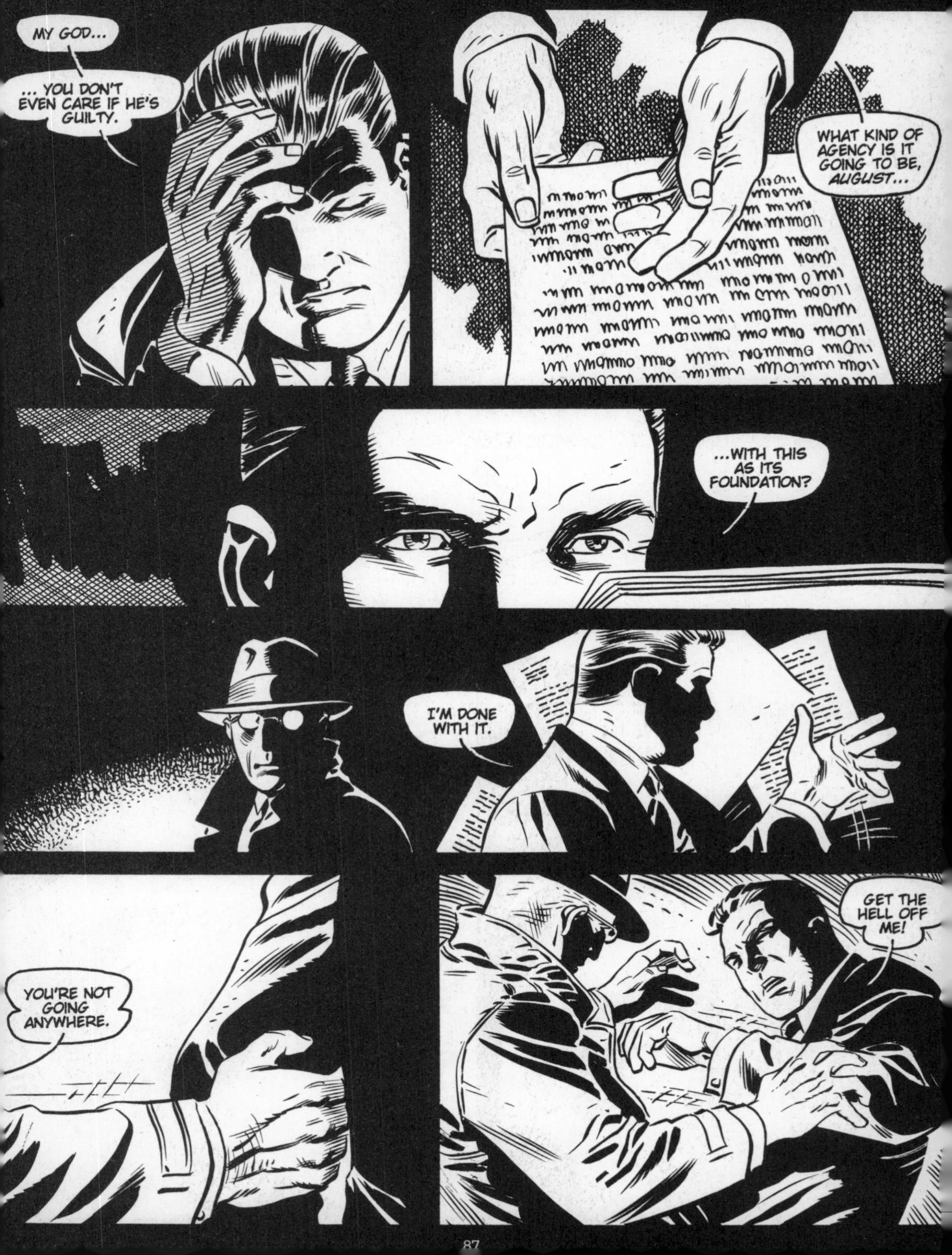
MY GOD...
... YOU DON'T EVEN CARE IF HE'S GUILTY.
WHAT KIND OF AGENCY IS IT GOING TO BE, AUGUST...
...WITH THIS AS ITS FOUNDATION?
I'M DONE WITH IT.
YOU'RE NOT GOING ANYWHERE.
GET THE HELL OFF ME!

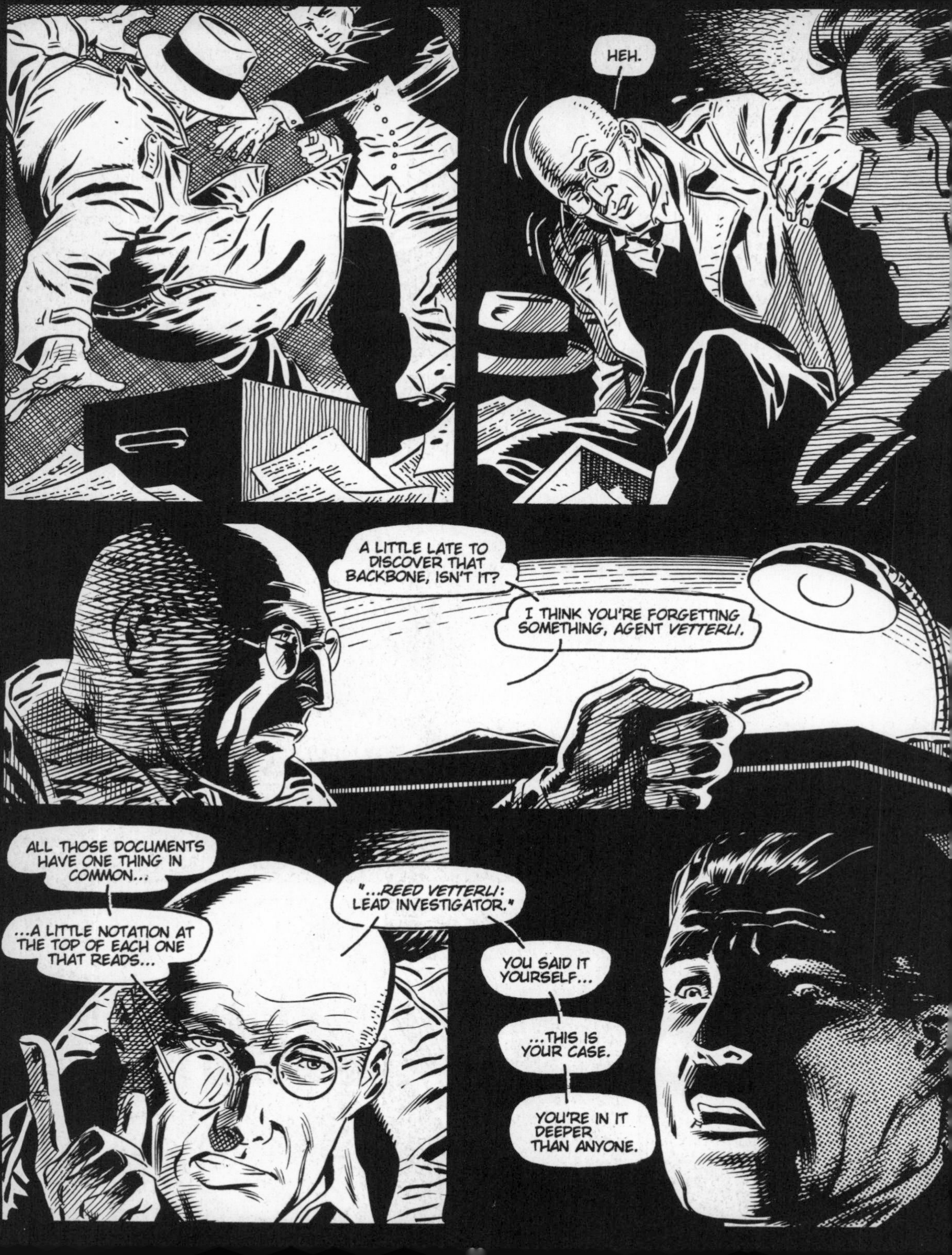
HEH.
A LITTLE LATE TO DISCOVER THAT BACKBONE, ISN'T IT?
I THINK YOU'RE FORGETTING SOMETHING, AGENT *VETTERLI*.
ALL THOSE DOCUMENTS HAVE ONE THING IN COMMON...
...A LITTLE NOTATION AT THE TOP OF EACH ONE THAT READS...
"...*REED VETTERLI*: LEAD INVESTIGATOR."
YOU SAID IT YOURSELF...
...THIS IS YOUR CASE.
YOU'RE IN IT DEEPER THAN ANYONE.

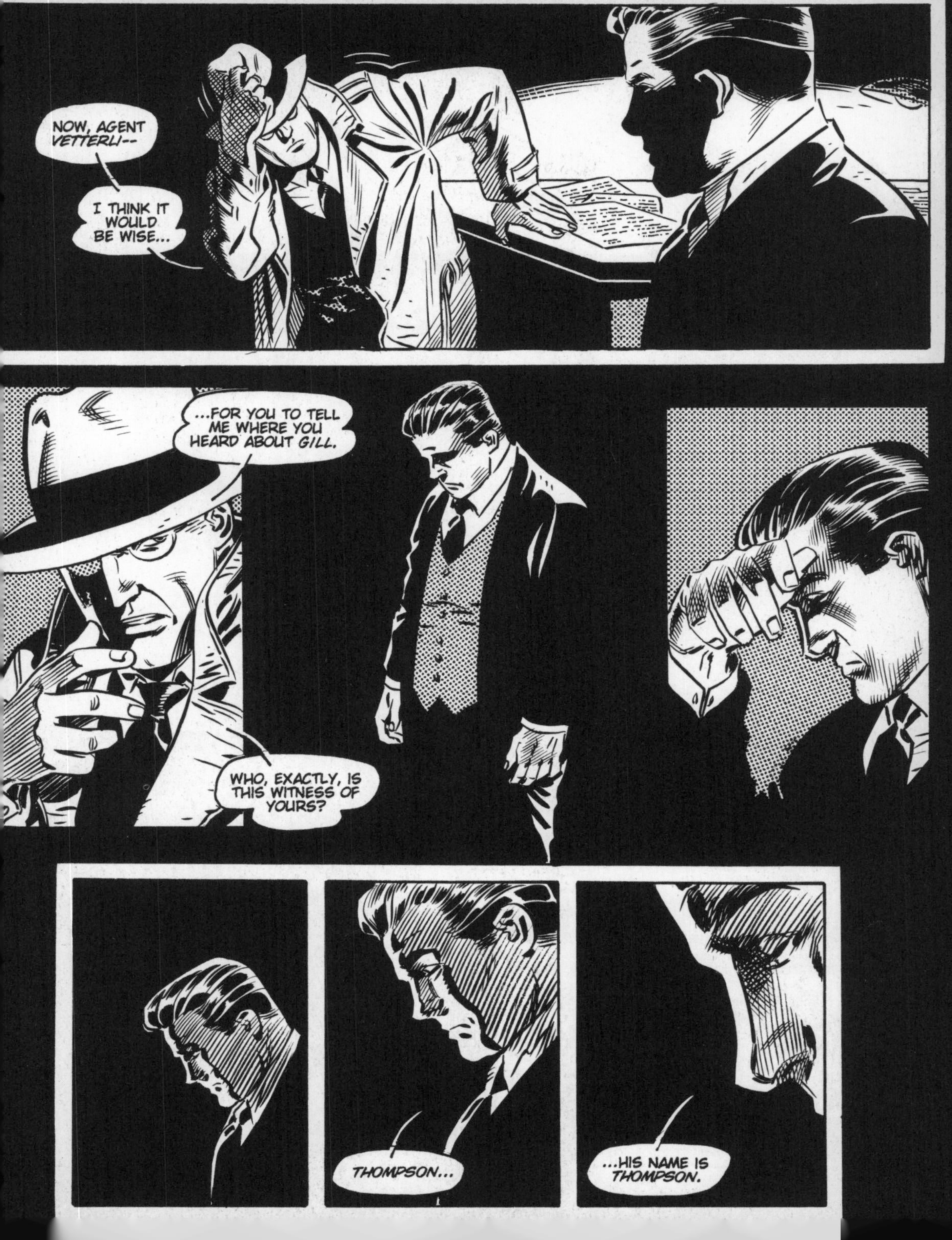
NOW, AGENT VETTERLI--
I THINK IT WOULD BE WISE...
...FOR YOU TO TELL ME WHERE YOU HEARD ABOUT GILL.
WHO, EXACTLY, IS THIS WITNESS OF YOURS?
THOMPSON...
...HIS NAME IS THOMPSON.

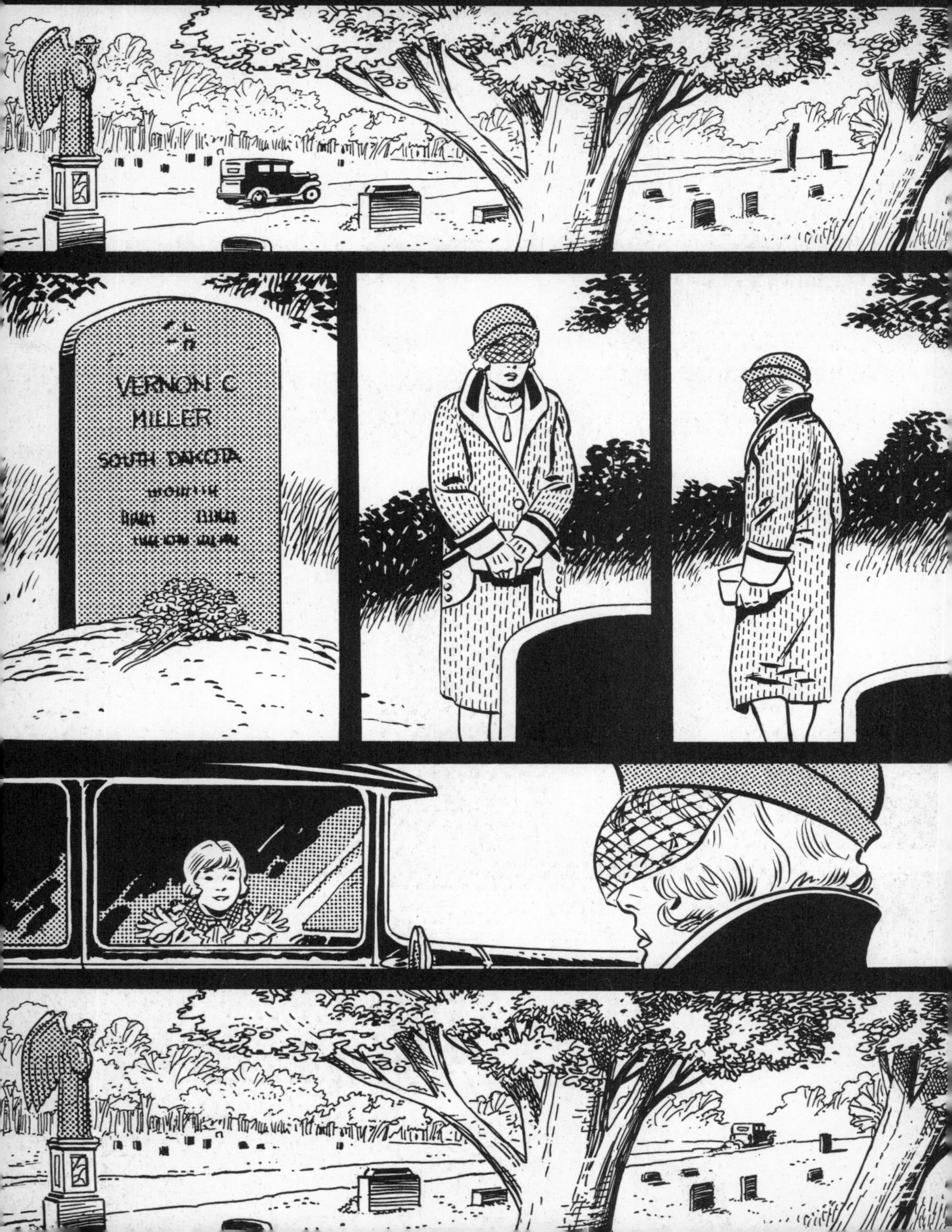
VERNON C
MILLER
SOUTH DAKOTA

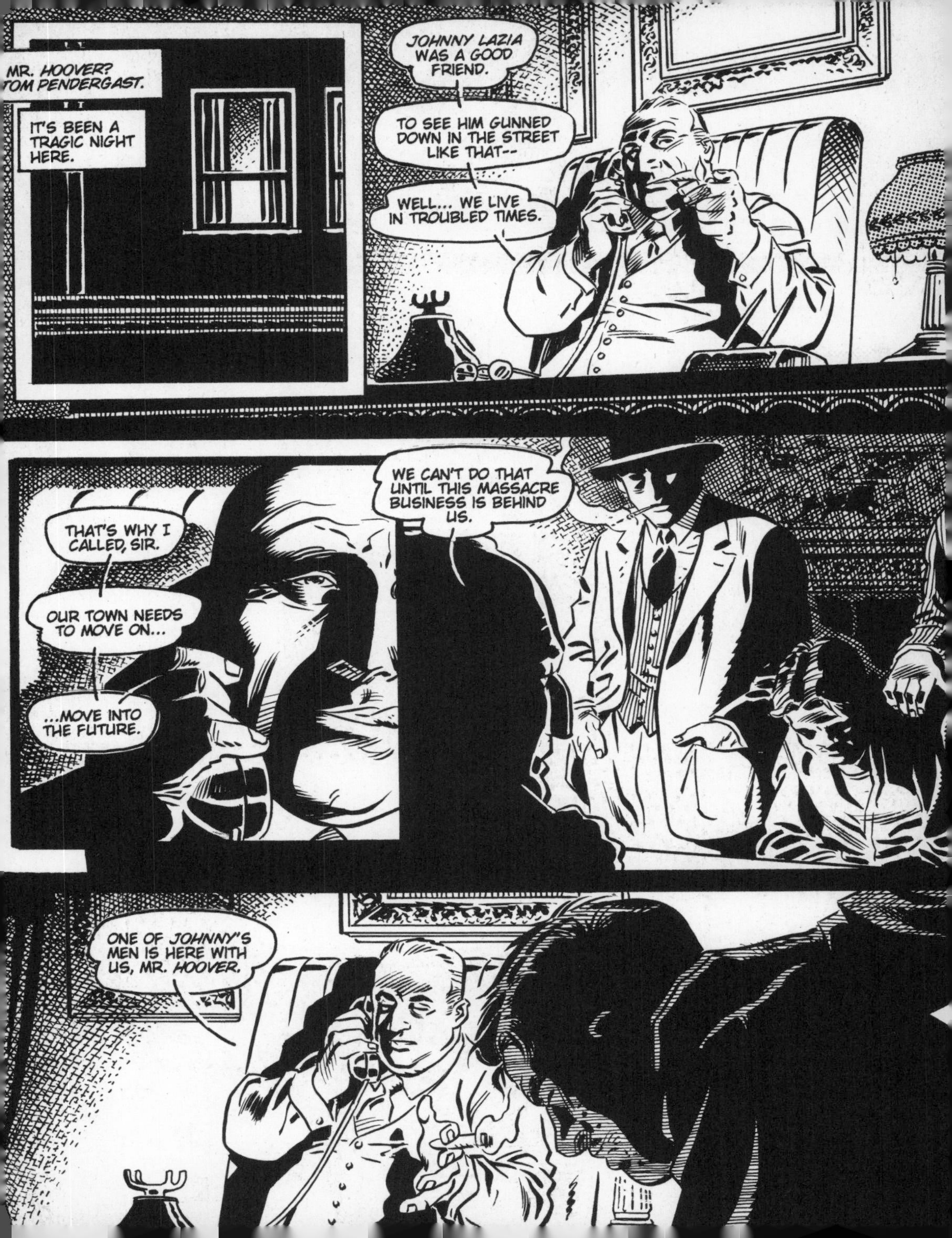
MR. HOOVER? TOM PENDERGAST.
IT'S BEEN A TRAGIC NIGHT HERE.
JOHNNY LAZIA WAS A GOOD FRIEND.
TO SEE HIM GUNNED DOWN IN THE STREET LIKE THAT--
WELL... WE LIVE IN TROUBLED TIMES.
THAT'S WHY I CALLED, SIR.
OUR TOWN NEEDS TO MOVE ON...
...MOVE INTO THE FUTURE.
WE CAN'T DO THAT UNTIL THIS MASSACRE BUSINESS IS BEHIND US.
ONE OF JOHNNY'S MEN IS HERE WITH US, MR. HOOVER.

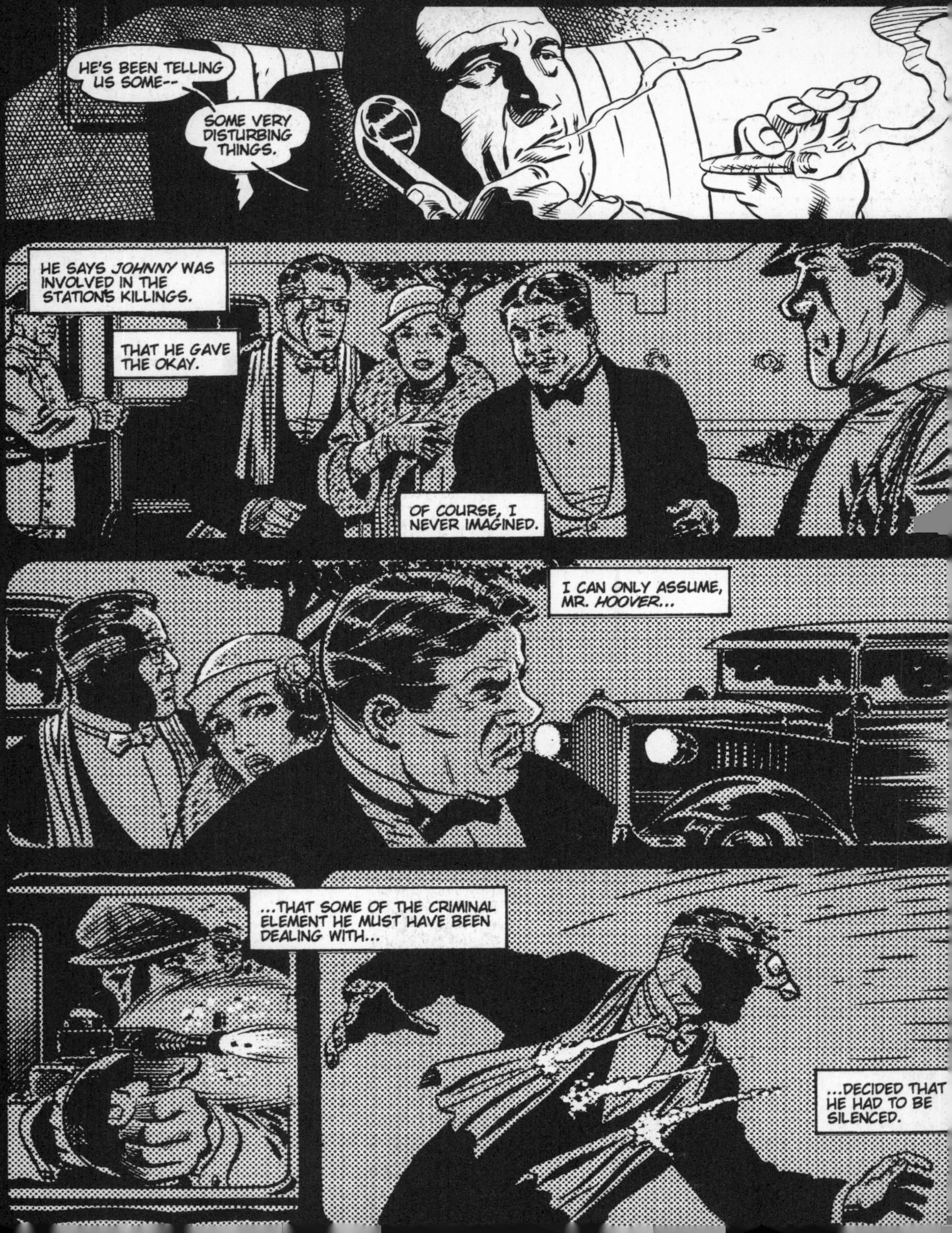
HE'S BEEN TELLING US SOME--
SOME VERY DISTURBING THINGS.
HE SAYS JOHNNY WAS INVOLVED IN THE STATION'S KILLINGS.
THAT HE GAVE THE OKAY.
OF COURSE, I NEVER IMAGINED.
I CAN ONLY ASSUME, MR. HOOVER...
...THAT SOME OF THE CRIMINAL ELEMENT HE MUST HAVE BEEN DEALING WITH...
...DECIDED THAT HE HAD TO BE SILENCED.

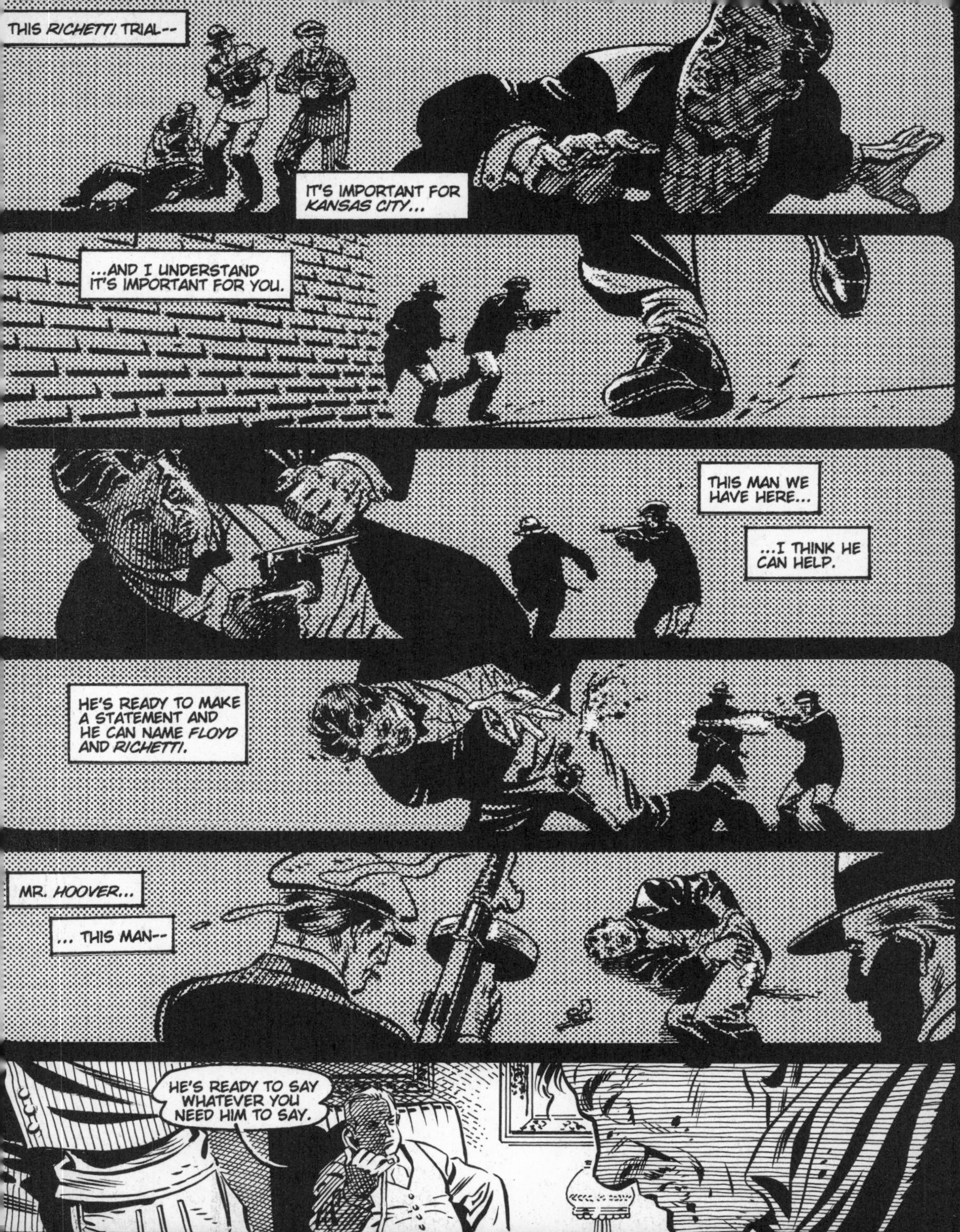

THIS RICHETTI TRIAL--
IT'S IMPORTANT FOR KANSAS CITY...
...AND I UNDERSTAND IT'S IMPORTANT FOR YOU.
THIS MAN WE HAVE HERE...
...I THINK HE CAN HELP.
HE'S READY TO MAKE A STATEMENT AND HE CAN NAME FLOYD AND RICHETTI.
MR. HOOVER...
... THIS MAN--
HE'S READY TO SAY WHATEVER YOU NEED HIM TO SAY.

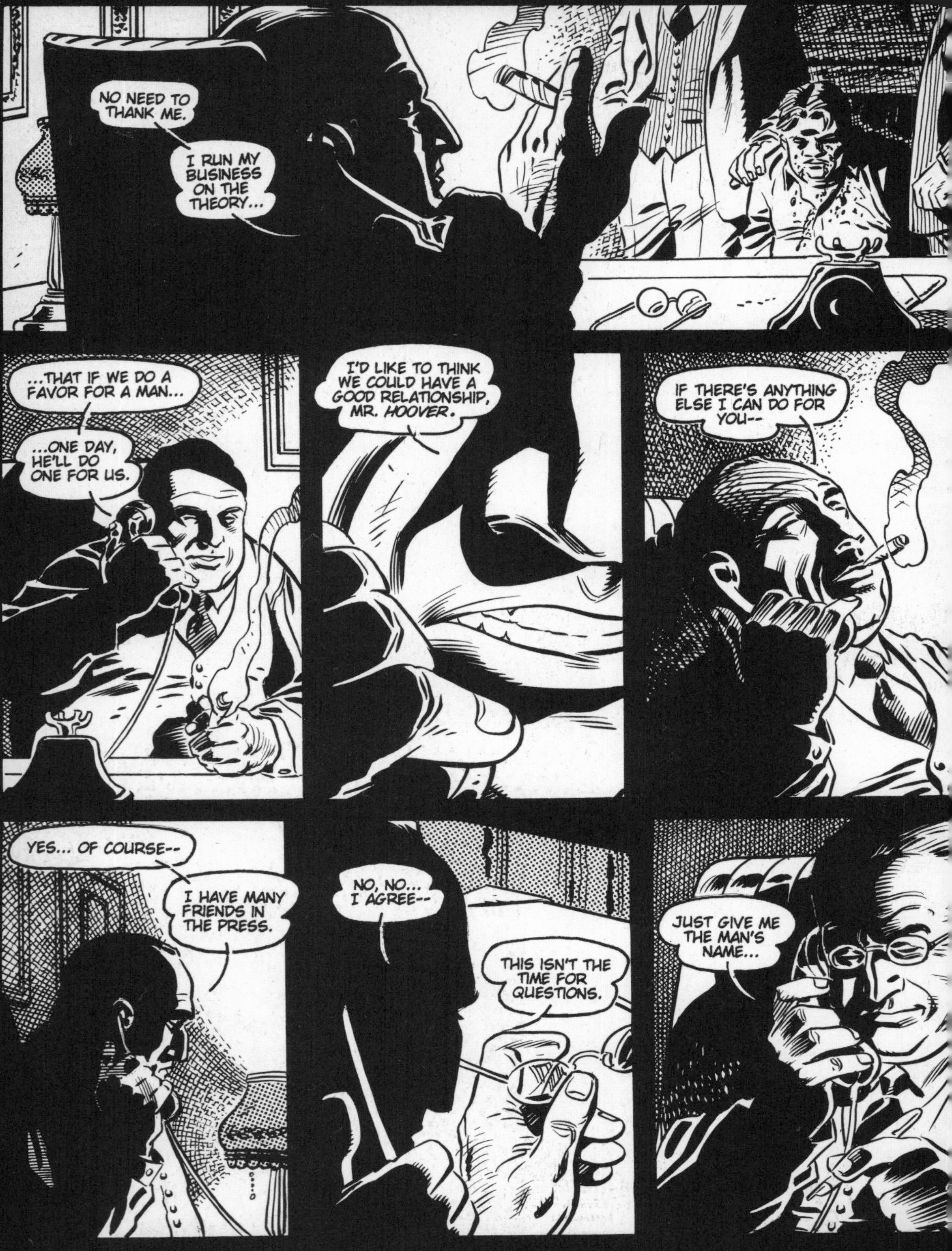
NO NEED TO THANK ME.
I RUN MY BUSINESS ON THE THEORY...
...THAT IF WE DO A FAVOR FOR A MAN...
...ONE DAY, HE'LL DO ONE FOR US.
I'D LIKE TO THINK WE COULD HAVE A GOOD RELATIONSHIP, MR. *HOOVER*.
IF THERE'S ANYTHING ELSE I CAN DO FOR YOU--
YES... OF COURSE--
I HAVE MANY FRIENDS IN THE PRESS.
NO, NO... I AGREE--
THIS ISN'T THE TIME FOR QUESTIONS.
JUST GIVE ME THE MAN'S NAME...

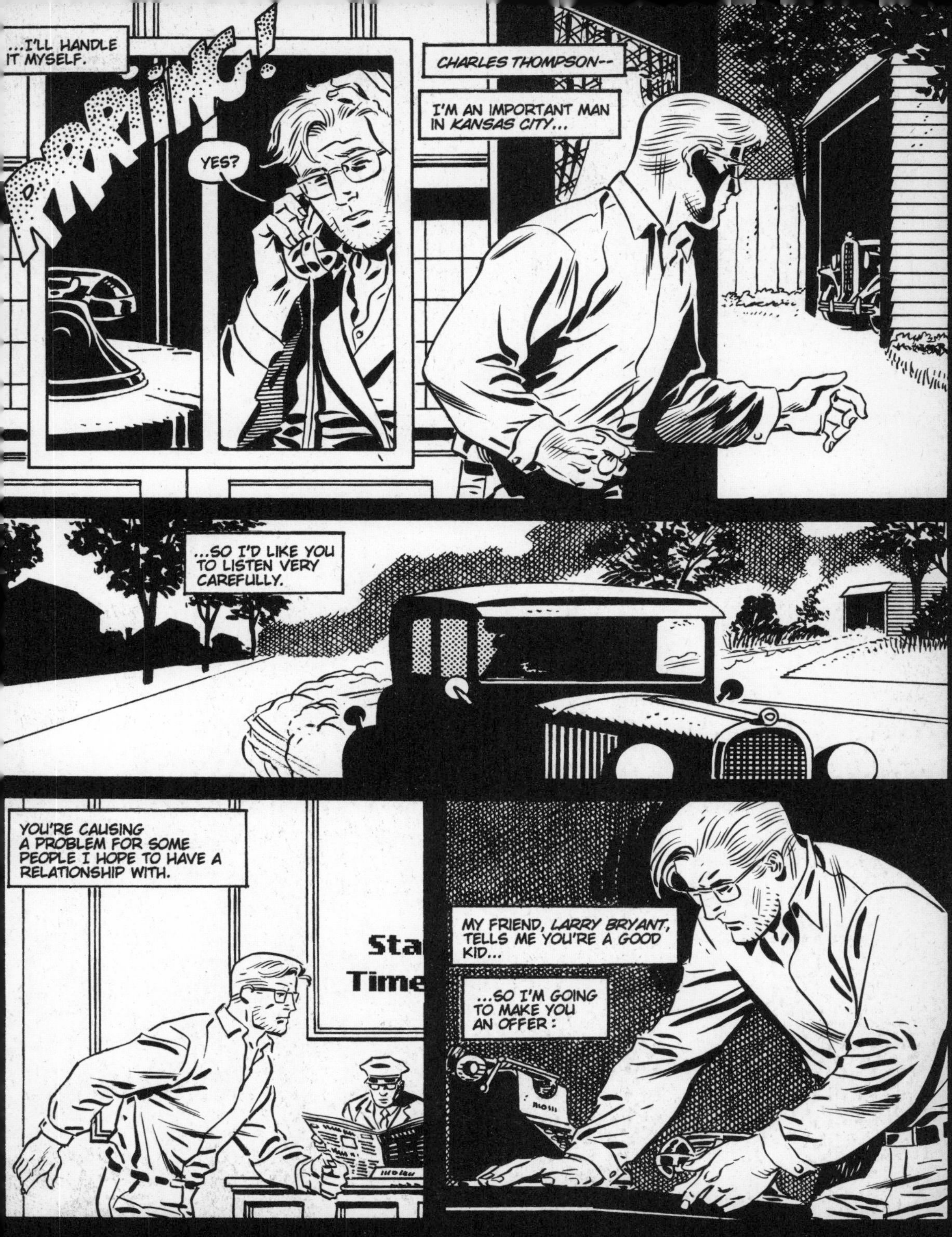

...I'LL HANDLE IT MYSELF.
RRRIIING!
YES?
CHARLES THOMPSON--
I'M AN IMPORTANT MAN IN KANSAS CITY...
...SO I'D LIKE YOU TO LISTEN VERY CAREFULLY.
YOU'RE CAUSING A PROBLEM FOR SOME PEOPLE I HOPE TO HAVE A RELATIONSHIP WITH.
MY FRIEND, LARRY BRYANT, TELLS ME YOU'RE A GOOD KID...
...SO I'M GOING TO MAKE YOU AN OFFER:

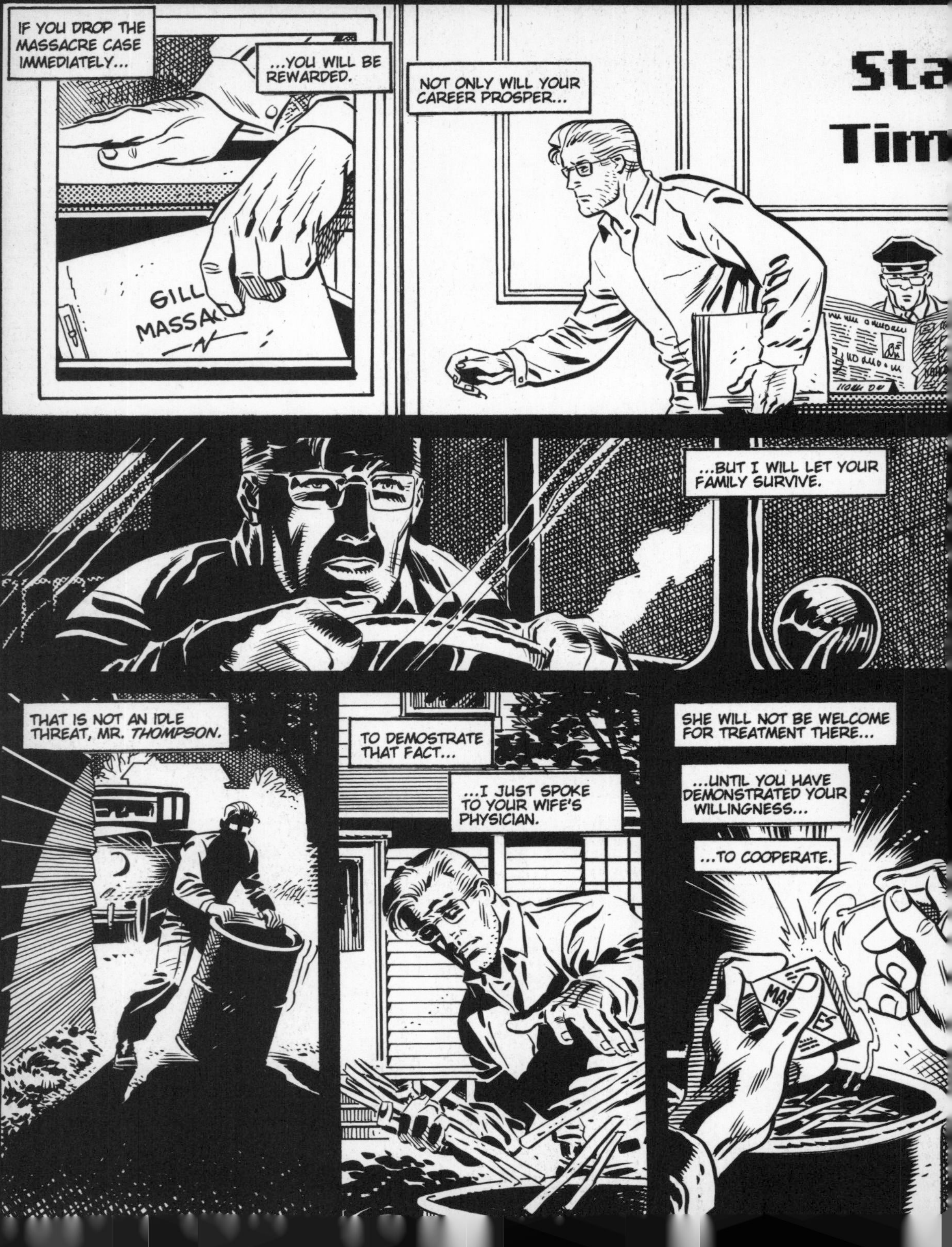

IF YOU DROP THE MASSACRE CASE IMMEDIATELY...
...YOU WILL BE REWARDED.
GILL MASSA
NOT ONLY WILL YOUR CAREER PROSPER...
Sta
Tim
...BUT I WILL LET YOUR FAMILY SURVIVE.
THAT IS NOT AN IDLE THREAT, MR. *THOMPSON.*
TO DEMOSTRATE THAT FACT...
...I JUST SPOKE TO YOUR WIFE'S PHYSICIAN.
SHE WILL NOT BE WELCOME FOR TREATMENT THERE...
...UNTIL YOU HAVE DEMONSTRATED YOUR WILLINGNESS...
...TO COOPERATE.

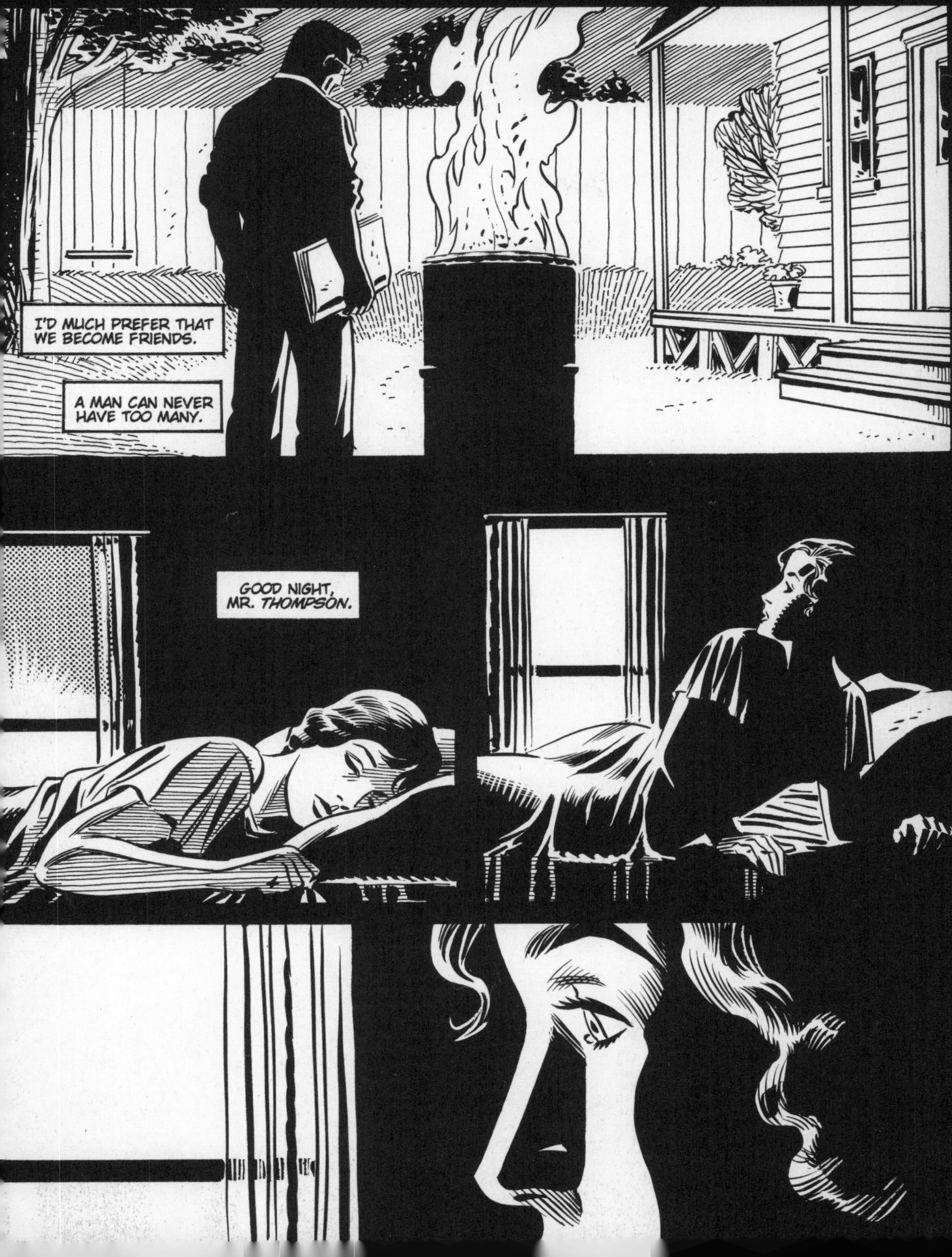
I'D MUCH PREFER THAT WE BECOME FRIENDS.
A MAN CAN NEVER HAVE TOO MANY.
GOOD NIGHT, MR. THOMPSON.

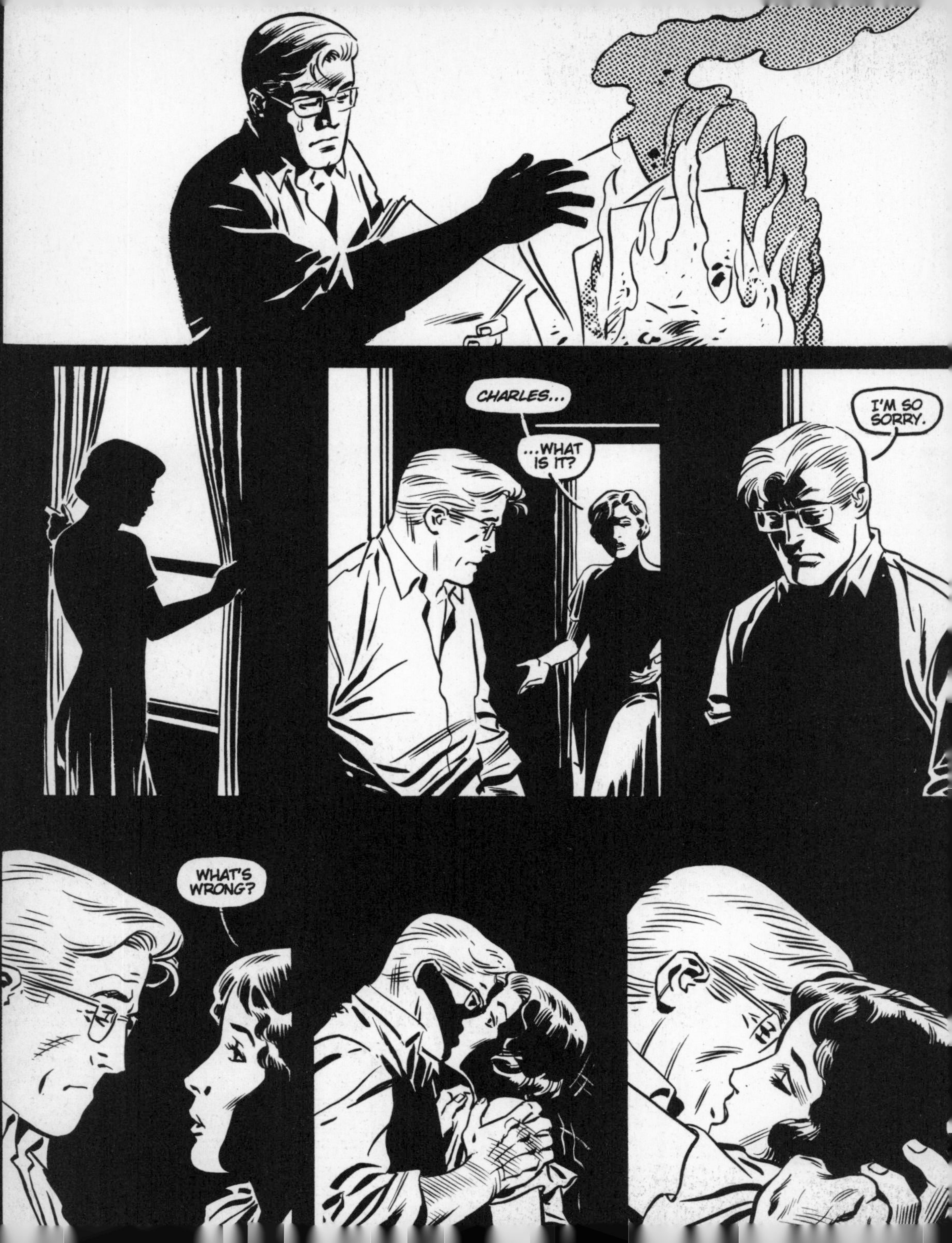
CHARLES...
...WHAT IS IT?
I'M SO SORRY.
WHAT'S WRONG?

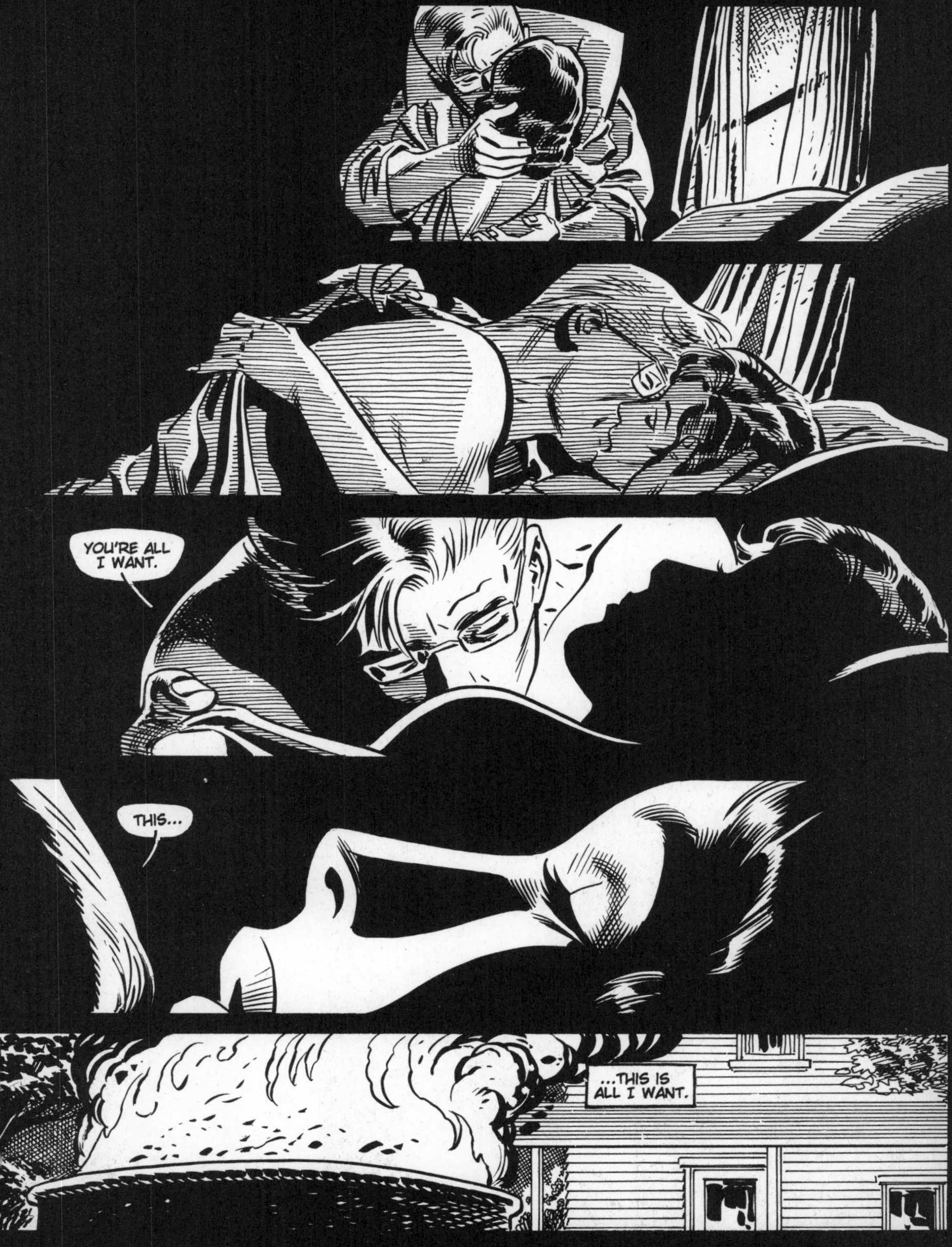
YOU'RE ALL I WANT.
THIS...
...THIS IS ALL I WANT.

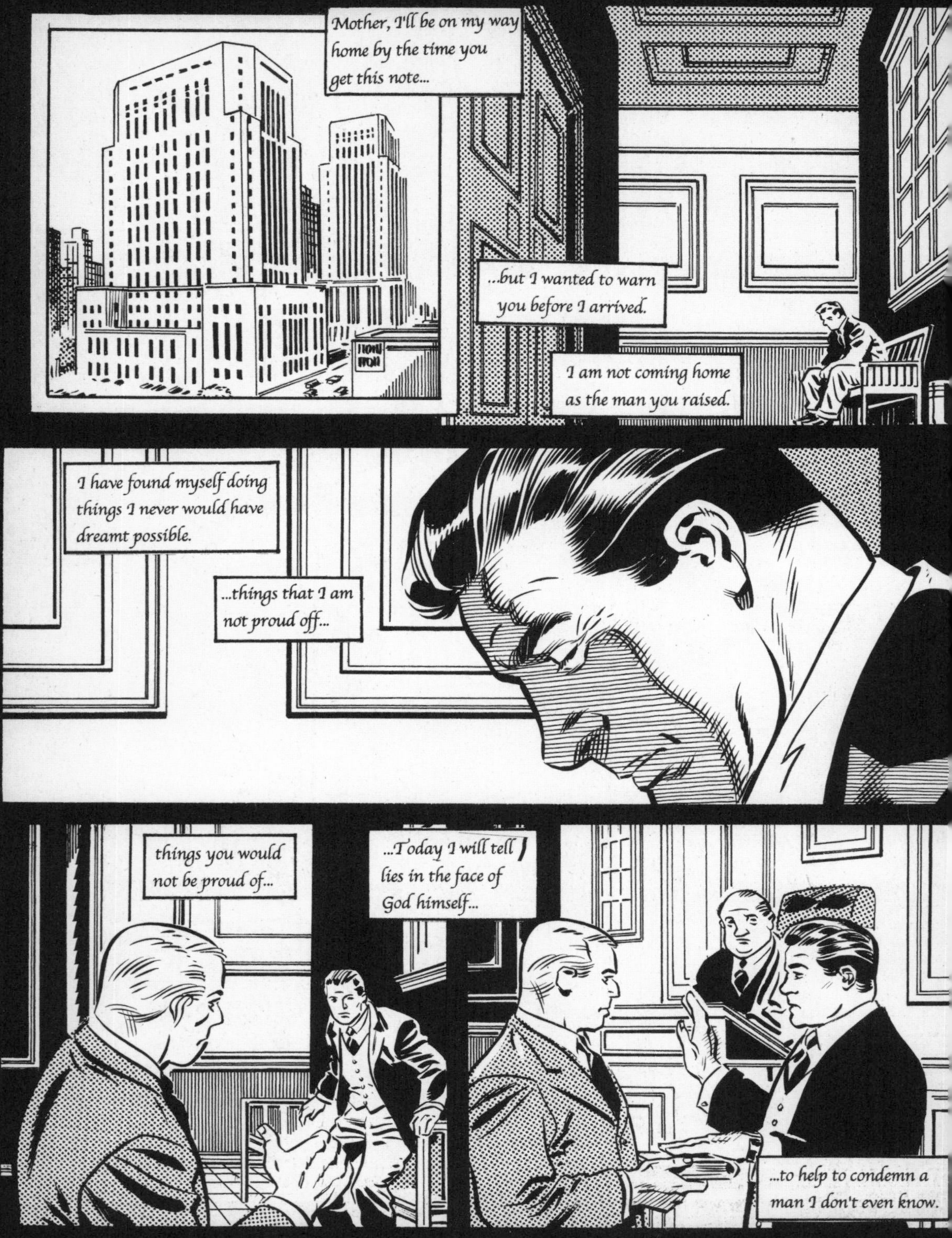
Mother, I'll be on my way home by the time you get this note...
...but I wanted to warn you before I arrived.
I am not coming home as the man you raised.
I have found myself doing things I never would have dreamt possible.
...things that I am not proud off...
things you would not be proud of...
...Today I will tell lies in the face of God himself...
...to help to condemn a man I don't even know.

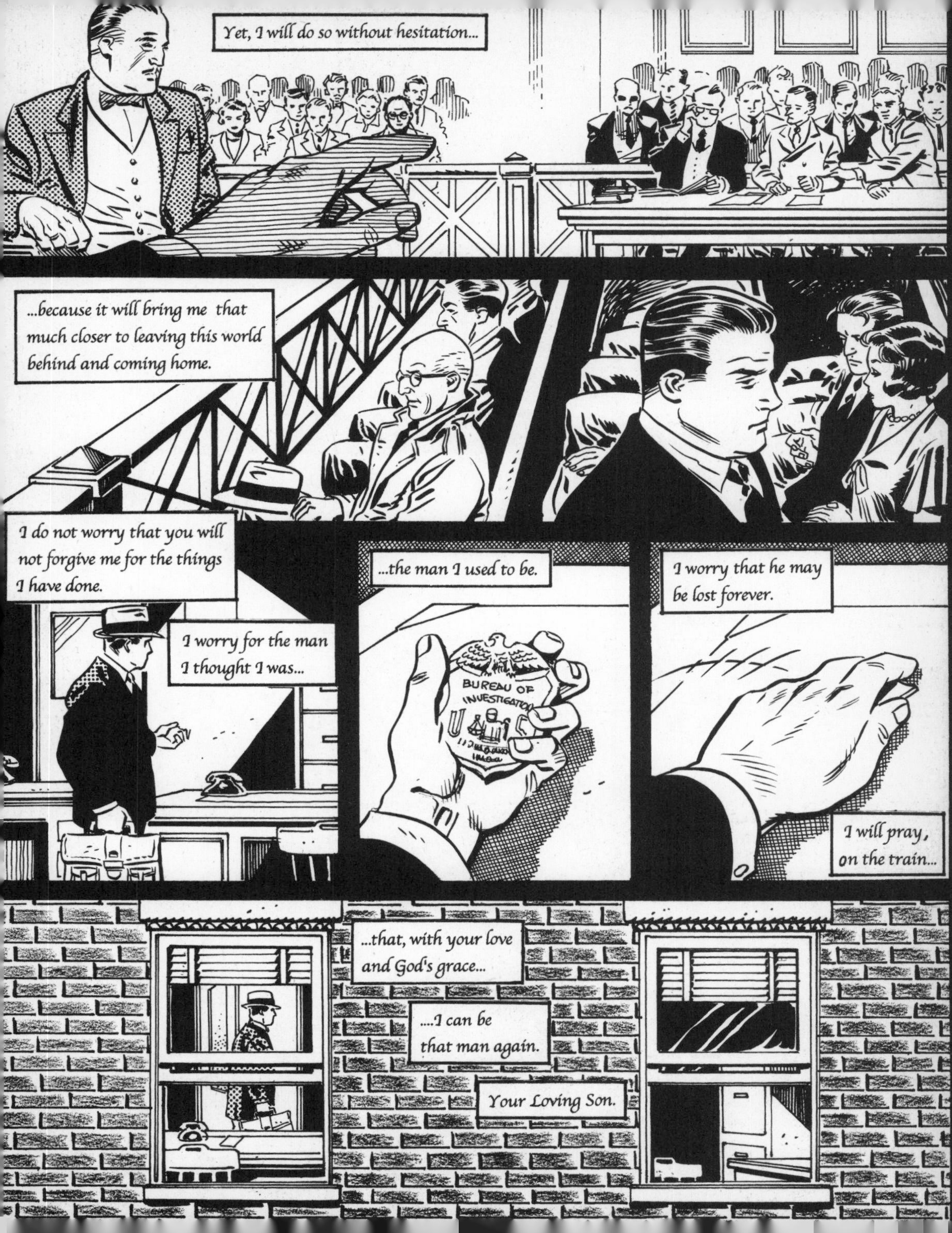
Yet, I will do so without hesitation...
...because it will bring me that much closer to leaving this world behind and coming home.
I do not worry that you will not forgive me for the things I have done.
I worry for the man I thought I was...
...the man I used to be.
BUREAU OF INVESTIGATION
I worry that he may be lost forever.
I will pray, on the train...
...that, with your love and God's grace...
....I can be that man again.
Your Loving Son.

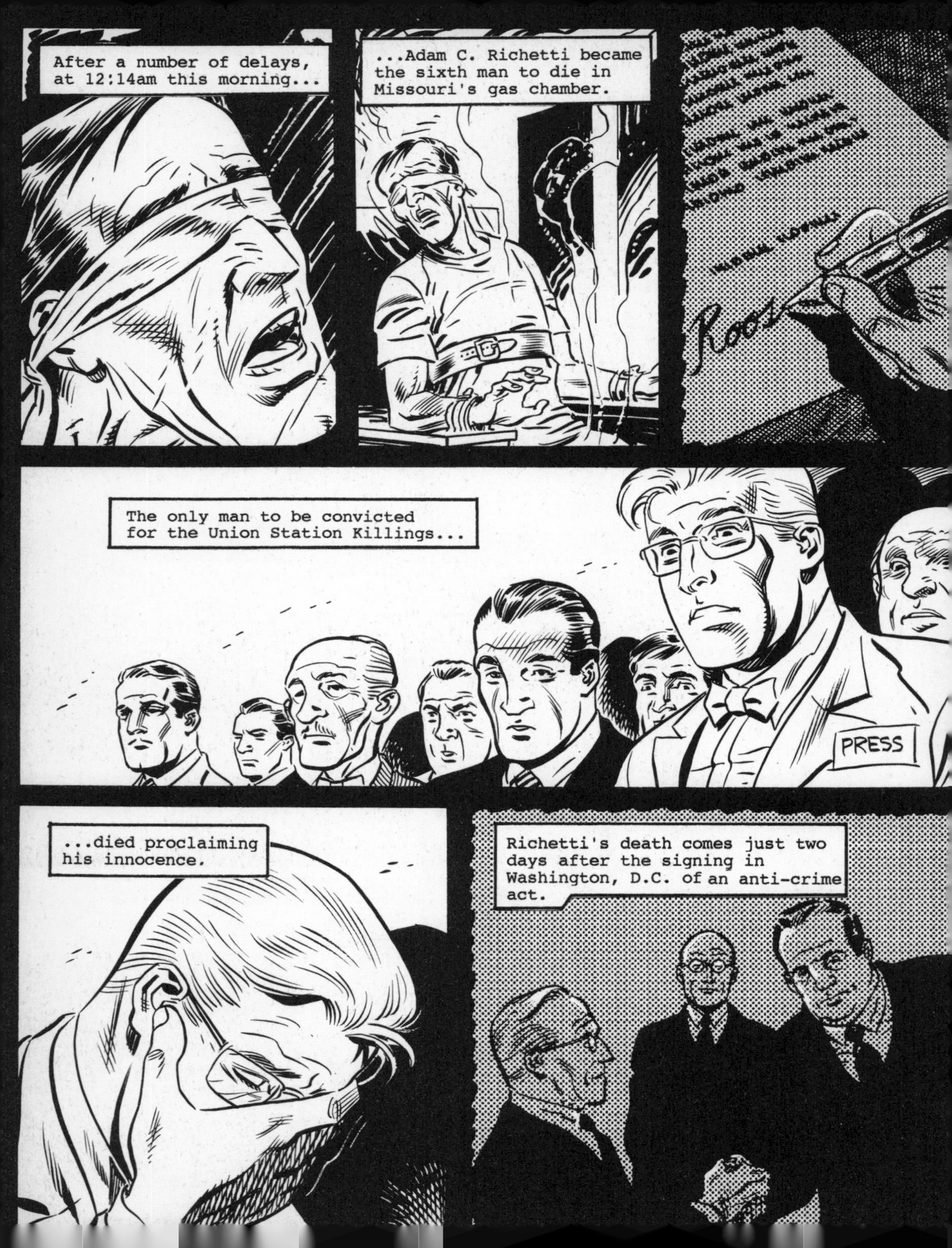
After a number of delays, at 12:14am this morning...
...Adam C. Richetti became the sixth man to die in Missouri's gas chamber.
The only man to be convicted for the Union Station Killings...
PRESS
...died proclaiming his innocence.
Richetti's death comes just two days after the signing in Washington, D.C. of an anti-crime act.

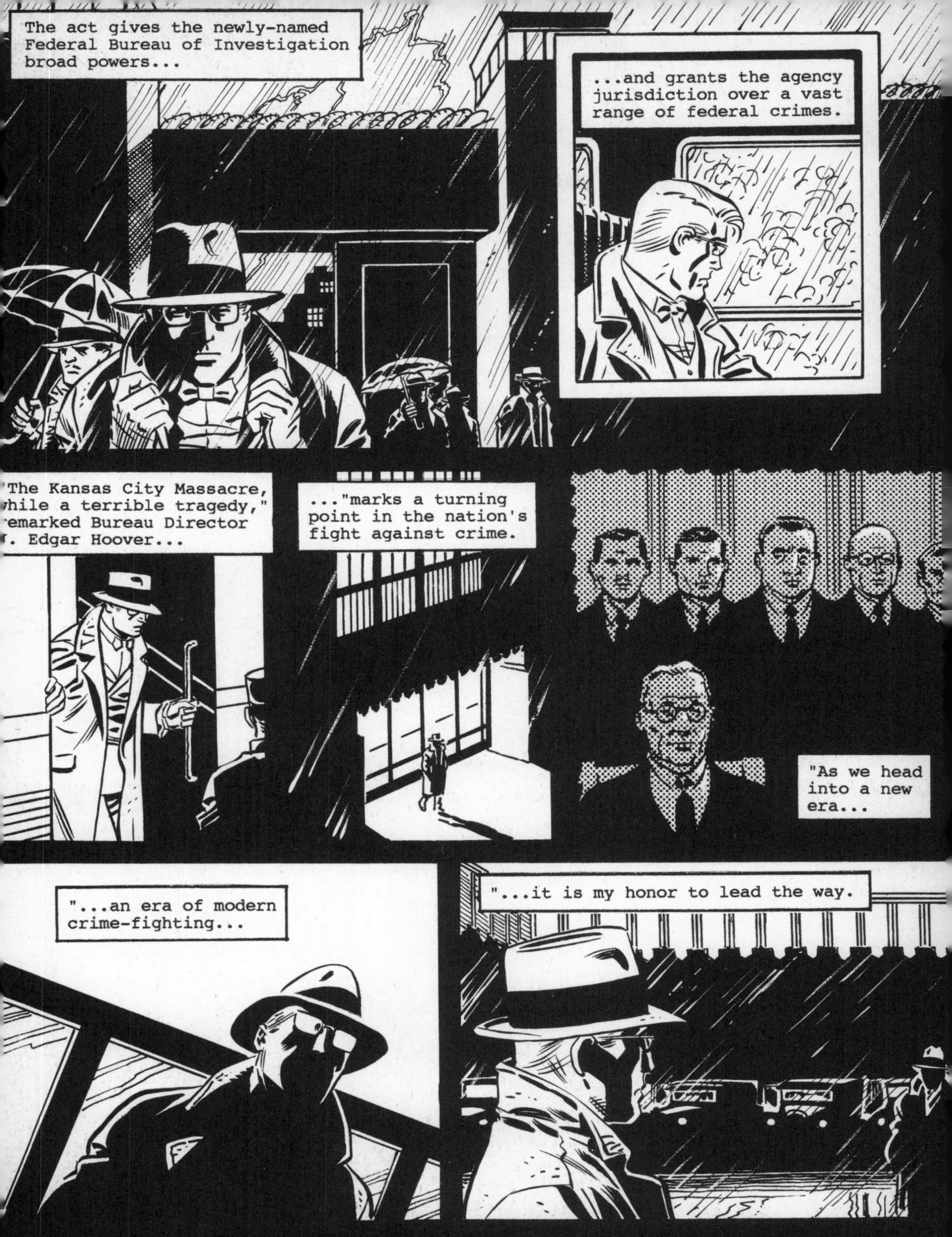
The act gives the newly-named Federal Bureau of Investigation broad powers...
...and grants the agency jurisdiction over a vast range of federal crimes.
"The Kansas City Massacre, while a terrible tragedy," remarked Bureau Director J. Edgar Hoover...
..."marks a turning point in the nation's fight against crime.
"As we head into a new era...
"...an era of modern crime-fighting...
"...it is my honor to lead the way.

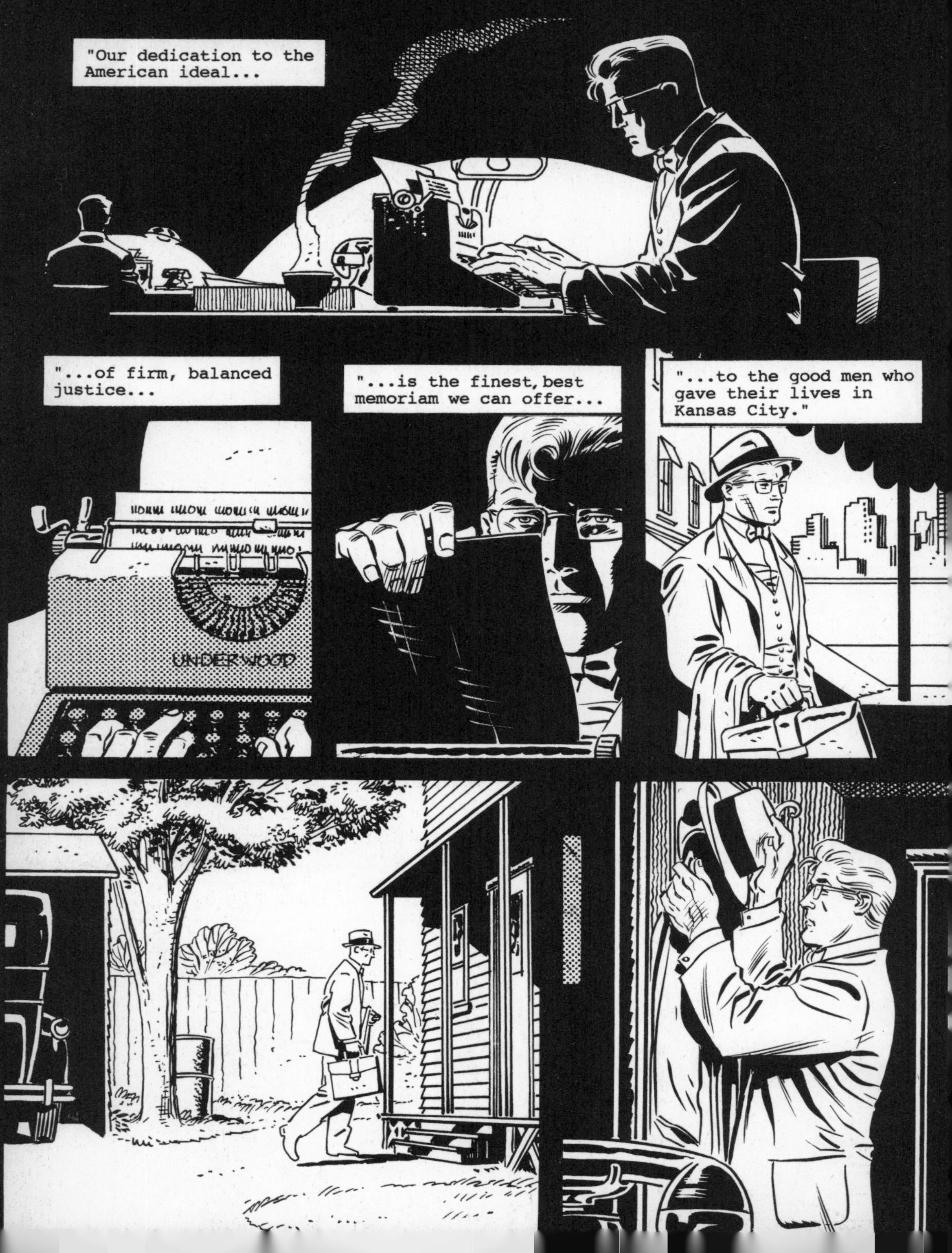
"Our dedication to the American ideal...
"...of firm, balanced justice...
"...is the finest, best memoriam we can offer...
"...to the good men who gave their lives in Kansas City."
UNDERWOOD

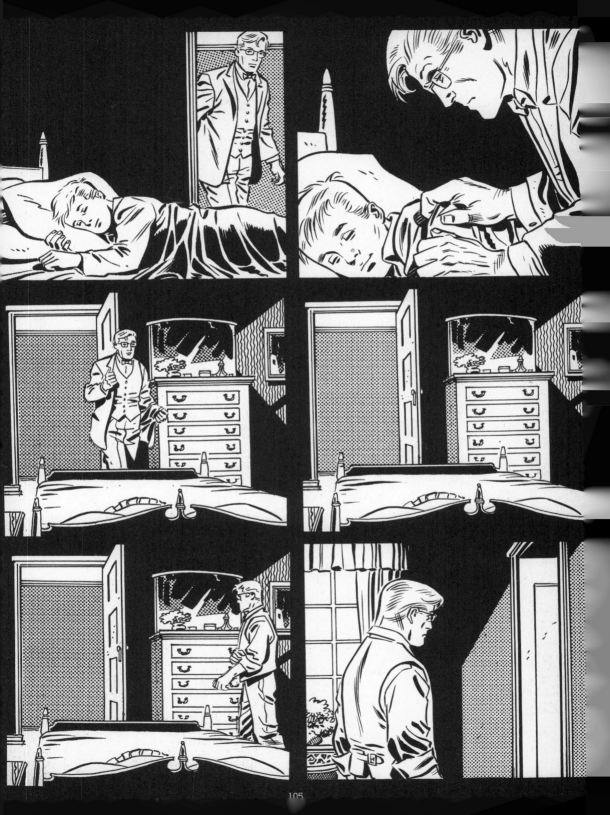

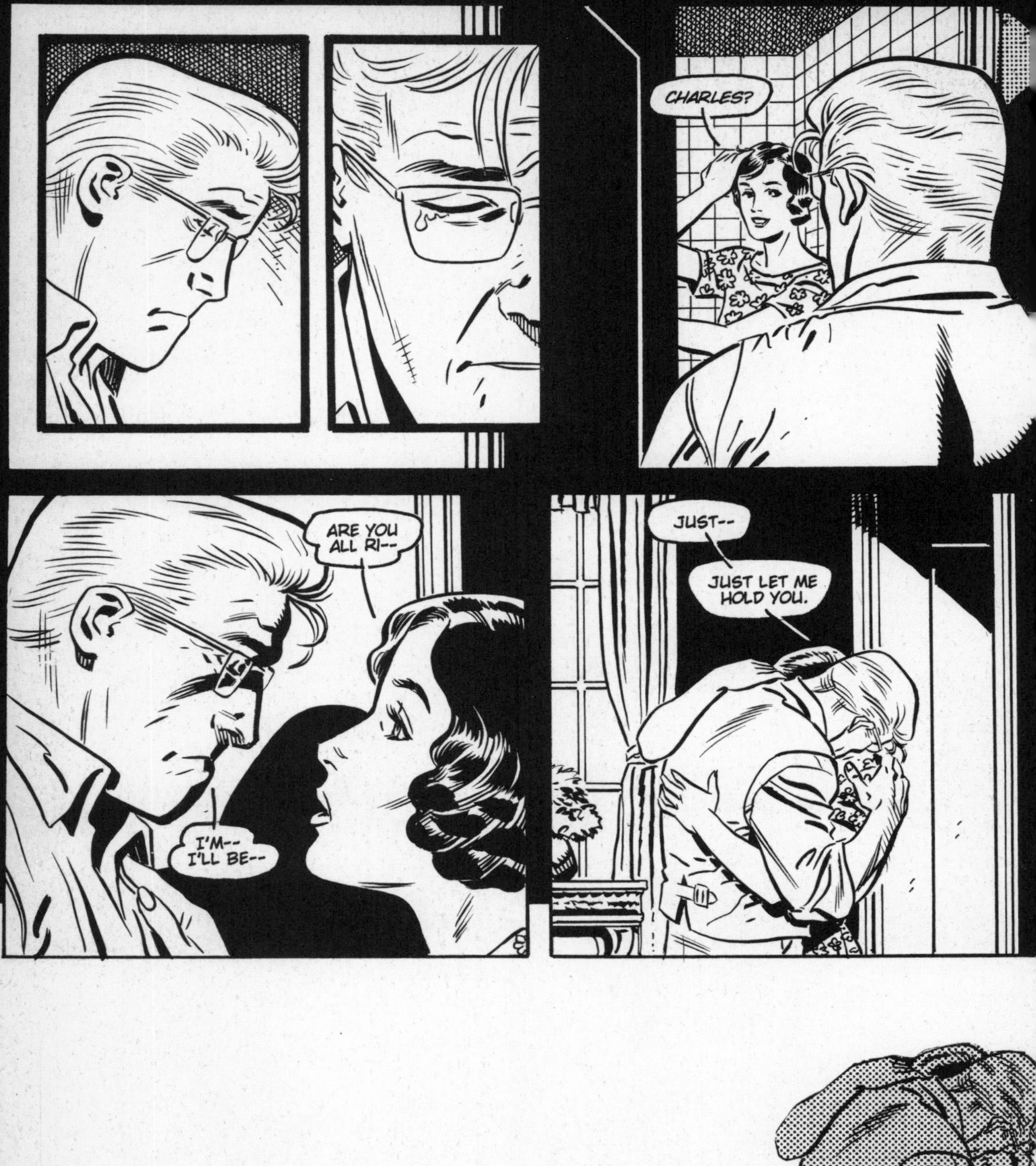
CHARLES?
ARE YOU ALL RI--
I'M-- I'LL BE--
JUST--
JUST LET ME HOLD YOU.

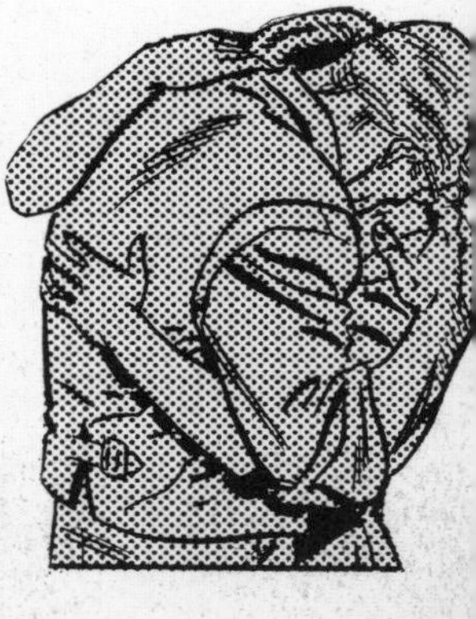

EDUARDO BARRETO
9-03

FOOTNOTES

Sources:

Union Station Massacre: The Shootout that Started the F.B.I.'s War on Crime
By Merle Clayton
Bobbs-Merrill, 1975
It took 40 years for a definitive book to appear on the massacre. Clayton is a capable writer, and his research skills are impressive. The attitude of the book, though, is quite conservative. Clayton draws a solid line between the good and bad guys, portraying the feds in a manner that would make Robert Stack proud.

The Union Station Massacre: The Original Sin of J. Edgar Hoover's F. B. I.
By Robert Unger
Andrews McMeel, 1997
The new definitive work on the subject. Unger is not only a great journalist, he is a wonderful writer... weaving facts gleaned from the FBI's files with the rich personalities of the case. While Clayton cemented the notion that Hoover used the massacre to catapult his agency to power, Unger pioneered the theory that Hoover's empire was built on a pack of lies.

Triple Cross Fire: J. Edgar Hoover & the Kansas City Union Station Massacre
By L.R. Kirchner
Janlar Books, 1993
Kirchner is not as polished a writer as Clayton or Unger, and some of his theories are far-fetched. That said, *Triple Cross Fire* is an interesting take. While I ended up using few facts provided by Kirchner, he did help inspire the connection I would build between the local political machine and the broader massacre investigation.

Union Station, Kansas City
By Jeffrey Spivak
Kansas City Star Books, 1999
A coffee table book, covering the history of the station, which is available in the bookstore of the restored station (if you live in the area and haven't visited the station since its rebirth, do so). There are a few pages concerning the massacre. No new facts, and the author relies on Unger for a massacre theory, but it's presented clearly and well-written. There's also a heartbreaking photo of Richetti behind bars that's worth the price of the book.

The Life and Death of Pretty Boy Floyd
By Jeffrey S. King
The Kent State University Press, 1998
A dry, but well-researched biography. Floyd's role in *Union Station* ended up being extremely limited, so I relied very little on this source. He did help, though, with Floyd's last words. For an entertaining, fictional take on Floyd, check out the novel, *Pretty Boy Floyd*, by Larry McMurtry and Diana Ossana.

Truman
By David McCullough
Simon & Schuster, 1992
A wonderful biography of Missouri's favorite son by one of our most accomplished historians. I relied on McCullough for biographical information on Boss Tom Pendergast.

In addition to these books, I spent several days poring over vintage newspaper articles from the *Kansas City Star* and *Times* (Kansas City supported two daily papers, one printed in the morning and one in the evening, until 1990). Thanks to the staff at the University of Kansas library for their patience as I learned to use those damn microfilm printers.

I looked through a number of internet sites pertaining to the massacre or its key players. Little factual information from these sources made its way to the final product, but there is some fascinating information available there. One site I particularly admire is dedicated to the history of the Richetti family (http://www.fortunecity.com/meltingpot/kuwait/55/index.htm). As with Floyd, Adam Richetti's role in this book ended up insignificant, and I cannot honestly list the site as a source, but it's a wonderful resource, nonetheless. For the most part, the web was used as a fact-checker. I found small tidbits such as what time the sun may have risen on a particular day in 1934 pretty easily.

Scene by Scene Notes
Act One
Scene One, Pages 3-4
The notion of Caffrey having a personal stake in the capture of Frank Nash comes from Clayton, who suggests that the agent had pursued the fugitive for some time. Caffrey resenting the presence of local police during the transfer is my invention, but it's based on the well-documented distrust between the two agencies. A number of sources claim that at least half of the KC police force was on the payroll or under the influence of the Pendergast political machine. During the massacre investigation, there were clear jurisdictional boundaries drawn, with little cooperation between the feds and the locals.

The mention of Pretty Boy Floyd by Vetterli foreshadows Floyd's involvement, and it's accurate. Floyd and his accomplice, Adam Richetti, had kidnapped a sheriff in Missouri earlier in the day, and their movements suggested Kansas City as their destination. The first draft of *Union Station* featured a scene between Floyd, Richetti, and their hostage, as well as a discussion between Vetterli and Caffrey as to Floyd's whereabouts. Limiting his role was a tough choice, but it allowed me to focus on my core group of players… Vetterli, Miller/Mathias, and the Thompsons. Had I been more directly involved with Floyd, I would have had to make clear my belief that he and Richetti were not involved in the shooting. I prefer the book's ambiguity on the subject.

I felt it important to present two things about one of my key players, Reed Vetterli, early on: he had no family save his parents in Utah, and he was a Mormon. Hence the phone call from his mother, which introduces both facts.

Scene Two, Pages 6-8
Most information about the suburban existence of Verne Miller and Vi Mathias comes from Unger, although both Clayton and the newspapers of the day documented their life in Kansas City, as well. The house Verne rented still stands, and has changed little. I was able to resist the temptation, while taking reference photos, to knock on the door and ask the current owners if they were aware of the home's history. Depending on whose story you believe, the floorboards of the house's attic had once been stained with the blood of Pretty Boy Floyd.

It seems that the couple enjoyed life in Kansas City. While it's hard to depict Verne Miller as a completely sympathetic figure, I do find some poignancy in the end of his relatively peaceful time with Vi and her daughter.

The call from Frances Nash represents the tip of the iceberg of a broad conspiracy involving associates and friends of Frank Nash, the full range of which is well documented by Unger. The investigation into this phone call marked the beginning of Reed Vetterli's trouble with Hoover. Vetterli ordered call logs from the phone company, but, according to Unger, did not give them a high priority. By the time the call logs led to the Miller house, Verne and Vi were long gone. While this incident did not make it into my story, it helped clarify for me that Vetterli, while capable, was in over his head with the massacre case.

Scene Three, Page 8-12
A lot of what is accepted as fact about the events immediately preceding the massacre comes directly from the statement of Jimmy "Needles" LaCapra, as documented by Clayton. It was his testimony that cemented Hoover's case against Adam Richetti, which we'll deal with in act three. LaCapra insisted that Floyd and Richetti were offered to Miller by Johnny Lazia the night before the killings. While *Union Station* does not directly address the guilt or innocence of Floyd and Richetti, I believe they were not present at the massacre

There is little credible evidence to make a great case either way, so this scene marks the beginning of my tightrope-walking. Clayton accepts LaCapra's statement as gospel. Unger views it as a desperate attempt by LaCapra, who feared for his life after Lazia's assassination, to please Hoover's agents.

According to LaCapra, the meeting between Miller and Lazia actually took place at Harvey's, in Union Station itself. I wanted to withhold the Station's appearance, so I moved the meeting to the historic Savoy Grill. You can still get a meal there, by the way, and it's a marvelous place...virtually unchanged since the turn of the last century.

Scene Four, Pages 13-14
The capture of Frank Nash deserves its own book. The lawmen had to practically kidnap Nash, who was enjoying a vacation in Hot Springs, Arkansas, under the protection of the local crime boss. Hot Springs was known as a safe haven for fugitives, and the agents had no real jurisdiction. Due to the constraints of a 100-page graphic novel, I have condensed the capture and journey to Kansas City into this train scene, which also gave me the chance to briefly introduce some of the victims of the massacre...not to mention the man for whose sake it all went down, Frank Nash.

Scene Seven, Pages 19-21
It's a safe assumption that Vetterli might have expected more firepower. I've dovetailed that expectation into the earlier scene between Vetterli and Caffrey. The inclusion of the missing machine gun also ties in with the earlier comments of Lazia. Grooms and Hermanson were known as honest, tough cops. Too honest, perhaps. I don't believe it was an accident that they ended up alone at Union Station that morning, without the machine gun they expected to find in their vehicle.

Scene Eight, Pages 22-32
A key witness in the case against Adam Richetti makes a cameo on page 24. Lottie West, who worked the station's information desk, would change her story a few times before Hoover was pleased. In the end, though, she would state that she clearly saw Floyd inside the station that morning.

With the exception of Miller, we keep the identities of the other shooters intentionally obscure. I wish I could definitely tell you who was there that day, but there is simply not enough evidence. To paraphrase Unger, it may well have been Floyd and Richetti, but you can't prove it by the case that was presented by Hoover's men. You can find a not-too-subtle clue as to whom I think may have been involved on page three of act one.

Frank Nash was seated behind the steering wheel when the shooting started to allow the lawmen to push the passenger seat forward, giving them access to the rear seat. Obviously, they weren't going to let Frank drive to Leavenworth.

Reed Vetterli's dash towards the station accounts for the famous bullet holes in the granite façade of the building. There is actually some credible evidence that they aren't bullet holes, after all, but whatever they are, you can still see them near the station's east doors.

Verne pulling the shotgun from the back seat and throwing it disgustedly to the ground is my invention. It foreshadows what we'll learn about that shotgun later on.

There is no evidence that Vetterli was in any way ashamed of his actions during the shooting. I have placed that shame upon him, to suit my own literary ends.

Act Two
Scene Two, Pages 39-42
There is no indication that Vetterli slept in the federal office building. It's a shortcut for me, done in an effort to show that, despite his lack of success, Vetterli was sincerely motivated to solve the case. The stakes were not only justice, but Vetterli's own career. In reality, a number of agents came and went in Hoover's desperate

attempts to find someone who could give him a location he could work with. I have condensed all of their efforts into Vetterli.

Along with the Thompsons, Dwight August is wholly my creation. I wanted to give Hoover a physical presence… a series of phone calls did not seem sufficient. There was no one on the scene to parallel August. He is simply my surrogate for the director.

Scene Three, Pages 43-45
Poor Verne Miller is about to suffer a slew of historical slanders at my hands. I feel a bit bad about it, but he was a cold-blooded killer, so fuck him. I have linked him here to the Karpis/Barker gang, which is possible, but completely unsubstantiated. It does make sense that he would have needed some cash if he had any hopes of picking up Vi and attempting to set up a new life. The mention of Verne's past career as a sheriff is accurate.

Scene Four, Pages 46-48
The view of Lackey as hero in the public mind is unquestionable, perpetuated not only by newspaper accounts of the day, but by Clayton, who presents the agent as a noble, wounded warrior. Clayton's book, in fact, is dedicated to Lackey.

Scene Five, Page 49
"Did You Ever See a Dream Walking" was a top hit for Eddy Duchin in 1933. Act two takes place in the fall/winter of that year, which compresses the actual timeframe.

Scene Six, Pages 50-54
The theories of Merle Gill are presented brilliantly by Unger. The real life of Gill is more complex than I had room for. He actually testified at Richetti's trial, although Hoover was clearly incensed by the forensic scientist's public declarations.

The notion of Lackey inadvertently firing the first shot comes from Unger, and is supported by Merle's public statements and the FBI's files. I have simplified his theory, which involved Lackey mistakenly carrying Otto Reed's weapon into the parking lot.

Scene Seven, Pages 55-61
According to Unger, there was a much larger group of agents waiting for Verne Miller in Chicago. The key difference between fact and fiction here, though, is that, in reality, the trap wasn't sprung until the morning after Verne and Vi actually were reunited. Undoing that meeting was a tough choice, but in the end, I found this near-miss more moving.

Again, Vetterli's role is greatly expanded here. He was not present at the ambush. Once I placed him there, it was easy to imagine his awkwardness with a weapon.

Scene Eight, Pages 62-66
More big-time history jumbling for Verne here. He actually died in Detroit, at the hands of mobsters…the motive unclear. It just served my purposes too well to have him meet with the Lazia organization again.

Scene Nine, Pages 67-68
Again, Vetterli was not present in Chicago, and he did not interrogate Vi Mathias.

According to Unger, I'm being far too kind to the feds both here and in the later interrogation scene.

Scene Ten, Pages 69-72
The Jackson Democratic Club, which served as Boss Tom Pendergast's office, still stands. It's about a four-block walk between the *Star's* office and 1908 Main Street, where Boss Tom held court. I do not know of any soup kitchen in the area, but I took the liberty of placing one here for dramatic effect.

Act Three

Scene One, Pages 77-78

The death of Floyd is presented accurately. I took some liberties, but his final words are pretty much as provided by King, via the FBI records. The only real stretch is that Richetti was not present. He was in a jail cell in the nearby town. Although not named here, the lead agent is Melvin Purvis, famous as the man who nabbed Dillinger. The death of Floyd was a victory for the agency, but not for Purvis. Hoover did not take well to agents getting more press than the director himself. Purvis would be out of the agency within a few years.

Scene Four, Pages 84-89

There is no evidence that Vetterli was kept in the dark by those working around him in the agency. He was likely as culpable as anyone else. His testimony at Richetti's trial certainly indicates as much. Vetterli's line about the foundation of the agency is inspired by Unger.

Scene Five, Page 90

There is precious little information to be found as to what happened to Vi Mathias after she signed the statement which named Miller, Floyd, and Richetti. I like to think she made a deal with Hoover that allowed her and her daughter to move far away, and to start a new life. Unger presents some evidence to support that notion.

Scene Six, Pages 91-94

While I gathered information on Pendergast's personality from McCullough, this scene is entirely my invention. I wanted to tie the local and federal interests, and it made sense to me that Pendergast might, detecting the scent of change in the air, approach Hoover in an effort to secure his position. Whether he did so or not, he did indeed remain a powerful figure until his indictment for income tax evasion in 1939. When he died in 1945, Vice President Truman caused considerable controversy by attending the funeral.

The assassination of Lazia is well-documented, and I have presented it fairly accurately. Insinuating that Pendergast was involved is a far stretch, however. The story of LaCapra and how he came to testify for the feds is much more involved than I had time for.

I wish I could have found a way to get Lazia's last words into the story, but great lines sometimes have to be sacrificed. In this case, I didn't think it would be appropriate to have Lazia speak during this flashback-style portion of Pendergast's scene. I can present them here, though. As he lay dying on the sidewalk, Johnny Lazia is reported to have said, "Why to me... a friend to everyone?"

Scene Eight, Pages 100-101

Vetterli did indeed testify, and if you believe Unger even a little bit, perjure himself at Richetti's trial. He did not immediately leave the agency, though. He was shuffled around by Hoover for a few years before heading home. He became Chief of Police in Salt Lake City. I did a lot of research on his later life, and as far as I can tell, he never married. He died in 1949.

Scene Nine, Pages 102-104

The portrayal of Richetti's behavior as he died is accurate. Again, I have compressed the time frame significantly.

The federal laws enacted in accordance with Hoover's newly-named FBI granted the agency the powers Hoover needed to become the pre-eminent law enforcement figure in the United States for the next 30 years or more. His record is somewhat subject to debate, but I think it's clear that Hoover used the massacre to launch a career that would see him treat the civil liberties of the American people with little respect.

Thank God it could never happen today.

Ande Parks
9-18-03